John Fraser

Chaucer to Longfellow

A choice selection of lectures on English literature; giving a comprehensive survey

of the Saxon language; and how to master it. Vol. 2

John Fraser

Chaucer to Longfellow
A choice selection of lectures on English literature; giving a comprehensive survey of the Saxon language; and how to master it. Vol. 2

ISBN/EAN: 9783337075293

Printed in Europe, USA, Canada, Australia, Japan

Cover: Foto ©Andreas Hilbeck / pixelio.de

More available books at **www.hansebooks.com**

CHAUCER TO LONGFELLOW

A CHOICE SELECTION OF

LECTURES ON ENGLISH LITERATURE

GIVING A COMPREHENSIVE SURVEY OF THE SAXON
LANGUAGE; AND HOW TO MASTER IT.

WITH CRITICAL REVIEWS ON

THE FIFTEENTH CENTURY ; SCOTCH POETRY ; CHAUCER ; SURREY ; WYATT ; SIDNEY;
RALEIGH; SPENSER; BACON; MARLOWE; SHAKESPEARE; WEBSTER; BEAUMONT;
FLETCHER; SHELLEY: BEN JONSON; MILTON; BURNS; HOOD; GEORGE
ELIOT; MRS. E. B. BROWNING; MME. DE STAEL; THE BRONTE
SISTERS; MARGARET FULLER; MRS. H. B. STOWE
AND THE MODERN NOVEL; TENNYSON;
LONGFELLOW; ETC., ETC.

BY

JOHN FRASER, A. M.,

Late Professor of Rhetoric and English Literature in the University of Chicago; Author of "History of Scottish
Chap-Books," "Archie Gascoigne; a Romance of Skye," "Youth's Golden Cycle,"
"History of Mormonism," Etc.

VOLUME II.

CHICAGO:
JOHNSON & ERSKINE, PUBLISHERS,
105 & 107 MADISON STREET.
1887.

TABLE OF CONTENTS.

SYNOPSIS LECTURE XVII.

1.—Rise of the English Drama. Beginnings of regular drama in reign of Henry VIII; rapid growth; Elizabethan dramatists nearly all scholars. Exuberance of every form of literature. Marlow, Peele, Lyly, Lodge, Kyd and Nash, the real founders of the English drama. John Lyly, the inventor of Euphuism; Thomas Nash, the most brilliant pamphleteer of the period; Thomas Peele, author of "King David and Fair Bethsabe;" Thomas Lodge, a physician, wrote "Rosalynde," from which Shakespeare derived "As You Like It;" Thomas Kyd, author of "Jeronimo" and the "Spanish Tragedy;" Robert Greene, author of five plays.

2.—Christopher Marlow, 1562–1593, son of a shoemaker; educated at Cambridge; led a wild life, and killed in a brawl; wrote early for the stage; greatest dramatic writer before Shakespeare; his "Tamburlaine the Great;" tragic conclusion of "Faustus ;" conclusion of "Edward the Second," much admired; his Barabus compared with Shylock, powerfully and splendidly drawn.

3.—Beaumont and Fletcher, dramatists nearest to Shakespeare, yet far below; they form one individuality. Francis Beaumont, the younger, and died first, 1585–1616; John Fletcher, born 1576, died 1625; the latter sole author of the "Faithful Shepherdess;" wrote thirty-seven or thirty-eight plays together; comedy of the "Woman Hater," the first published in 1607. Knowledge of stage effect and brilliance of dialogue; analysis of "The Maid's "Tragedy," a powerful but repulsive drama, a noble moral; "Philaster; or, Love Lies a Bleeding," well written and interesting, but with a needlessly complicated plot; "A King and No King," ingenious and entertaining, but with an unfortunate plot;

377

"The Scornful Lady" has some good situations and sprightly dialogue, affords insight into fashionable life and morals; "The Custom of the Country," an objectionable drama.

4.—PHILIP MASSINGER, 1584–1639, son of a retainer of the Earl of Pembroke; received a classical education; shy, reserved and inclined to melancholy; has characteristics as a dramatist; knew Shakespeare's writings well, but does not plagiarize. "The Roman Actor," well conceived, with strong characters and rapid action, language dignified and noble; "The Great Duke of Florence" ought still to be a good acting play, altogether unobjectionable; "The Maid of Honor," well conceived and told, on the whole, a pure play; "The Picture," ingeniously contrived, humor sprightly and abundant; "The Emperor of the East," artistically unsatisfactory, and more than usually objectionable; "A New Way to Pay Old Debts," in some respects the most complete and satisfactory; Sir Giles Overreach; "The City Madam," meant to ridicule the airs and extravagance of city ladies; "Luke;" "The Guardian," ingenious and pleasing.

5.—JOHN FORD, 1586–1639, a gentleman of means, bred to the law; tragic power, tenderness and pathos; weak in comedy; choice of subjects unfortunate. "The Broken Heart," a noble drama; "Perkin Warbeck," pure and wholesome; "The Elder Brother," sketchy, but the main idea pleasantly developed; "Rule a Wife and Have a Wife," an admirable play, but immoral; "The Queen of Corinth" illustrates the triumph of purity over vice— a parody of Don Quixote; "The Double Marriage," unsatisfactory and unnatural. Other plays; Gifford's criticism.

End of the Elizabethan drama.

DRAMATISTS AROUND SHAKESPEARE.

MARLOW, BEAUMONT AND FLETCHER, MASSINGER, FORD.

The greatness of Shakespeare has caused the utter eclipse of many sons of genius, who might otherwise have remained visible in the literary heavens. He is like the sun before whose presence the planets pale and vanish. In the popular mind, it may be said, so far as literature goes, the reign of Elizabeth means only Shakespeare. He is a lofty mountain, towering mid-ocean in a waste of waters. Such a conception is, however, altogether false, and the same evolution is distinctly descernible in the English drama, that scientists have noted elsewhere. If we would figure to ourselves its rise and decline, we might do so by imagining a gradually ascending mountain range, rising peak above peak, till it culminates in a height that pierces the heavens, and descending step by step again, until it is lost in cloud and gloom. Thus from the miracle play, in which we find the origin of the English drama, we proceed to the moral play, and thence to the interlude, a species of farce, and so on until, in the reign of Henry VIII., we meet with the beginnings of the regular drama. After its inception its growth was marvelously rapid. It is worthy of note that nearly all the dramatists of the Elizabethan period were scholars—Oxford and Cambridge men. It seems as if a passion, or craze if you will, had suddenly sprung up for this species of composition. It was, in fact, a consequence of the extraordinary life and energy of the time. Everything seemed to conduce to awaken and stimulate the imagination of men. Old shackles had been thrown off, and new ideas filled men's minds. A new world had been discovered, the spirit of freedom was in the air, and visions of boundless glory dawned on the eyes. There was peace and prosperity in the land. A long "winter was past, the rain was over and gone; the flowers appeared on the earth, and the time of the singing of birds was come." It was not the drama alone that found a new berth and grew sturdily, but every form of literature flourished. If we retain the figure of a mountain range, we can imagine a stately river of poesy flowing in the fair valley below, with countless tributary streams, brooks and rills, while

"All the air is filled with pleasant noise of waters."

Ellis said that nearly a hundred names of poets belonging to the reign of Elizabeth might be enumerated, besides many who left no memorial except their songs, and Drake has made a list of more than two hundred. Nor is the prose literature of the period less worthy of note.

Marlow, Peele, Greene, Lyly, Lodge, Kyd and Nash, were the precursors of Shakespeare, and they are the real founders of the English drama. If he transcended them all immeasurably, it was most of all because in the alembic of his mind his characters became so real, and living, that they have remained immortal creations. His predecessors either had not the power, or lacked the patience to fashion complete and consistent characters, having that vitality which makes us recognize them as no mere bundle of qualities, or skillfully constructed automatons, but living creatures whom we love or hate, inspiring all the emotions aroused by the men and women around us. The life of those early dramatists was all hurry-skurry. They had too much wealth of material, and they did not know well what to do with their riches. Their days and nights were full of brawl and licence. It is a sad record that has come down to us of those men. Greene dying in a garret of a surfeit of red herring and Rhenish wine; Marlow killed in a tavern quarrel. They, almost none of them, saw half their days. Nor should we judge them harshly. The circumstances of the time will account very much for all that we might be inclined to censure, just as the vices of the West Indian slaves, on their emancipation, may quite rationally be explained. They were probably neither better nor worse than an equal number of their fellow mortals would have been under the same conditions.

JOHN LYLY is an exception to the foregoing remarks, his life not being remarkable for its excesses. He is called the *Euphuist* from his prose work, "Euphues, or the Anatomy of Wit." An example of euphuism, of which he was the inventor, and which consists in an absurdly high-flown way of speaking, is to be found in Sir Piercie Shafton, one of the characters in Scott's "Monastery." Lyly was an able writer, and, notwithstanding the affectations that may be laid to his charge, he did some service in the way of euphony to the English language. He was also a dramatist and a poet. Some of his songs are well known, particularly the delicate little anacreontic beginning:

> Cupid and my Campaspe played
> At cards for kisses.

THOMAS NASH, a scholar of Cambridge, was the most brilliant pamphleteer of the period. A series of pamphlets directed against the Puritans in 1589, exhibit him as a satirist of extraordinary vigor and fertility. His chief claim to notice as a dramatist is the share he had in the composition of Marlow's tragedy " Dido, Queen of Carthage." Of GEORGE PEELE, whose best drama is his " Love of King David and Fair Bethsabe," Campbell says it is " the earliest fountain of pathos and harmony that can be traced in our dramatic poetry. Peele was a shareholder with Shakespeare and others in Blackfriars' theatre. THOMAS LODGE, a distinguished physician, wrote a number of plays, notably one entitled, " The Wounds of Civil War, lively set forth in the true tragedies of Marius and Sylla." He is placed by Collier " in a rank superior to Greene, but. in some respects inferior to Kyd." In conjunction with Greene he wrote " A Looking-Glass for London and England," an attempt to counteract the puritanical outcry against the stage. Lodge wrote poetry and tales, as well as plays. His prose novel, entitled " Rosalynde," Euphue's Golden Legacie, found in his cell at Silextra, afforded Shakespeare the materials for " As You Like It."

THOMAS KYD, called by Jonson, Sporting Kyd, is the author of "Jeronimo," and the " Spanish Tragedy," the latter of which contains fine passages, whose authorship, however, is disputed, being generally ascribed to Jonson.

ROBERT GREENE, of unhappy memory, wrote five plays. He wielded an extremely facile pen. His friend Nash says of him: " In a night and a day would he have yarked up a pamphlet as well as in seven years; and glad was that printer that might be so blessed to pay him dear for the very dregs of his wit." Greene was a man of large and varied experience, as well as of good education, and he has, even when hurried and careless, that valuable quality in a writer of being interesting. Especially notable are the writings which refer to his own unhappy life. His attack on Shakespeare in his " Groatsworth of Wit," is often quoted. " There is an upstart crow, beautified with our feathers, that, with his tiger's heart wrapt in a player's hide, supposes he is as well able to bombast out a blank verse as the best of you; and, being an absolute *Johannes Factotum*, is, in his own conceit, the only *shake-scene* in the country."

Marlow, Peele and Greene are the three most noted dramatists belonging exclusively to the reign of Elizabeth, but by far the greatest of these is

MARLOW.

He was the son of a shoemaker, but was educated at Cambridge, where he graduated. He led a wild, irregular life, and met his death in a brawl, when only a little over thirty years of age. What he might have accomplished had he lived longer, and perhaps settled down, we can only imagine. He wrote for the stage when twenty-four years old, when, if not earlier, his "Tamburlaine the Great" appeared. His fame among his contemporaries ranked high, and he is undoubtedly the dramatic writer first in rank before Shakespeare. Jonson speaks of "Marlow's mighty line," and Drayton, in his "Polyollion," sings:

> Next Marlow, bathed in the Thespian springs,
> Had in him those brave translunary things
> That the first poets had; his raptures were
> All air and fire, which made his verses clear;
> For that fine madness still he did retain,
> Which rightly should possess a poet's brain.

"Tamburlaine the Great" is remarkable as having been the first play in blank verse exhibited on the public stage. It is not free from the bombastic and turgid, but it is at the same time replete with tragic excellency. The inflated style was no doubt deemed appropriate in the mouths of oriental tyrants. In the "Life and Death of Dr. Faustus," Marlow perhaps reaches his greatest height. The conclusion is splendidly awful, if one may be permitted the expression. Realistic in the extreme, there is yet nothing revolting in the scene in which the

> Scholar, once admired
> For wondrous learning in our German schools,
> Meets his fearful doom.

The conclusion of his tragedy of " Edward the Second " has been even more admired. "The reluctant pangs of abdicating royalty in Edward," says Charles Lamb, "furnished hints which Shakespeare scarce improved in his " Richard the Second; " and the death-scene of

Marlow's king moves pity and terror beyond any scene, ancient or modern, with which I am acquainted." In "The Rich Jew of Malta," the character of Barabas has been compared, but not so justly, with that of Shylock. It is, however, powerfully and splendidly drawn. Marlow has also bequeathed us some beautiful lyrics. One feels inclined to apply to him the words of the chorus in his own Faustus, thinking of his melancholy and early death:

> Cut is the branch that might have grown full straight,
> And turned as Apollo's laurel bough,
> That sometime grew within this learned man.

BEAUMONT AND FLETCHER.

If we pass to the other side of the mountain range which we took as our illustration, we shall find that, next to Shakespeare's, rise the creations of Beaumont and Fletcher. Their plays stand higher than those of Ben Jonson. And yet the descent from Shakespeare is a great one. The singular partnership which existed between the two writers is itself interesting and attractive. It has had its parallel in some respects in our own times. Beasant and Rice afford an example of a literary bond not altogether dissimilar. In the case of the dramatists the fusion of their individual genius is so complete that it cannot be satisfactorily determined what share each had in the composition of their plays. For all practical purposes, then, they must be regarded as forming one individuality.

Of the two, Francis Beaumont was the younger by ten years, and he appeared first in the world of letters. His first venture was a translation from Ovid's Metamorphoses, which appeared when he was only in his seventeenth year. In 1612 was produced his "Masque of the Inner Temple and Gray's Inn." He wrote several poems,—"True Beauty;" a sonnet, beginning, "Like a Ring without a Finger"; one on "The Tombs in Westminster Abbey."

> Here are sands, ignoble things,
> Drop't from the ruin'd sides of kings.

There is also a famous letter of his to Ben Jonson, beginning "What things have we seen done at the Mermaid". Beaumont died in 1616, the same year as Shakespeare and Cervantes, at the age of thirty-one.

John Fletcher, a Scotchman, was born in 1576. He is the sole author of the pastoral drama of the "Faithful Shepherdess."

The number of plays which they may have written together, during the ten years of their co-partnery, is estimated at thirty-seven or thirty-eight, whilst other fourteen pieces may be credited exclusively to Fletcher. The first published of the pieces, which have been ascribed to the two associated together, the comedy of the "Woman Hater," appeared in 1607.

It must be admitted that Beamont and Fletcher fall very far below the immortal bard. They lack his intensity, his grasp, his breadth and depth. Their plays are much spoiled by their licentiousness, and most of them bear the marks of carelessness and haste. What is very noticeable, however, is their knowledge of stage effect, and, in their happier scenes, the flow and brilliance of their dialogue. "It is the richest stream of real conversation, edged with the fire of poetry." One can well understand that in an age which could endure their grossness, their popularity was greater than Shakespeare's, for they had precisely those qualities which enlist the sympathies and maintain the interest of an every day audience. Two of their plays, Dryden tells us, were acted in his time for one of Shakespeare's. Some examples may be given of their skill in plot and incident, in which they excelled.

The scene of "The Maid's Tragedy" is laid in Rhodes. The drama is singularly powerful, but repulsive. It is illustrative of the terrible consequences brought by unrestrained and unlawful lust, not only upon the immediate criminals, but on a wide circle of connections and friends. The King, to possess Evadne, and protect her character, forces a noble and too loyal gentleman, Amintor, troth-plighted to the beautiful and hapless Aspatia, to marry her. On the marriage night she reluctantly confesses her crime, and Amintor, in turn, is forced to reveal it to her brother, and his bosom friend, the brave Melantius. The latter, whose fierce passion less easily brooks the restraints of loyalty, plots revenge, and, by an ingeniously managed ruse (which is artfully worked out) compels his enemy, old Calianax, father of the wronged Aspatia, to deliver up the fort which commands the city. Before he has consummated his revenge, however, Evadne, moved to repentance, alike by her brother's passion and her awakening love for Amintor, who scorns her unpurified affection, stabs her royal seducer to death, and rushing into Amintor's chamber, finds him lamenting over the dying form of a youth, whom he has mortally wounded, after first suffering gross insults, and who had passed herself off as the brother of

Aspatia, but who is Aspatia herself. She shows him the bloody evidence of her crime, and, on her now trebly horror-stricken husband repulsing her with loathing, kills herself. Aspatia, momentarily recovering, and having revealed herself in time to hear Amintor's vain protestations of love, expires, vowing undying affection (in a finely moving scene). Amintor finally stabs himself, immediately on which Lysippus, the new king, and brother of the dead monarch, enters with Melantius, courtiers, etc , and the play ends with his warning words:

> May this a fair example be to me
> To rule with temper ; for, on lustful kings,
> Unlooked-for, sudden deaths from heaven are sent ;
> But curst is he that is their instrument.

The language of this drama is powerful, the passion is nobly expressed, and the characters vividly distinguished and drawn. There are touches of fine pathos and feeling interspersed. The plot is well conceived, the incidents are dramatic and the action is rapid. The noble, self-restrained, and superstitiously loyal nature of Amintor is finely contrasted with that of his hardly less noble—though less governable friend Melantius; while the variable moods and conflicting passions of the two hapless heroines are also finely portrayed; and, though but a sketch, the weak, foolish old man, Calianax, has a distinct if not altogether satisfactory, or vigorous personality of his own. Although the portrayal and development of lust is necessarily so essential an element in the play, being essential, it is to that extent pardonable and artistic, and is never unnecessarily obtruded, while the moral is noble, and is driven home with almost appalling force.

The death of Aspatia is infinitely beautiful and sad.

Asp. I shall surely live. Amintor, *I am well:*
A kind of healthful joy wanders within me.

Amin. The world wants lives to excuse thy loss !
Come let me bear thee to some place of help.

Asp. Amintor, thou must stay; I must rest here;
My strength begins to disobey my will.
How dost thou, my best soul? I would fain live
Now, if I could : *wouldst thou have loved me then?*

Amin. Alas !
All that I am's not worth one hair of thee.

Asp. Give me thy hand ; *my hands grope up and down.
And cannot find thee; I am wondrous sick;*
Have I thy hand, Amintor?

Amin.   Thou greatest blessing of the world, thou hast.

Asp.   I do believe thee better than my sense,
          Oh! I must go.   Farewell.   [*Dies.*

Amin.   *   *   *   *   *

          Some hidden power tell her, Amintor calls,
          And let her answer me !   Aspatia, speak !

               *   *   *   *   *

          The soul is fled forever ; and I wrong
          Myself so long to lose her company.
          Must I talk now?   Here's to be with thee love !

                              [*Stabs himself.*

In "Philaster, or Love Lies a Bleeding," the scene is laid in Messina.   Pharamon, Prince of Spain, a worthless libertine, is, by the King of Messina, espoused to his daughter Arethusa, who loves and is loved by the brave and gallant Philaster, the wronged heir of the crown, and the people's favorite.   He presents his mistress with a supposed boy, Bellaris, as page, who is, however, Euphrasia, the lovely daughter of Dion, a noble courtier.   Prince Pharamon is caught by the King in a liason with a court lady Megra, who, in self-defense, threatens the King, that, if he harms her, she will make public his daughter's lewdness with the page Bellaris.   Certain suspicious circumstances, and the false stories of honestly designing friends, cause an estrangement between Philaster and Arethusa.   Both fly the court, though in different ways, as also does poor Bellaris; and Philaster, being captured, is condemned to death.   The people rise *en masse* and save him.   Bellaris, suddenly freed in some way from an oath of secrecy, revealing herself to be a girl, the King makes a virtue of necessity, and the two lovers are made happy; the play winding up with the somewhat indefinite moral:

                    Let princes learn
          By this, to rule the passions of the blood,
          For what herein wills can never be withstood.

There is no marked character in this play, and, though, well-written and interesting, the plot is needlessly complicated, and ill-put together. Philaster is a noble, brave and upright gentleman, and Bellaris a really lovely and pathetic picture.

"A King and No King" has its scene laid in Armenia, and the capital of Iberia.   It is very ingenious, and with many drawbacks, entertaining, though it is unfortunate that the plot should turn on an offensive crime, which, after all, has not been committed.   The character of

Poressus, and that of Arbaces, King of Armenia, greatly detract from the interest; the former's cross stupidity being greatly exaggerated, and obtruded so much, and the latter's fitfulness and unmethodical madness, together with his frequent changes of passion and opinion, being unnatural. Mardonius, however, is a splendid type of strong manhood, brave, noble and loyal. The women, as usual, are only so-so.

Arbaces, a vain-glorious, brave and unnaturally variable-tempered king, having overcome in a duel, and made captive, the gallant Tigranes, King of Armenia, wishes the latter to marry his sister Parthea, whom he has not seen since she was in her cradle. On meeting her, however, he is smitten with love, and the self-conflict which ensues is powerfully described, giving rise, as it does, to a thousand sudden fits of passion and demeanor on the King's part. After a little she returns his love, but they combine to fight against it. All is confusion and despair, until at the most critical stage, Gobrias, the lord-protector, discovers to the King that his supposed majesty was not the real king, being the son of himself Gobrias, and not of his supposed father, the late king. Arane, the queen-mother, fearing she would never bear child to her old husband, had prevailed upon Gobrias to pass off his own son as hers, but the king dying soon after, she found herself with child, and bore Panthea. The whole ends happily with the marriage of Arbaces and Panthea, and of the queen-mother and Tigranes.

"The Scornful Lady" has its scene in London. It is an ill-contrived, inartistically complicated play, with some good situations and sprightly dialogue, valuable chiefly for its vivid picture of contemporaneous fashionable life and morals.

Sir Roger, curate to the anonymous "Scornful Lady," is a curious bit of character painting. The other personages have little originality, being all—notably Morecraft, the usurer; Young Loveless, the prodigal, and Mrs. Younglove, the abigail—very conventional.

The "Lady" is wooed persistently but vainly by the elder Loveless, whom at heart she loves, and the play is mainly occupied with the various devices he employs to force from her an avowal of love, and promise to marry. Perhaps the most striking of these is his giving over his house, etc., under the charge of his steward, Saul, to his dissolute brother, while he himself is supposed to travel, and how, under cover of pretended drowning, he practices on his mistress' affection, and watches in disguise the debauchment of his steward, and the drunken orgies of his brother and friends.

Among the many improbabilities of the play is the quietness with which the supposed to be drowned Loveless, the Elder, is received when he surprises his brother, the steward, and the rest, carousing.

The plot of yet another play, entitled "The Custom of the Country," the scene of which is laid in an Italian town and in Lisbon, is too complicated to be briefly recited. However, it is so very filthy that it is perhaps better left alone. Yet the prologue opens thus:

> So free this work is, gentlemen, from offence,
> That, we are confident, it needs no defence
> From us, or from the poets. We dare look
> On any man, that brings his table-book
> To write down what again he may repeat
> At some great table, to deserve his meat.

PHILIP MASSINGER.

As a dramatist, Philip Massinger is next in rank. He was born in 1584, at or near Wilton, the magnificent seat of the Earl of Pembroke, of which family his father was a retainer, as the poet informs us in his dedication to "The Bondman," to Philip, Earl of Pembroke and Montgomery. He probably roamed through the princely halls of Wilton, where Sidney composed his "Arcadia." Somewhere or other he obtained a classical education. All the great wits of that time, however poor, seem to have been equally fortunate this way. He entered a commoner of St. Albans' Hall, Oxford, May 14, 1602, quitting the university abruptly without a degree about 1606. Probably he went to London, and, falling in with play writers and actors, joined them. It was an exciting time in the metropolis. The visit of the King of Denmark to his august brother filled court and city with pageants, revellings and masques. "Macbeth" was then first performed, and King James is said to have written a letter of compliment to Shakespeare on it.

Massinger was shy, reserved, and inclined to melancholy. The first we hear of him definitely is between 1612 and 1614, in company with Field and Daborne, composing a nameless drama. He wrote many plays, eighteen of which survive. "The Virgin Martyr," "Bondman," "Fatal Dowry," "A New Way to Pay Old Debts," and "The City Madam," are his best known; he is skillful in the construction of his plots, but is remarkable, although eloquent, neither for imagination or pathos, and still less for wit or humor. Eight of his plays collected by John Warburton, were destroyed by his cook.

The rest of Massinger's story is little more than a list of his works, and the dates of their production. Probably he never married, and there is no hint that he ever loved. Perhaps he met Shakespeare and *sacked* with him at the Mitre or the Mermaid, though Shakespeare had retired some years before he produced his first extant play. Certainly he greatly admired and was deeply versed in Shakespeare, but he never plagiarizes.

He was always complaining, as we gather from his dedications. He felt the humiliation of patronage bitterly. He was buried in St. Saviour's churchyard, the comedians being his only mourners. No stone marked the spot, but the parish register contains this: March 20, 1639-40, buried Philip Massinger, a stranger.

The plot of many of the plays will not bear the telling, but that of "The Roman Actor" is, in respect of decency, of a better description. The scene is laid at Rome. The plot is well conceived, the characters strong, and the action very rapid. Cæsar compels Lamia to divorce Domitia, whom he makes empress, and slays Lamia. Incidently he provokes Parthenius to treason, by killing his miserly father, Philargus, and the empress to hate by killing her lover, Paris, the actor, whom he has discovered in her company. His own death is prophesied, and, though he does all he can to avoid it, he is murdered at the very time predicted by Parthenius and the empress. All throughout we are conscious of the cold shadow of fate. The language is dignified and noble; the speech of Paris in defence of actors admirable; the immorality, if equally obtrusive, is less repulsive—as being with purpose and meaning—than in other plays. The device is employed of play within play, as in "Hamlet."

"The Great Duke of Florence," the scene of which is principally in Florence, ought to be a good acting play yet. It is perfectly clean. Prince Giovanni, nephew and heir of Duke Cozmio, brought up with Lidia, fair daughter of his tutor, Charamanti, loves her. She is praised to the Duke so highly that he is smitten, and sends his favorite Sannazaro to report upon her. Sannazaro, loving her at sight, reports falsely, and prevails on Giovanni reluctantly to back him up. The Duke, puzzled by the conflicting reports, knows not what to think, until his suspicions are aroused on his niece, in love with Giovanni, and, at his request, petitioning him to permit her to have Lidia as her companion at court. She gives as her reason Giovanni's high praise of her. Suspecting a plot, the Duke suddenly visits Charamanti, to judge for himself. Giovanni and Sannazaro, in great fear, do the same, contriv-

ing to get to Charamanti's just in time to warn Lidia, and contrive
some means further to deceive the Duke.   Accordingly Petronella
(Lidia's maid) personates her mistress and at table takes too much
wine.   The Duke, disgusted, complains to her father, who, not being
in the plot, is greatly surprised, and going to his daughter, who pretends
illness, leads her to the Duke, when the ruse is discovered.   Ultimately
all ends well, as the Duke, who, in his turn, is bewitched by Lidia's
charms, on being reminded of his vows of fidelity to his late wife, considerately gives way, and pardons the scapegrace prince, etc.

Much might be made of the various complications, particularly of
Petronella's personation of her mistress, but Massinger had little sense
of humor, and misses the opportunity.   The conduct of Petronella in
the dinner scene, is so gross as to be highly offensive, and materially to
detract from the pleasure of the piece.

"The Maid of Honor," scene Sicily and the Siennese, is another
pure play, except for some slight lapses here and there.   It is well conceived and told, though the interest drags occasionally.   Bertoldo's
repeated recreancy is unnatural in such a man.   The conclusion,
though, perhaps, really all we could expect, is unsatisfactory, and "huddled up with a lame denouement."   Bertoldo, natural brother of the
king, loves in vain Camiola, "The Maid of Honor," who refuses to
accept the attentions of a knight of Malta, vowed to celibacy.   Bertoldo
makes war against the Duchess of Sienna,—the king only not openly
approving,—and is taken captive, being allowed to languish in prison,
unaided by king or friends, till Camiola ransoms him by payment of
50,000 crowns, on his promising to marry her.   Meanwhile the Duchess
of Sienna falls in love with him, returns his ransom, and succeeds in
making him promise to marry *her*.   All meet at the King's court to
celebrate the nuptials, when Camiola appears and prefers her prior
claim; whereupon the Duchess, touched by her story, resigns Bertoldo
(nothing loath) to her, and a priest is fetched to marry them, when
Camiola surprises all by renouncing the world, and wedding the Church;
first leaving one-third of her fortune to a nunnery, one-third to pious
uses, and one-third to her faithful admirer Adorni, who, spite of his
passion, had faithfully performed her instructions in pleading her suit
to Bertoldo, and ransoming him.   Finally, Bertoldo repents, is received
back into the knighthood of Malta, and again vows himself to celibacy.
It is delicately hinted that the King and Duchess may marry.

The Picture" is ingeniously contrived; the humor is sprightlier,
freer and more abundant.   The scene is laid in Hungary and Bohemia;

the situations are striking, and the picture of the two fine courtiers, spinning, reeling and hungry, in their shirts, very comical.

Mathias, a poor Bohemian nobleman, seeks his fortune in foreign war, all for the sake of his dear wife Sophia, whose magic portrait he takes with him, which its maker, the scholar Baptista, assures him will turn yellow when its original turns lustful, and black when she actually sins. Mathias so distinguishes himself in battle that king Ladislaus and his vain (but really good) and imperious Queen wish to retain him at court. The latter also loads him with jewelry, but he only asks to be allowed to go home. Piqued at his preference of his wife to herself, and that he glories in Sophia's chastity, the Queen determines to undermine the purity of both. So, by a ruse, she gets Mathias to consent to stay one month at Court, while she dispatches Ricardo and Ubalda to tempt Sophia, she herself meanwhile straining every art to seduce Mathias. These two courtiers tell Sophia that the jewels her husband sends her by them had been given him by various ladies, with whom he had been intimate. She is so enraged that she burns to be revenged, and, for a brief time, almost makes up her mind to yield to the importunings of the two knaves.

Meanwhile, Mathias, who at first rejects the Queen's overtures, enraged at seeing the magic portrait turn yellow, finally agrees to accede to her wishes, and an interview is arranged for next day. The Queen informs the King, and it is so arranged that he and his friends shall, unseen, witness the triumph over the Knight's virtue. But, when the Queen next day seeks Mathias, that gentleman has reconsidered the matter, rejects her offers of love, and reads a wholesome and richly deserved lecture to the now humiliated and penitent Queen. Seized with remorse, and realizing the silliness and wickedness of her conduct, her Majesty, with king, courtiers and all, rides post haste to Mathias' castle, to prevent, if possible, the success of the plot against Sophia's virtue. On arriving there she meets with fresh humiliation, and all the company with a ludicrous surprise; for Sophia, having, like her husband, reconsidered the matter, has had the two courtiers stripped to their shirts, and compelled to save themselves from starvation by carding, spinning and reeling, at a pittance a day, like two old women.

"The Emperor of the East," the scene of which is at Constantinople, is artistically unsatisfactory, besides being more than usually objectionable on moral grounds; yet the Prologue, spoken at "Court," says:

He durst not, Sir, at such a solemn feast,
Lard his grave matter with one scurrilous jest;
But labour'd that no passage might appear
But what the Queen without a blush might hear;
And yet this poor work suffered by the rage.
And envy of some Catos of the stage;
Yet still he hopes this Play, which then was seen
With sore eyes, and condemned out of their spleen,
May be by you, the supreme judge, set free,
And raised above the reach of calumny.

"A New Way to Pay Old Debts," the scene of which is laid in Nottinghamshire, is, in some respects, the most complete and satisfactory of all Massinger's works. Sir Giles Overreach ruins his nephew, Wellborn, through the latter's own loose life, and Wellborn, repenting in rags, by the aid of Lady Allworthy and Sir Giles' selfish and villainous steward, Marall, succeeds in recovering his lands out of which Overreach had (legally) swindled him; while the poor page to Lord Lovel weds Margaret Overreach, her father thinking she has married his lordship. Overreach goes mad, whilst Wellborn obtains a company, and begins a new life.

The device by which Wellborn recovers his lands is as bad as that by which Overreach had robbed him of them. There is less that is objectionable in this play than in the others; the characters are powerfully drawn and self-consistent. That of Sir Giles Overreach is splendidly sustained in his magnificently audacious villany ; but Greedy, on the other hand, is overdrawn and tiresome, humor not being Massinger's forte.

"The City Madam,"—scene, London, is ill-conceived, though not without ingenuity. It is meant to ridicule the airs and extravagance of would-be fashionable city ladies, astrologists, etc.

Sir John Frugal, vexed at the airs of his wife and three daughters, and believing his broken-down brother Luke to be a hypocrite, pretends to retire to a monastery, and leaves all his estates, etc., to Luke. The daughters, advised by their mother, and the astrologer, Stargazer, insult their honest lovers by their preposterous pretensions, but, on Luke assuming the reins, all is changed. In place of fine clothes and dainty dishes, they are meanly clad and poorly fed. Finally, Sir John quietly reappears, when Luke is deposed in disgrace; mother and daughters are humble and repentant; these last are reconciled to their lovers, and all ends well. To his wife and daughters, Sir John, in the concluding lines, drives home the moral—

> Make you good
> Your promised reformation, and instruct
> Our city dames, whom wealth makes proud, to move
> In their own spheres ; and willingly to confess
> In their habits, manners and their highest port,
> A distance 'twixt the City and the Court.

"The Guardian" is one of the most ingenious and pleasing of Massinger's plays; though some of the incidents,—as poor Calipso taking Iolante's place, and having her nose cut off by Severnio,—are highly improbable. The scene is laid in Naples.

Calista, daughter of Iolante and Severino (banished for the supposed murder of his brother Monteclaro, and turned high-minded bandit), loves, but is rejected as wife by, the libertine Adoris. She is loved, however, by Caldoris, whose lustful, but good-natured and hot-tempered uncle, Durazzio, seconds him. At last Adoris agrees to elope with and marry Calista, the same night that Iolante is to receive at supper a strange Frenchman, Laval. Accidentally, in the dark, Calista's maid is carried off in mistake for her mistress by Adoris, with whom she is secretly in love, while Calista, stumbling into Caldoris' arms, rides off, in mistake, with him. The same night, Severino, on whose head is a reward, secretly visits his house, to find Iolante, loosely and voluptuously dressed, at the sumptuously furnished supper table. He binds her, puts out the lights, and retires for a knife. Calipso, her maid, takes her place, and, in the dark, is slashed and hacked by the madly jealous Severino, while Laval is dismissed by Iolante. In the morning she relieves her maid, and, obtaining the forgiveness of Severino, by the pretended miracle of an instantaneous recovery from her wounds, accompanies him back to the forest. His banditti capture the rest of the *dramatis personæ*, including the disguised King Alphonso, who, moved by Severino's generous conduct (which he proves by a stratagem), pardons all. Laval turns out to be the supposed dead brother, Monteclaro; Calista is discovered to be well-born, and the curtain is rung down on a double marriage.

In this play we have recalled to mind "Two Gentlemen of Verona."

Massinger's blank verse is graceful and flowing, but feeble in the endings; sometimes degenerating into very indifferent prose. The extreme suddenness of love is common to all the plays, which it will be observed are always made to end happily, Massinger probably not being of a robust enough nature to contemplate a purely tragic ending. The finish is invariably two or four lines of moral in rhyme, as:

> So, all ends in peace now,
> And, to all married men, be this a caution,
> Which they should duly tender as their life
> Neither to dote too much, nor doubt a wife.

JOHN FORD.

This dramatist, who was born in 1586, and died in 1639, came of a good Devonshire family; was bred to the law, and had the singular good fortune to be of independent means, rather scorning to live by his pen, and only writing to please himself. Charles Lamb considered him of the first order of poets. His blank verse as soft and musical. He excelled in depicting scenes that awaken tenderness and pathos. In tragedy he is often terrible, but in comedy, weak. His choice of subjects was unfortunate. Hartley Coleridge says of him, that "he delighted in the sensation of intellectual power; he found himself strong in the imagination of crime and agony; his moral sense was gratified by indignation at the dark possibilities of sin, by compassion for rare extremes of suffering. He abhorred vice, he admired virtue; but ordinary vice and virtue were to him as light wine to a dram drinker. His genius was a telescope—ill adapted for neighboring objects, but powerful to bring within the sphere of vision what nature has wisely placed at an unsociable distance. Unquestionably he displayed great *power* in these horrors, which was all he desired; but had he been of the first order of poets, he would have found and displayed superior powers in familiar matters of to-day—in failings to which all are liable, virtues which all may practice, sorrows for which all may be the better." His titles frequently suggest the modern sensational novel, "Brother and Sister," "Love's Sacrifice," "The Broken Heart," "The Lovers' Melancholy." He is the author of about a dozen plays that have survived.

"The Broken Heart," the scene of which is laid in Sparta, is in many respects a noble drama, informed by a lofty purpose, and a sublime morality. The story is well told, and the characters, though too much alike, are firmly drawn.

Penthea is forced against her dead father's wish, by her brother Ithocles (otherwise a noble soul, who bitterly repents this action afterward) to marry the insanely jealous Bassanes, and give up her lover Orgilus. The latter finally pretends a friendship for Ithocles, who is enamoured of the Princess Calantha. Penthea, going mad, starves herself to death. Orgilus leads Ithocles on his marriage day to her bedside, and, as he sits, his chair fastens upon him like a vise. Thus fixed he is stabbed by Orgilus, and dies nobly. The king dying at this crisis, Calantha becomes queen, and, sentencing Orgilus to lose his life, he chooses to bleed himself to death. Calantha disposes of the kingdom, and dies of a broken heart upon the body of Ithocles, on whose finger she has placed her mother's wedding ring.

"Perkin Warbeck," the scene of which is laid in England and Scotland, is a noble play, pure and wholesome. Warbeck's character is greatly planned and greatly executed. Impostor or not (he was never an impostor consciously), he was a hero and died a king. Kate's constant love is touchingly described, as also the noble Dalzel's hopeless constancy to her. Edward Seventh's character is true to tradition, and well presented. King James, having less individuality (perhaps because artistically less prominent), is a less successful effort. The subordinate characters are firmly sketched, and Huntley's hearing to his daughter, when he stays her in her constancy to her husband, whom all the time he believes to be a pretender, is nobly conceived. Warbeck's speeches and bearing uniformly princely.

The scene of " The Elder Brother " is laid in France; the plot and *motif* are both sketchy, but the main idea—the change of Charles from a book-worm into a man of action, and of his brother from a fashionable fop and libertine, into a gallant gentleman, by the force of circumstances acting upon them—is pleasantly developed. The generous, level-headed, out-spoken and quick-tempered old Miramont, though conventional [see "The Lady of Lyons"] is a vigorous portraiture, and the characters of the two brothers are distinctly drawn and happily contrasted. Old Andrew, also, is a life-like character, full of color and life. The remaining figures are too subordinate to call for notice, or are unsatisfactory.

Though many of the characters bear French names, and the scene is laid in France, they are English to the backbone, notably Brisac, a justice of the peace, and his serving man Andrew.

Brisac, having two sons, Charles, the elder, a book-worm; and Eustace, an affected courtier, whose native nobility has been dwarfed and led astray by the influence of depraved courtiers, espouses Eustace to Angellina, daughter of Lewis, a French lord. To provide a suitable marriage portion he has arranged to disinherit Charles, in spite of the vigorous remonstrances of his rich brother Miramont. When asked, however, to sign the deed of renunciation, Charles demands to be confronted with the bride, whom seeing, he loves right off; and love, awakening in him ambition and native energy, he promptly asserts his rights, and, by the moving magic of his tongue, wins the affections of Angellina.   Disowned by their parents, the lovers escape to Miramont's house, and Lewis and Brisac quarrel.   The latter turns Eustace and his courtier friends out of doors for cowards, bidding them go bring back Angellina.   They surprise the lovers at night, in the absence of Miramont, only, however, to be ignominiously defeated and driven forth by Charles.   Awakened to a sense of his position and degradation by the gross cowardice of his courtier friends, Eustace drives them from him, and, determined to regain his reputation and bride, waylays Charles, when they fight.   Miramont returning, interferes, when news comes that Lewis, with law officers, has captured and carried off both Brisac and Angellina.   Eustace and Charles shake hands, and all start off in pursuit.   On overtaking Lewis and company, the arguments of old Miramont prevail, and all ends happily.

Charles' speeches are full of fine feeling and imagery.

" Rule a Wife and Have a Wife," the scene of which is Valladolid, is an admirable play; spirited, full of life, intrigue, manners, morals and incidents.   The character of Leon is boldly and vigorously drawn; his wit quick, fertile and to the occasion apt; his action noble; his language dignified and manly.   The prologue faintly and half-heartedly apologizes, and not without need, for the poet's slipping aside lasciviously, if not too wide; advising the ladies of the audience to " hold your fans close, and then smile at ease; " and carefully remarking that, the scene being laid in Spain, no reflection is meant to be made on English ladies and manners, for " no such gross errors in your kingdom reign."

As usual in the plays, though the *locate* is foreign, the personages are native; their names are Spanish, they themselves are English.   The only novelty in the way of character-drawing is that of Cacafrago, a rich usurer, who is fat and a glutton.

"The Queen of Corinth " illustrates the triumph of purity over vice. " The Knight of the Burning Pestle " is a stupid attempt to imitate or parody Don Quixote.   The best part of it, and this is very good, is the dramatic and life-like characters of the critics, citizen and his wife, who sit among the spectators and accompany the play with a running fire of amusing criticisms, suggestions and orders.

" The Double Marriage," the scene of which is laid in Naples, is most unsatisfactory and unnatural, yet not without a strain of high nobility and purity. It opens nobly. "The Knight of Malta," is, in some respects one of the best of these plays, the incidents being so rapid and exciting that the reader has no eye for the absurdities, and conflictings of situation and character, but is hurried breathless to the happy conclusion. A noble spirit animates the whole, the moral being the superiority of temperance and self restraint, and the degrading and demoralizing effects of yielding to passion. "Love's Cure; or the Martial Maid," scene Seville, has the humorous element strong, and, for a miracle good; in some parts being full of Shakespearian breadth, variety, quickness, ease and point.

Regarding Ford, Gifford says, "I know few things more difficult to account for than the deep and lasting impression made by the more exalted portions of Ford's poetry."

Other names which may be mentioned, and with which this most brilliant period closes, are Webster, author of the "Duchess of Malfi," a wholesale dealer in murders and ghosts. Chapman, notable as the first English translator of Homer, and last of all Shirley, the author of some forty dramatic pieces that have come down to us.

By an act of the Long Parliament, September 2, 1642, theatrical entertainments were put an end to.

SYNOPSIS LECTURE XVIII.

SUBJECT—TOM HOOD—1799-1845.

INTRODUCTORY.—Hood's strong hold on the sympathies of his country-men was his intense humanity and genuine humor. Short names given to those we love best.

Lives of authors, apart from their books, barren in incident and romance. That of Hood a record of suffering and trouble, with stray gleams of sunshine, home pleasures and a happy nature to relieve the dark outline of his life.

HIS LIFE.—Born in London, the son of a Scotchman, at his father's death apprenticed to an engraver, which trade not agreeing with his health he went to Scotland, where he made his first appearance as an author. His success greatly influenced his after life. In 1821, as sub-editor of "The London Magazine," he wrote his first verses, entitled "To Hope." Three years later he married, and in 1834, becoming involved in pecuniary difficulties, he removed to the continent where he stayed six years. In 1841 he was appointed editor of "The New Monthly Magazine," and on January 1, 1844, he started a magazine of his own entitled "Hood's Magazine," which, through lack of funds had to be given up. May 3, 1845, Hood died, in his forty-sixth year.

CHARACTERISTICS OF HIS GENIUS.—Style, simple and forcible. The prince of wits. The magician of words. Main features of his humor, good nature, ease and naturalness. His fame as a wit hurt his reputation as a poet. Verse clear and musical, his language direct and strong, his poetry, like his heart, was fresh. In Hood were united the intellect of a man, the heart of a child, the glowing fancy and airy imagination of the poet, and the practical common sense of a man of business.

TOM HOOD.

We give short names to those whom we love best. It would sound as oddly to talk of Sir Richard Steele or Mr. Thomas Hood, as to call Milton "Jack," or Browning "Bobby." Our admiration for the writings and genius of the author of "Paradise Lost," is, of course, greater than what we entertain for those of Steele or Hood, yet we love the latter as men more than we love Milton. Dante, Bacon, Kant and Goethe are elevated by their strength of genius beyond the range of our complete sympathies. Our admiration of them is more of the intellect than of the heart. Steele, Lamb and Hood, on the other hand, are more like ourselves; we love them for their intense humanity; for the very weaknesses that help to draw them within the circle of our affinities. Tom Hood is one of ourselves, an intimate friend, a member of our family, with whom we can laugh and be merry, and to whom we can tell our secrets and chat in pleasant, homely fashion. We visit him in our ordinary clothes, not being compelled to put on full dress. In his company we are at home, as if we had been intimate with him from boyhood, and can fancy at times that we hear his quiet laugh, his merry quip, and see the pleasant smile that lit up his pale, solemn face.

The lives of authors, apart from their books, each successive publication of which may be likened to a great battle, are proverbially barren of incident and romance, and that of Tom Hood is but a record of suffering and trouble, unrelieved by aught save a few stray gleams of sunshine, by the affectionate caresses of a loving wife and children, and by the never-failing halo of a happy nature which served to brighten the dark outlines of his life.

Tom Hood was born 1799, in London. His father was a native of Scotland, who had traveled southward in search of fortune, and, like most Scotchmen of a migratory nature, never returned to his native country. Scotchmen, it has been said, are only at home when abroad, and Hood was a typical Scotchman. He was, from all accounts, a good man of business, and held in respect for his social and moral

virtues. His family consisted of James, Thomas and four daughters.
James died at an early age, of consumption, which ultimately carried
off his mother and two sisters. The lines entitled "A Deathbed,"—
among the most touching in the language—were written by Hood on
the death of his sister Anne, and originally appeared (less one verse) in
a Glasgow University Album. They are full of the fine tenderness
and sweet affectionateness which in later years developed into such
rare perfection; a tenderness and sympathy that were constantly gushing over into rhythmical expression at the sight of a wretched needle-
woman, or a drowned Magdalen, as at the recollection of a dying
friend or sister.

> " We watched her breathing through the night,
>   Her breathing soft and low;
> As in her breast the waves of life
>   Kept heaving to and fro.
>
> So silently we seemed to speak,
>   So slowly moved about;
> As we had lent her half our powers
>   To eke her living out.
>
> Our very hopes belied our fears,
>   Our fears our hopes belied;
> We thought her dying when she slept,
>   And sleeping when she died.
>
> For when the morn came, dim and sad,
>   And chill with early showers,
> Her quiet eyelids closed; she had
>   Another morn than ours."

The elder Hood died not long afterward, leaving his widow and
children slenderly provided for, and Tom, not to encroach on their
scanty means, was articled to his uncle, Mr. Sands, an engraver. The
knowledge and experience acquired while there proved of great use in
after life, enabling him to illustrate his own jokes with cuts, rude and
inartistic, it is true, but very characteristic, and sometimes only less
comical than the jokes themselves. The confinement and drudgery of
the business, however, soon told upon his health, and he was shipped
off to some relatives in Dundee. How he spent his time in Scotland is
not known; but pleasantly enough, we have reason to believe, and
greatly to the benefit of his health. While in Dundee he made his first
appearance as an author in the *Dundee Advertiser*, now one of the most

influential and enterprising of British journals. He gives a pleasant account of his boyish delight on first seeing himself in print, which contrasts rather sadly with some remarks on the same subject which he let fall many years afterward, in a letter to his friend, Mons. de Franck, half-pay officer in the Prussian army. The latter had been accusing Hood of laziness in writing, on which the poet replies: "What a noise you make about my silence! Why didn't *you* write in the interval? You, you, you who have half-pay for doing nothing, whereas I am only half-paid for doing everything. Besides, I have to write till I am sick of the sight of pen, ink and paper; but it *must* be a change to you to scribble a bit after your fishing, shooting, boar-hunting, and the rest of your idle business at Antonine. *You* know what leisure is; I don't."

To him who can read between the lines, these words are full of suggestive pathos, revealing how great the difference between their writer's ideas of authorship in 1843, when he had reached the topmost round of the ladder, and his ideas on the same point some twenty years before, when stealthily, and with trembling hand, he dropped his first verses into the editorial box of a provincial newspaper?

His small literary success in Dundee greatly influenced his after life, for from this time he gradually drifted—like most literary men—into authorship, to which he had naturally a strong leaning; his father having been a man of cultivated taste and literary attainments, a partner in the publishing firm of Vernor & Hood, and himself the author of two novels.

In 1821 Hood returned to London, and was soon installed as subeditor of the "London Magazine." He eagerly took advantage of the opening afforded him, and was soon busily engaged in the duties of a literary life. His first original paper appeared in the July number for 1821, in some verses "To Hope," and he shortly afterwards became a regular contributor. His turn for humor shows itself in his answers to correspondents, some of which are very amusing, *e. g.*: "H. B.'s sonnet to the 'Rising Sun' is suspected of having been written for *a lark*;" "'The Echo' will not answer;" "W. is informed that his 'Night' is too long, for the moon rises twice in it," and so on. Hood's connection with the "London" was the means of introducing him to many friends, among his fellow-contributors being bright-eyed, loving, stuttering Charley Lamb, with his small spare body and finely-shaped head; fair-faced Coleridge, with his waving hair, grave smile and girlish complexion; poor Clare, in bright green coat, and seedy yellow waistcoat; De Quincey, with his dreamy eyes and pinched face, "sicklied o'er with a

pale cast of thought;" Hazlitt, whose fine spirit disappointment was fast
souring, and the pink-and-white purity of whose complexion gave the
lie to the pointless sneer of pimple-nose, with which the Blackwood
bullies were never tired of pelting him; the large-browed Barry Cornwall, Allan Cunningham, Judge Talfourd, Horace Smith, and other
literary celebrities.   Amongst his closest friends was John Hamilton
Reynolds, who wrote some pleasant articles in prose and verse, under
the *nom de plume* of "Edward Herbert."   This friendship, unfortunate
in the end, had an important bearing on Hood's life, for through it he
became acquainted with his friend's sister, Jane Reynolds, whom he
married on May 5th, 1824.   Authors, and particularly poets, are proverbially unfortunate in their marriages.   Socrates, Job, Milton, Byron,
Shelley, with many others, have been unhappy in their wives.   It js
pleasant, therefore, to know that Hood's case was a bright exception.
Despite the sorrows, hardships, and life-long disease that crippled his
energies and marred his life, the union was a singularly happy one.
Mrs. Hood was a woman of cultivated mind, great moral worth, and
literary sympathies.   She was her husband's constant nurse through
an illness that never left him; cheered him when heavy of heart, acted
as amanuensis, and during the last few years of his life, so devoted to
him her time and thought that latterly Hood became restless and unable to write unless she were near.   Seldom have the words of the great
novelist, who was almost a great poet, been more nobly exemplified
than in the person of Mrs. Hood:

> "O, woman!   *   *   *
> When pain and anguish wring the brow,
> A ministering angel thou!"

She needed a sweet temper to put up with a husband so brim full of fun
and practical jokes as Hood.   Nothing seemed to ruffle her temper,
and she was always ready to join in the laugh, even when against herself.   Strange still, no matter how often or how badly her husband
fooled her, she was always ready to trust him blindly again, and again
he fooled more outrageously than ever.   The reason was that she knew
him so well and loved him so dearly.   Nothing could shake her confidence in him, and he knew it and took advantage of the fact.   She had
to keep a strict watch on every letter she wrote, for if she left it for any
time in Hood's presence, he would take advantage of her absence to
change the 't's' into 'l's', the 'l's' into 't's', and after interlining here
and there the most extraordinary statements, to add, by way of climax,

some ludicrously absurd postscript. Their children tell us that she was a capital subject for his fun, for she believed implicitly in whatever he told her, however improbable, and though seriously vowing not to be taken in again, she was sure to be caught. Her innocent face of wonder and belief added greatly to the zest of the jokes. On one occasion, when living at the coast, Hood gave his wife some useful hints on buying fish. "Above all things, Jane," said he, "as they will endeavor to impose upon your inexperience, let nothing induce you to buy a plaice that has any appearance of red or orange spots, as they are sure signs of an advanced stage of decomposition." Accordingly Mrs. Hood, on the faith of her newly-acquired knowledge, was quite prepared to do battle with the crafty fisherwoman, one of whom called shortly afterwards. As it happened the woman had nothing but plaice, which she turned over and over, praising their freshness and beauty. Mrs. Hood was too sharp; *she* was not be taken in; the obnoxious spots were there. In vain the fisherwoman protested that they were fresh from the water. The cautious buyer gravely shook her head, and with a look of satisfied wisdom, not without a certain sad pity for the woman's supposed dishonesty, observed, "My good woman, it may be as you say, but I could never think of buying any plaice with those very unpleasant red spots." "Lor' bless yer eyes, Mum!" ejaculated the astounded fisherwoman, "who ever seed plaice *without* spots?" A suppressed giggle on the stairs behind her revealed the joke, and, turning her head hastily, Mrs. Hood caught sight of her husband's coat-tails, as the owner hurriedly disappeared in an ecstasy of laughter leaving her to appease the angry sea-nymph as she could.

The most careless reader of Hood's life cannot help being being struck with the happiness of the poet and his family in the midst of continual difficulties and broken health. Mrs. Hood is constantly talking of her husband. Her private letters teem with sentences beginning "Hood said this;" "Hood did that;" "Hood took me to such a place." The lovableness of the man manifests itself in his life and poetry. He was essentially a family man; joking with his wife, contriving all sorts of tricks and games for his children, and after a severe night's work stealing into their bedroom to leave upon their pillow some comical sketch to amuse them on waking.

The first few years of his married life were the most unclouded Hood ever knew, and he much needed some little happiness to hoard up against the bitter years that were fast coming. The young couple lived for some years in Robert street, Adelphi. Hood was a thorough

Cockney, and though doomed by the fault of others to pass the best part of his life on the continent, was never at home out of London. Only a city-bred man, one familiar with the misery and squalor of city life, could have written the "Song of the Shirt." His first child did not long survive its birth. The parents felt the disappointment keenly, for, on turning over some old papers after Hood's death, his children came upon a tiny curl of golden hair, wrapped in a yellow, time-worn paper, on which were inscribed, in their father's handwriting, these lines:

> " Little eyes that scarce could see,
>   Little lips that never smiled,
>   Alas! my little, dear, dead child,
> Death is thy father and not me,
> I but embraced thee, soon as he! "

About this time, conjointly with his brother-in-law, Hood published anonymously his "Odes and Addresses to Great People." The little work had a large sale, and much speculation was excited as to its author; Coleridge, with others, attributing it to Charles Lamb. In 1826 appeared the first series of "Whims and Oddities," which took so well that a second edition followed next year. In the same year appeared his "Plea for the Midsummer Fairies," in which the author's exquisitely delicate fancy runs riot in very prodigality of wit. The poem, however, failed to hit the public taste, and sold so badly that the author bought up the remainder of the edition "to save it," as he himself ruefully remarked, "from the butter shop."

In 1829 he removed with his family to the country, first to Winchester, and next to the Lake House, which latter place suggested some of the best descriptions in his novel of "Tylney Hall." In 1830—the year in which Tom Hood, the younger, was born—appeared the first "Comic Annual," which proved a success, and was the means of widening the author's circle of admirers. Among those to whom it introduced him was the Duke of Devonshire, who wrote Hood a kindly letter, with the request that he would supply him with a set of titles for a door of sham books. Among those sent were these: "Dante's Inferno; or, a Description of Van Demon's Land;" "On Cutting off Heirs with a Shilling," by Barber Beaumont; "Percy Vere," in 40 vols.; "Lamb, on the Death of Wolfe;" "Pygmalion," by Lord Bacon; "Memoirs of Mrs. Mountain," by Ben Lomond; "Rules for Punctuation," by a thoroughbred Pointer; "Cursory Remarks on Swearing;" "Recollections of Bannister," by Lord Stair; "Life of Jack Ketch," with cuts of his own execution; "Tadpoles,

or Tales out of my own Head;" Barrow on the Common Weal," etc.
From this time the "Comic Annual" appeared regularly, and by 1833
its author had become pretty well known to the general public. At the
end of 1834, by the failure of a firm, Hood became involved in pecuniary
difficulties. He strove hard to recover himself, but resisted the advice
of his friends to have recourse to the Bankruptcy Court. Emulating
the example of another illustrious Scotchman, he determined to wipe
out his debts with his pen, with which view, leaving his all to his cred·
itors, he sailed for the continent. In the face of failing health, a
doubtful future, and his wife's being left behind through illness, Hood
kept up a brave heart, resolved to see nothing but the bright side of the
picture. The letters which he wrote Mrs. Hood at this time are very
touching:

"I saw a vision of you, dearest, to-day," he writes, "and felt you
leaning on me, and looking over the Moselle at the blue mountains and
vineyards. I long but to get to work with you and the pigeon pair by
my side, and then I shall not sigh for the past. Only cast aside sea
fears and you will find your voyage a pleasant one. * * * * *
Get yourself strong, there is still a happy future; fix your eyes forward
on our meeting, my best and dearest. Our little home, though homely,
will be happy for us, and we do not bid England a very long good-night
—good-night, too, my dearest wife, my pride and comfort!"

He then goes on in a postscript to make suggestions as to the best
mode of traveling, and closes:

"May God have all those I love, or who love me, in his holy keeping, is the prayer of the subscribed,

THOMAS HOOD.

Mrs. Hood followed in March, 1839, and in the lovely little town of
Coblenz, with its vineyards and ruin-crested mountains, and the broad
Rhine and blue Moselle flowing pleasantly through, Hood settled down
to hard work. His spirits were singularly elastic, and each fresh misfortune served to stimulate his energies. He had set before him an
honorable task—the payment of his debts—and he was determined that
nothing should hinder him in his work. The Germans—with whom,
although cousins, he was not on "speaking" terms—afforded a capital
butt for his wit. His private letters to friends in England are filled
with the drollest accounts of how he got on abroad. Hood is the
"Mark Tapley" of letters; never so happy as when he should be most
wretched. His German neighbors swindled him on every side. The
fact of his being English was sufficient reason for charging him thirty

or thirty-five per cent on everything. "I had some shirts," he writes, "made here, and they not only changed the cloth I had bought for them, but sent me home some so laughably short, I could only make *shift* with them; yet this was a respectable shop." Indeed, he was afraid that if many more Englishmen came over there would be a revolution, not that "they would desire to remove their king, but that they would wish their *sovereign* to go farther." "He was even surprised," he remarks, "to get sweet milk, the Germans having such a *turn* for everything *sour*." The climate, too, affected his health unfavorably. He was constantly suffering from violent spasms of the chest, coughing, ague, and blood-spitting, and, to crown all, the doctors proved themselves to be leeches indeed. Like the rest of their countrymen, they bled him so unmercifully that he grew weak and thin. "I heard the other day," he writes, "of a man who had no fewer than thirty-five leeches on his thigh. The man who bled me, and there are several bleeders here, told me he had attended eighty patients that month! One of the blisters would *draw* a wagon." He made at least one pleasant friend during his first summer at Coblenz, in the person of the young Prussian officer to whom I have already referred—Mons. de Franck—a brave, kindly, handsome young fellow, who was Hood's constant companion in all his fishing rambles, and was in the habit of dropping in of an evening in a friendly way to play cribbage with the poet and his wife. Through all his ill-health Hood worked hard. The public at home, that laughed over the quaint quips and cuts which the never-failing "Comic" brought them, little thought with what pain and difficulty its mirth-inspiring pages were written. Yet, day by day, and often far into the night, the scratch of the pen was heard in his little room, and when, as often happened, the writer was so exhausted as to be unable to hold it, propped up by pillows, he still dictated to his wife the never-failing flow of fancy and wit. Some of Mrs. Hood's letters home are amusing: "Did you," she writes, "ever hear of bathing in malt? It is a German remedy. You see written up here: 'Beer, Brewery and Bath House;' Hood (always Hood) will have it they bathe in beer; he thinks the little children may be done in small beer." In 1836 the monotony of the poet's life was pleasantly varied. His friend De Franck, with his brother officers—for Hood was a favorite everywhere—prevailed on him to accompany the regiment on their march to Bromberg. His account of his military life is very humorous, and although the accommodations was often very bad—one house, where an officer was billeted, being so ruinous that his dog simply stood and

howled at it—Hood enjoyed himself thoroughly. He was much delighted to find that his clerical appearance exempted him from the payment of tolls, the tollkeepers all taking him for a chaplain. In the
beginning of 1837 he finally made up his mind to leave Coblenz. It
was high time. The air of the place was killing him, and after his
friend De Franck had left he felt lonely. For the first time he grew
really alarmed, and through all his fun at this time there runs an under-
note of sadness. At Ostend, whither he removed next, he lived for
some time, and found the place pleasant enough, but its miasmatic
swamps and mists were worse even than the alternated extremes of
heat and cold at Coblenz. Still he liked Ostend (as he tried to like
every place), and one feels almost angry at his contentedness in a
country whose climate was killing him by inches. His friend Dr.
Elliott at length prevailed on him to return to England in 1840, and
was thus the means of prolonging his life a few years more. From this
time the shadows deepen round him. One attack of illness succeeded
another. He was often so weak as to be unable to move, and not un-
frequently was attacked by several ailments at once.

In 1841 a gleam of sunshine gladdened his life. On the death of
Theodore Hook he was appointed editor of the "New Monthly Magazine," at a salary of £300 a year, independently of what his own articles might bring. Shortly before, in the same periodical, he wrote his
famous poem, "Miss Kilmansegg and her Golden Leg." At the close
of the same year he removed to St. John's Wood, where he now and
then gave cosy little dinner parties to his literary friends. We met him
in the July of '42, at a dinner given to Dickens, at which he was to
have presided, but modestly gave way, on the plea of ill-health, in favor
of Captain Marryatt. Among the company were Monckton, Milnes,
Charles and Tom Landseer, Barry Cornwall, Ingoldsby (Barham),
Cruikshank, Father Prout and Ainsworth. The dinner went off happily.
Dickens made a speech in which he hinted that the great advantage of
going to America was the pleasure of coming back; Ingoldsby chanted
a Robin Hood ballad; Cruikshank sang a comical burlesque; Father
Prout sang the "Deep, Deep Sea," in a deep, deep, voice; and a Manchester friend of Ainsworth sang a Manchester ditty so full of trading-
stuff that, as Hood remarked, it really seemed to have been, *not composed*, but manufactured, and everybody was *quite at home in dining out*.
Upon his own health being drunk, Hood explained that a certain
trembling of his hand was not from palsy or ague, but an inclination
to shake itself with every one present.

Meanwhile he was working merrily, and, on his health and fortune improving, he paid a second visit to Scotland, where he met William Chambers, and passed some happy hours with Blackwood, Moir and Lord Jeffrey. Unfortunately it was vacation time in the University, and he had not the good fortune to meet Napier and Professor Wilson, but, on the whole, he was greatly pleased with the land of his fathers. In the Christmas number of *Punch* for 1843 appeared the "Song of the Shirt." For the first time Hood really caught the ear of the world as a singer. The song went straight to the heart of the nation; it was copied into every paper, the verses were on every tongue, and little boys sang it in the streets. Who is not familiar with its simple and intense pathos. Next to "The Bridge of Sighs" it marks the highest limit of Hood's genius, and its moral is of a kind that, unfortunately, needs enforcement today quite as much as it did fifty years ago. Let me once more recall to you the pitiful picture of the poor London needlewoman as she croons to herself the heart-broken refrain:

Stitch, stitch, stitch.

Hood's connection with the "New Monthly" soon ceased, and he started a magazine of his own entitled "Hood's Magazine," which appeared on January 1, 1844. His new speculation promised well; the list of contributors comprised most of the well-known literary men of the day, and the magazine had a large sale, yet owing to failure of funds on the proprietor's part it came to a sudden end. So great was the esteem in which Hood was held that many acquaintances came forward at this juncture, with offers of gratuitous service. Mrs. S. C. Hall, at that time an entire stranger, offered to send him sketches for his magazine only stipulating that she should name her own terms, the payment to be the pleasure she would feel in assisting, however humbly in the success of his periodical, as a tribute of veneration to the author of the 'Song of the Shirt.'" Nor was the failure of the magazine the only blow. His health gave way under the vexations, never to return. Yet, in the midst of all his illness and troubles, like a nightingale singing in the stormy dark, he composed many of his best songs; the "Haunted House," the "Lady's Dream," "The Laborer's Lay," and "The Bridge of Sighs," having appeared in rapid succession. Towards the close of the year the clouds lifted momentarily. Sir Robert Peel proposed that a yearly pension of £100 should be conferred on him. The pension was granted but came too late. The brave heart that had kept up so long, and made a very music of its sadness, at last gave in. The Xmas num:-

ber of the magazine had come out, sparkling with fun and merriment. "Mrs. Peck's Pudding," and its grotesque illustrations, afforded seasonable Xmas amusement at every fireside but the author's own. *His* family knew too well the state of his health to enjoy his jokes. He was so ill that he did not even attempt to be cheerful, but growing silent as he felt the shadows of the unseen steal over him, he prepared to meet his end. On Xmas Day he crawled into his little dressing-room for a few hours, that his family might be cheered on that day at least by signs of returning health, but it was a painful mockery of enjoyment. Shortly after he rallied once more at the call of the January number of the magazine, and, with the determination to die in harness, wrote some of his best sketches propped up in bed. At the beginning of the year '45 he was so sure of his end, and withal, so resigned, that he wrote farewells to his most intimate friends. "Among these," writes his son, "one to the late Dr. Moir (better known as Δ) is so touching and simple, and so characteristic of his patience and resignation," that we cannot help quoting it.

"DEAR MOIR:—God bless you and yours, and good bye! I drop these few lines as in a battle from a ship water-logged, and on the brink of foundering, being in the last stage of dropsical debility; but, though suffering in body, serene in mind. So, without reversing my union jack, I await my last lurch, till which, believe me, dear Moir,

Yours most truly,
THOMAS HOOD."

In the February number of his magazine appeared the last verses Hood ever wrote, verses not unworthy a dying poet.

> "Farewell, Life! my senses swim;
> And the world is growing dim;
> Thronging shadows cloud the light,
> Like the advent of the night,—
> Colder, colder, colder still,
> Upward steals a vapor chill—
> Strong the earthly odor grows,
> I smell the Mould above the Rose.
>
> Cloudy fears and shapes forlorn
> Fly like shadows at the morn,—
> O'er the earth there comes a bloom—
> Sunny light for sullen gloom,
> Warm perfume for vapors cold,
> I smell the Rose above the Mould!"

"We shall never forget," write his children, "one night, when his mind was wandering, his repeating the lovely lines by Lady Nairn:"

> "I'm wearin' awa', Jean, [His wife's name.]
> Like snow weather in thaw, Jean!
> I'm wearin' awa'—
>   To the land o' the leal !
> But weep na, my ain Jean,—
> The world's cares are vain, Jean,
> We'll meet and be fair,
>   In the land of the leal!"

Even in his last moments, in a letter to Sir R. Peel (in which, by the way, the irrepressible pun breaks out), he advocates the cause of humanity, and expressed his sorrow, *not* at dying, but at his inability to do anything to lessen the moral gulf that separates rich and poor,—a gulf which some of his own writings might seem tended to widen. All that affection could prompt, or science do for him was done. Dickens and Ward, with other literary friends, proffered him assistance. Game, fruit and wine came from unknown hands, and among other touching proofs of esteem, was an envelope enclosing a bank note for £20, and bearing these words, in a foreign hand:

> "A Shirt,
> And a sincere wish for health."

A stranger sent his coachman daily to lift the invalid to his easy chair, and a lady sent violets from the country, on hearing that he loved their odor. All was of no avail. Spring came with her quiet balm and beauty, and just when the flowers were struggling into blossom, and nature was astir with life, the gentle spirit that had loved her so well, and embalmed her praises in choicest verse, passed away:

> "His quiet eyelids closed; he had
> Another morn than ours."

As the hour of final parting approached the dying poet kissed his children, and clasping his wife's hand said, "Remember, Jane, I forgive all—*all*—as I hope to be forgiven." He lay for some time peacefully breathing, slowly and with difficulty. His wife, bending over him, heard him murmur faintly, "O Lord! say 'Arise, take up thy cross and follow Me!'" His last words were, "Dying—dying!" as if glad to realize the rest implied in them. He then sank into what seemed a deep slumber, which lasted till Friday, and at noon on Saturday, May 3, 1845, he breathed his last without a struggle or a sigh.

His funeral was quiet and private, and the weary brain that had given to the world so many gentle fancies and immortal songs, lay still for ever 'neath the sod of Kensal Green Cemetery. I shall conclude this hasty sketch of the life of one of the truest, kindliest and most manly characters in history, with the exquisite sonnet in which he himself contrasts False Poets and True:

"Look, how the lark soars upward and is gone,
  Turning a spirit as he nears the sky!
  His voice is heard, but body there is none
    So fix the vague excursions of the eye,
    So, poet's songs are with us, though they die.
  Obscured and hid by death's oblivious shroud,
    And earth inherits the rich melody,
  Like raining music from the morning cloud,
    Their voices reach us through the lapse of space;
  Yet few there be who pipe so sweet and loud;
  The noisy day is deafened by a crowd
    Of undistinguished birds, a twittering race;
  But only lark and nightingale forlorn
  Fill up the silences of night and morn."

Thomas Hood was the prince of wits. His nature was so steeped in the choicest spirit of humor that it constantly bubbled up and over in quip and jest. He was the magician of words, ruling language with a despotic sway, and compelling it to perform the strangest antics. His style is the perfection of simplicity and force. The words are mostly Saxon words with which we are all familiar, and they are chosen with consummate taste. Hood wrote like a child—from the heart; artlessly, naturally; yet, with what wisdom and wit, and "tears and laughters for all times!" The continued popularity of his humorous writings is wonderful, if we bear in mind the evanescent nature of wit, and especially of that form of it which we call "punning." A flash, a sudden contrast, a laugh, and all is over; the heartiness of the laughter being proportionate to the suddenness of the surprise, and we can only be surprised once. The best joke misses fire on repetition. Like champagne, its virtues escape in the effervescence. Yet, for all this, Hood's works are more generally read and admired to-day than ever. Wherein, then, lies the secret of their popularity? Other comic annuals grow stale; time robs them of their flavor and steals their charm, but "Hood's Own" is as fresh and mirth-inspiring to-day as when it

first appeared.   The secret lies here.   Through all Hood's comicalities
we are conscious of an under current of truth, modesty and fresh, child-
like humor, and, paradoxical as it may appear, of an intense spirit of
sad earnestness.   This man, who was wont to tickle the world into
laughter, was yet not always merry himself.   His tears were as often
tears of pain as of joy, and he sometimes put on a sunny face to hide
from his friends the agony that gnawed within.

With all his modesty, too, Hood was conscious, as no great nature
can help being, of his great powers, and their partial though necessary
misapplication.   He felt that he was meant to be something better than
an inspired jester, and because the world denied him leisure to indulge
his aspirations he fretted silently.   His writings, bristling with merriment, his comic sketches, his inimitable puns, are but the by-play of a
soul fitted for nobler things; for though

> " *   *   *   His wit was like Ithuriel's spear,
>   Yet 'twas mere lightning from the cloud of his life
>   Which held at heart most rich and blessed rain
>   Of tears melodious, that are worlds of love;
>   And rainbows, that would bridge from earth to heaven;
>   And light that should have shown like Joshua's sun
>   Above our long death-grapple with the wrong;
>   And thunder-voices, with their words of fire,
>   To melt the slave's chain and the tyrant's crown—
>   His wit?—a kind smile just to hearten us!
>   Rich foam-wreaths on the waves of lavish life,
>   That flasht o'er precious pearls and golden sands."

His real work lay in another direction, and it was chiefly because
he had hungry mouths to feed, and a family to support, that he so often
wore the jester's cap and bells.   His flashes of humor were not un-
frequently but the outcome of a mind ill at ease, and seeking relief
from pain; the spindriff of his soul's agony.

The world was quick to discover and appreciate his wealth of wit,
and, regardless of the author, insisted upon drawing upon it; more
willing, as it ever is, to pay highly for what would make it laugh than
for what would make it think and weep.   What could poor Hood do?
He knew that he was meant for other and nobler work, but the public,
and, in consequence, the publishers, would have it; and in the background were near ones and dear ones needing to be fed and clothed.
Yet how worthily he fulfilled his task!   It is hard to exaggerate the
temptation which a writer who is constantly expected to be witty, must

often have to overstep the limits of good taste. Yet in all Hood's writings there is not a line which could offend the most fastidious taste. The main feature of his humor, like his nature, is its good-nature, ease and naturalness.   There is nothing sour in his philosophy or his verse; his wit is never ill-natured, always kindly, considerate, humane.   His best jokes, too, are so simple that it is often difficult to detect them at once.   He tells his stories with so. grave a face, that the rogue imposes on us for a moment.   What could be simpler, for instance, than the following straightforward matter-of-fact statement?

> "And Christians love in the turf to lie,
> Not in watery graves to be;
> Nay, the very fishes would *sooner die*
> On the land than in the sea."

Of course they would "die sooner", but they would sooner not die at all.   Or take this little quartette on a " Picture of Hero and Leander"

> "Why, Lover, why
> Such a water rover?
> Would she love thee more
> For coming half seas over?
>
> Why, Lady, why
> So in love with dipping?
> Must a lad of Greece
> Come all over dripping?
>
> Why, Cupid, why
> Make the passage brighter?
> Were not any boat
> Better than a lighter?
>
> Why, Madame, why
> So intrusive standing?
> Must thou be on the stair
> When he's on the landing?"

Or the so well-known "pathetic ballad":

FAITHLESS NELLY GRAY.

> Ben Battle was a soldier bold,
> And used to war's alarms;
> But a cannon-ball took off his legs,
> So he laid down his arms!

Now as they bore him off the field,
  Said he, "Let others shoot,
For here I leave my second leg,
  And the Forty-second foot!"

The army-surgeons made him limbs;
  Said he,—"They're only pegs,
But there's as wooden members quite,
  As represent my legs!"

Now Ben he loved a pretty maid,
  Her name was Nelly Gray;
So he went to pay her his devours,
  When he'd devoured his pay!

But when he called on Nelly Gray,
  She made him quite a scoff;
And when she saw his wooden legs
  Began to take them off.

"O Nelly Gray! O Nelly Gray!
  Is this your love so warm?
The love that loves a scarlet coat,
  Should be more uniform!"

Said she, "I loved a soldier once,
  For he was blithe and brave;
But I will never have a man
  With both legs in the grave!

Before you had those timber toes,
  Your love I did allow,
But then, you know, you stand upon
  Another footing now!"

"O Nelly Gray! O Nelly Gray!
  For all your jeering speeches,
At duty's call I left my legs
  In Badajos' *breaches!*"

"Why then," said she, "you've lost the feet
  Of legs in war's alarms,
And now you cannot wear your shoes
  Upon your feat of arms!"

"O, false and fickle Nelly Gray:
  I know why you refuse:—
Though I've no feet—some other man
  Is standing in my shoes!

I wish I ne'er had seen your face;
  But, now, a long farewell!
For you will be my death;—alas!
  You will not be my *Nell!*"

Now when he went from Nelly Gray,
  His heart so heavy got—
And life was such a burthen grown,
  It made him take a knot!

So round his melancholy neck
  A rope he did entwine,
And, for a second time in life,
  Enlisted in the Line!

One end he tied around a beam,
  And then removed his pegs,
And, as his legs were off—of course,
  He soon was off his legs!

And there he hung till he was dead
  As any nail in town,—
For though distress had cut him up,
  It could not cut him down!

A dozen men sat on his corpse,
  To find out why he died—
And they buried Ben in four cross-roads,
  With a stake in his inside!

So inextricably were the lines of tragedy and comedy inter-woven in the web of his mind that even his most serious powers have sometimes a suspicion of the grotesque. An occasional verse, or phrase, or line reminds us very remotely of the laughing face lurking behind the mask, and we sometimes pause to ask ourselves is it indeed the mask or the face? His genius was so constantly hover-ing between the two that it is not easy at times to say which it meant favor.

Let us take this to ourselves, and when we grow querulous, and fret because of some little grief or passing pain, call to mind how this brave heart kept on singing and making merry in the midst of trials such as it falls to the lot of few of us to encounter. As an example of this delicate intermingling of airy humor and pathos, let me read you

I REMEMBER, I REMEMBER.

I remember, I remember,
　The house where I was born;
The little windows where the sun
　Came peeping in at morn;
He never came a wink too soon,
　Nor brought too long a day;
But now, I often wish the night
　Had borne my breath away.

I remember, I remember,
　The roses, red and white,
The violets, and the lily cups,
　Those flowers made of light!
The lilacs where the robin built,
　And where my brother set
The laburnum on his birth-day,—
　The tree is living yet!

I remember, I remember,
　Where I was used to swing,
And thought the air must rush as fresh
　As swallows on the wing;
My spirit flew in feathers then,
　That is so heavy now,
And summer pools could hardly cool
　The fever on my brow!

I remember, I remember,
　The fir-trees dark and high;
I used to think their slender tops
　Were close against the sky.
It was a childish ignorance,
　But now 'tis little joy
To know I'm farther off from heav'n
　Than when I was a boy.

Sickness in Hood's case becomes the subject of side-splitting fun, and his nimble wit can extract pleasure even from the gout. At one time, on the sudden cessation of a violent blood-spitting, he writes, in the inevitable P. S.: "Can my spitting blood have ceased because I have none left? What a subject for a German romance, 'The Blood-less Man!'" On another occasion, being prevented by illness from delivering a lecture on "The Pleasures and Advantages of Literature," to the members of the Manchester Athenæum, he wrote to the directors as follows:

"Poisoned by the malaria of the Dutch marshes, my stomach for many months resolutely set itself against fish, flesh and fowl; my appetite had no more edge than the German knife before me. But, luckily, the mental palate and digestion were still sensible and vigorous; and whilst I passed untasted every dish at the Rhenish *table d'hote*, I could still enjoy my 'Peregrine Pickle,' and the feast after the manner of the Ancients. There was no yearning toward calf's head à-la-tortue, or sheep's heart; but I could still relish Head-à-la-Brunnen, and the 'Heart of Mid-Lothian.' * * * Denied beef, I had Bulwer and Cowper; forbidden mutton, there was Lamb; and, in lieu of pork, the great Bacon or Hogg. Then, as to beverage; it was hard, doubtless, for a Christian to set his face, like a Turk, against the juice of the grape. But, eschewing wine, I had still my Butler, and in the absence of liquor, all the choice spirits, from Tom Browne to Tom Moore. * * *
Of evils, great and small, Providence has allotted me a full share; but still, paradoxical as it may sound, my *burthen* has been greatly lightened by a *load of books*. Everybody has heard of the two Kilkenny cats, who devoured each other; but it is not so generally known that they left behind them an orphan kitten, which, true to its breed, began to eat itself up, till it was diverted from the operation by a mouse. Now, the human mind, under vexation, is like that kitten; it is apt to prey upon itself, unless drawn off by a new object, and none better for the purpose than a book. For example, one of Defoe's; for who, in reading his thrilling 'History of the Great Plague,' would not be reconciled to a few little ones ?"

Children and dogs are proverbially fond of good men, and, with both, Hood was a favorite. Like Shelley in some things, he resembled him in this, that he never outgrew his boyhood. He delighted in contriving puzzles with which to amuse the little ones, and his appearance in their midst was always the signal for noisy happiness. He stole into their hearts on all fours. He—whose word commanded the ear of the world—could yet adapt his thoughts and language to the comprehension of the youngest, and write just such a letter as a child might write if it only had Hood's wit. Witness those charming letters of his to the children of his friend, Doctor Elliott. In a letter to the youngest, he writes :

"MY DEAR MAY:—How do *you* like the sea? Not much, perhaps; it's so 'big.' But shouldn't you like a nice little ocean that you could put into a pan? Have the waves run after you yet, and turned your two

little shoes into pumps full of water? Have you been bathed yet in the
sea, and were you afraid? I was, the first time, and, dear me, how
I kicked and screamed! or, at least, meant to scream, but the sea—
ships and all—began to run into my mouth, and so I shut up. Did
you ever try, like a crab, to run two ways at once? See if you can do
it, for it is good fun; never mind tumbling over yourself a little at
first. It would be a good plan to hire a little crab for an hour a day, to
teach baby to crawl if he can't walk, and if I was his mamma I would,
too. Bless him! But I must not write on him any more—he is so soft,
and I have nothing but steel pens. And now, good-bye! The last fair
breeze I blew dozens of kisses for you, but the wind changed, and, I am
afraid, took them all to Miss H——; or somebody that it shouldn't.''

And to another sister the following very characteristic letter:

"MY DEAR JEANNIE:—So, you are at Sandgate! If you should catch a
big crab, with long claws, and like experiments, you can shut him up in
a cupboard with a loaf of sugar, and see whether he will break it with
his nippers. Besides crabs, I used to find jelly-fish on the beach, made,
it seemed to me, of sea-calves' feet, and no sherry. There were star-
fish, also, but they did not shine till they were stinking. I hope you
like the sea; I always did when I was a child, which was about two years
ago. Sometimes it makes such a fizzing and foaming I wonder some of
our London cheats do not bottle it up and sell it for ginger pop. When
the sea is too rough, if you pour the sweet oil out of the cruet *all* over
it, and wait for a calm, it will be quite smooth—much smoother than a
dressed salad. Some time ago *exactly*, there used to be large white
birds, with black-tipped wings, that went flying and screaming over the
sea. Do you ever see such birds? We used to call them "gulls" but
they didn't mind it.

Well, how happy you must be! Childhood is such a joyous merry
time, and I often wish I was two or three children; and wouldn't I pull
off my three pairs of shoes and socks, and go paddling in the sea up to
my six knees; and oh, how I should climb up the downs and roll down
the ups on my three backs and stomachs.''

Hood's fame as a wit has hurt his reputation as a poet. For ten
who can appreciate his puns, not one can appreciate his poetry. Men
were slow to believe that a man who could joke so well could succeed
in aught else, forgetting that sorrow and joy, gravity and wit, are but
the complements of each other; reverse sides of the same coin.

Hood's verse is clear and musical; at times recalling Shelley, as in the fragment "Verses in an Album."

"Far above the hollow
    Tempest and its moan
Singeth bright Apollo
    In his golden zone ;
Cloud doth never shade him,
Nor a storm invade him
    On his joyous throne.

So when I behold me
    In an orb as bright,
How thy soul doth fold me
    In its throne of light !
Sorrow never paineth,
Nor a care attaineth,
    To that blessed height."

His mind was steeped in the spirit of Elizabethan literature. In his verse we catch once more an echo of a by-gone age; the fresh, quaint flavor of times when thought was simpler; the strong, clear, tinkling language of a people who spoke their mind. His verse is clear and ringing as a bell; it falls on the ear like pleasant music—not a note but is in tune. At times, especially in his early poems, we light on some pretty conceit or affectation, reminding us of Herbert or Quarles, but generally his language is strong, direct and simple. The terseness of his lines is often Shakespearian, and his "Hero and Leander" has the true Spenserian ring. His poetry, like his heart, was fresh:

"His hymns, bright noted as a bird's,
    Arousing these song-sleepy times
With rhapsodies of perfect words,
    Ruled by returning kiss of rhymes."

I have left myself no space for criticism of his poems *seriatim*, but would recommend to your perusal the " Plea of the Midsummer Fairies," that exquisite poem of Elf-land; "Miss Killmansegg and her Precious Leg," and the " Haunted House," one of the most perfect pictures of still life to be found in poetry. But what, after all, was Hood's finest poem was his life, and his noblest monument the forward place he occupied in the war of that great army of reformers, that, always swelling, marches grandly on to ever-increasing victories over prejudice and wrong. The simple record of Tom Hood's life by his

children is a nobler monument even than that erected to his memory
in Kensal Green by a sorrowing public.   His life was poetry:

> "Not a lyric, sudden-flashing from the frenzy of the strife,
> But an Epic swelling grandly onward to the close of life;
> Noble Epic! but the prelude of a nobler song to come,
> That shall peal when all the nations of the universe are dumb.

It has been maintained, with some show of justice, that poets, because of their keener sensibilities and finer tastes, are necessarily thin-
skinned and irritable.   And, to some extent the charge is true.   They
are more keenly alive than ordinary men to joyous as to saddening influences.   "The slings and arrows of outrageous fortune," that fall
back blunted from the thicker hides of their neighbors, sting their's
with exquisite pain.   But that this is at best only a half-truth is sufficiently attested by the life of Hood, which shows that a man may combine the most delicate fancy, the tenderest heart, and the nimblest wit
with a strong, healthy contempt of danger; a sturdy perseverance in
the face of odds, a fearless heart that never knows defeat, and a happy
nature that, ever welling up through pain and sorrow, keeps fresh and
cool the dusty paths of life.   In Hood were united the intellect of a
man, the heart of a child, the glowing fancy and airy imagination of
the poet, and the practical common sense of a man of business.   The
world was to him one large family, of which his own was the central
point, from which his sympathies radiated to every airt.

Beyond an amiable weakness for titles, and a slight tendency to
sentimental sensationalism which tinges some of his best poems, we can
find nothing to blame in Hood, unless it be the occasional aimlessness
of his wit, and the folly of frittering away his powers in jest and pun;
and this, as I have already said, was not so much his fault as the
public's.

To such of you as may think this praise extravagant, all I can say is
"study his life for yourselves."   However much we may admire Hood
as a man and humorist, his claims on the suffrages of the future rest on
surer and higher grounds.   His life, though noble, would have been
forgotten; his stores of wit and humor, his comical cuts and side-splitting ballads would, in the process of years be quickly swept aside, had
he not arisen at a critical moment to give voice to the inarticulate cry
of wretchedness, ignorance and want, and gather up in one sublime
ode, and direct aright the hazy sentimentalism and ill-directed philanthropy that were floating about in society.   While some were dis-

cussing Utopian schemes for the social reform of far-distant savages, forgetting that charity begins at home; and others, disgusted by the mass of wretchedness and vice that festered hourly before their eyes, folded their arms and looked sadly on in dumb despair—this man went straight to the root of the matter, and by a divine instinct, succeeded in touching the great common heart of humanity that throbs and beats beneath all distinctions of race, class, politics and caste.

Finally, Hood was not one of those men of commanding intellect, who arise but once or twice at most in a nation's history. He did not signalize himself by being the first to climb the slippery steps of Pisgah and catch sublime glances of the promised land, with which to gladden men's hearts. He is no cold, unapproachable idol of the intellect, to be worshipped from afar with awe and trembling. Rather is he enshrined amid the Oliver Goldsmiths, and Charles Lambs, and Philip Sidneys, and Walter Scotts, and Henry Wadsworths, and Longfellows; a kind, genial, honest-headed man of genius, whom one feels it is good to have known and pleasant to remember; whose laugh has a hearty ring wherewith to blow away the cobwebs of sorrow and care; and the shake of whose hand does one's heart good. There have been three or four greater writers in English literature, and a few more as great, but there has been no one whose efforts on behalf of the poor, the outcast, and the fallen have embalmed his memory in a kindlier affection and regard than Thomas Hood, the darling of the English heart.

SYNOPSIS LECTURE XIX.

SUBJECT—GEORGE ELIOT—1819–1880.

HER LIFE.—Born at Arbury Farm. Character of father. Removal to Griff; character of country about Griff. Mother's character and delicacy. Sent to school when very young. Her love for her brother. Subject to nightmare. Her father's pet; drives with him about the country. First journey to Staffordshire. Education; religious impressions. Riot at Nuneaton. Mother's death. Marriage of sister; gets sole charge of house. Letters to Miss Lewis. First visit to London with brother. Objections to fiction reading. First poem. Removal to Foleshill Road, Coventry. New friends. Excursion with the Brays. Makes translation of Strauss' "Leben Jesu;" joy at finishing; pleasure in Strauss' letter. Visit to Dover with father. Letters to Miss Sara Hennel. Strain of father's illness and death in 1849. Goes abroad with Mr. and Mrs. Bray, staying at Geneva until following spring; returns to England and takes up her abode at Rosehill with the Brays. Meets Dr. Chapman; goes to London as assistant editor of the *Westminster Review*, meets all the literary men of mark; amongst whom Mr. Lewes, with whom she goes to the continent; returning to England, they travel and live together, Mr. Lewes inducing her to begin her life work of novel writing. Her great love for him. Mr. Lewes' death. Married to J. W. Cross May 6, 1879, died December 22, 1880.

AS A NOVELIST.—Chief characteristics, perfect intelligence; immense flexibility of sympathy, perfect power of reproducing the surface of things. A wonderful power of writing effective dialogue. A quiet undercurrent of half sympathetic, half contemptuous humor; and lastly, great accuracy and beauty of style. Most of her writings autobiographical.

As a Humorist.—Her reputation rests on her realistic pictures of the humorous of the old generation before the time of railways or telegraphs, as in McGilfil, etc.

As a Poet.—The idea subordinates the matter to its will; her foundation is conscience, the moral perceptions and the moral will. Abstract the ethical interest from her poems and there is a total collapse of design, characters and incident.

GEORGE ELIOT.

A talk, not a lecture,—and at the outset I am conscious of a strong
sense of diffidence—George Eliot is not an ordinary writer, to be dismissed after a brief study and in a short hour's talk. I approach her
with something of the feeling of embarrassment and almost veneration
with which, with unsandaled feet, I venture to touch the hem of Shakespeare's garment.

Embarrassment, because her works present so many points for criticism; can be approached from so many sides,—the artistic, the narrative, the romantic, the poetic, the philosophic, the tragic, the pathetic,
the humorous and what not.

What I should like to do—would be to give four lectures. As it is
I shall briefly study her as:

First. A woman—her life.

Second. As a novelist, humorist and poet.

And lastly, as an influential and potent factor in the forces that
influence men's lives, and help to shape the character of coming
generations.

Mary Ann Evans was born November 22, 1819, at Arbury Farm,
Chilvers Coton, afterwards immortalized by its Sheperton church. Her
father, Robert Evans, was land agent and surveyor to five estates in
Warwickshire. In this capacity he was highly respected, and his reputation for trustworthiness may be said to have been proverbial. Mary
Ann was the youngest of three children by a second marriage, Mr.
Evans having also a son and daughter by his first. In 1820 removed to
Griff—charming, red brick, ivy-covered house on the Arbury estate
where George Eliot spent the first twenty-one years of her life. The
house stood at a bend of the highroad between Coventry an . Nuneaton, and within two miles of the mining village of Dedworth,—the
landscape and scenes around have been transfigured into many an
idyllic picture by George Eliot.

"Here were powerful men walking queerly, with knees bent outward
from squatting in the mine, going home to throw themselves down

in their blackened flannel and sleep through the daylight, then rise
and spend much of their high wages at the alehouse with their fellows
of the Benefit Club; here the pale, eager faces of handloom weav-
ers, men and women, haggard from sitting up late at night to finish the
week's work hardly begun to the Wednesday. Everywhere the cottages
and small children were dirty, for their languid mothers gave their
strength to the loom; pious dissenting women, perhaps, who took life
patiently, and thought that salvation depended chiefly on predestina-
tion, and not at all on cleanliness. The gables of dissenting chapels
now made a visible sign of religion, and of a meeting place to counter-
balance the ale-house, even in the hamlets.   *   *   Yet there
were the gray steeples too, and the churchyards with their grassy
mounds and venerable headstones, sleeping in the sunlight; there were
broad fields and homesteads, and fine old woods covering a rising
ground, or stretching far by the roadside, allowing only a peep at the
park and mansion which they shut in from the working-day world." In
these midland districts the traveler passed rapidly from one phase of
life to another; after looking down on a village dingy with coal dust,
noisy with the shaking of looms, he might skirt a parish all of fields,
high hedges and deep-rutted lanes; after the coach had rattled over
the pavement of a manufacturing town, the scene of riots and trades-
union meetings, it would take him in another ten minutes into a rural
region, where the neighborhood of the town was only felt in the
advantages of a near market for corn, cheese and hay, and where men,
with a considerable banking account, were accustomed to say "they
never meddled with politics themselves." Two coaches passed the
door daily and were the chief connecting links between the household
at Grif and the outside world. Otherwise life went on with that monotonous regularity which distinguishes the country from the town. And
it is to these circumstances of her early life that a great part of the
quality of George Eliot's writing is due, and that she holds the place
she has attained in English literature. Her roots were down in the
pre-railroad, pre-telegraphic period—the days of fine old leisure—but
the fruit was formed during an era of extraordinary activity in scientific
and mechanical discovery. Her genius was the outcome of these conditions. It would not have existed in the same form deprived of either
influence. Her father was already known for his knowledge and judgment in all matters relating to land, and for his general trustworthiness
and high character, so that he was always busy. His position cannot
be better summed than in the words of his daughter written in regard

to some one who had written of her, after the appearance of "Adam Bede," as a "self-educated farmer's daughter."

"My father did not raise himself from being an artisan to be a farmer; he raised himself from being an artisan to be a man whose extensive knowledge in very varied practical departments made his services valued through several counties. He had large knowledge of building, of mines, of plantations, of various branches of valuation and measurement—of all that is essential to the management of large estates. He was held by those competent to judge as *unique* among land agents for his manifold knowledge and experience, which enabled him to save the special fees usually paid by land owners for special opinions on the different questions incident to the proprietorship of land."

Mr. Evans was also noteworthy for physical strength and determination of character. With all this strength, however, he seemed to have combined a certain self-distrust, owing perhaps to his earlier imperfect education. His second wife was a woman with an unusual amount of natural force; a shrewd, practical person, warm-hearted and affectionate. She came of a race of yeomen and her family are, no doubt prototypes of the Dodsons in the "Mill on the Floss." Her health having broken down, the children were sent at an early age to school. As characteristic of George Eliot's childhood the following anecdote is related by Mr. Charles Lewes. When four years old she recollected playing on the piano, of which she did not know one note, in order to impress the servant with her abilities. This was the time when the love for her brother grew into the child's affections. She used always to be at his heels, insisting on doing everything he did. She was not, in these balmy days, in the least precocious in learning. Mere sharpness was not a characteristic of her mind, hers was a large, slow-growing nature. In her moral development she showed the absolute need of some one who should be all in all to her, and she to him. It is to this happy period of her life she refers in the brother and sister sonnet:

"But were another childhood's world my share,
I would be born a little sister there."

When her brother was eight years old he was sent to school at Coventry, and her mother continuing in very delicate health, she was sent along with her sister to school at Attleboro, where they continued as boarders for three or four years, occasionally getting home to Griff on Sundays. The other girls in the school, who were all, naturally, very much older, made a great pet of the child, and used to call her "little mamma." At this time she began to be subject to fears at night—"the susceptibility to terror"—which she has described as haunting Gwendolen Harleth in her childhood. This nightmare influenced her whole life. Her brother's chief recollection of this period is the delight of the little sister at his home-coming for holidays, and her anxiety to know all he had been doing and learning. She was her father's pet, and from a very early age he was in the habit of taking her with him in his drives about the neighborhood.

Her fondness for reading at this time became a passion with her, and was deepened by the fact that her brother had a pony given to him, so that he cared less for his sister's company. Her first journey from home took place in 1826, when she accompanied her father and mother into Derbyshire and Staffordshire. In her eighth year she was sent to a larger school at Nuneaton with her sister. The principal governess was Miss Lewis, who became her most intimate friend, and afterwards principal correspondent. Every book she could lay hands on she now read, and it must have been about this time that the episode occurred in relation to "Waverley," which is given in the *Century Review* of June, 1881: "Somewhere about 1827, a friendly neighbor lent 'Waverley' to an elder sister of little Mary Ann Evans. It was returned before the child had read to the end, and, in her distress at the loss of the fascinating volume, she began to write out the story as far as she had read it for herself; beginning naturally where the story begins with Waverley's adventures at Tully Veolan, and continuing until the surprised elders were moved to get her the book again." A very pointed reference to this is the following lines from the motto of the fifty-seventh chapter of "Middlemarch":

> " They numbered scarce eight summers when a name
> Rose on their souls and stirred such motions there
> As thrill the buds and shape their hidden frame
> At penetration of the quickening air :
> His name who told of loyal Evan Dhu,
> Of quaint Bradwardine, and Vich Ian Vor,
> Making the little world their childhood knew
> Large with a land of mountain, lake and scaur,
> And larger yet with wonder, love, belief
> Towards Walter Scott, who, living far away,
> Sent them this wealth of joy and noble grief—
> The book and they must part, but, day by day,
> In lines that thwart like portly spiders ran,
> They wrote the tale, from Tully Veolan."

We know, too, from the "Mill on the Floss," that the "History of the Devil," by Daniel Defoe, was a favorite. "The Pilgrim's Progress," also, and " Rasselas " had a large share of her affections.

At school the growing girl soon distinguished herself, and, on her returning home, she and her brother acted charades very cleverly. She was now recognized in the family circle as no ordinary child. In her thirteenth year she was sent to a Miss Franklin's school at Coventry. She was probably then very much what she has described her own Maggie at the age of thirteen.

"A creature full of eager, passionate longings for all that was beautiful and glad; thirsty for all knowledge; with an ear straining after dreamy music that died away and would not come near to her; with a blind, unconscious yearning for something that would link together the wonderful impressions of this mysterious life, and give her soul a sense of home in it. No wonder, when there is this contrast between the outward and the inward, that painful collisions come of it.

This year, 1832, was not only memorable for the change to a new and superior school, but it was also much more memorable to George Eliot for the riot which she saw at Nuneaton, on the occasion of the election for North Warwickshire, after the passing of the great reform bill, and which subsequently furnished her with the incidents for the riot in "Felix Holt." In the summer of 1836 her mother died, after a long illness, and in the following spring her sister was married to a surgeon, practicing at Meriden, in Warwickshire; thus the entire charge of the Griff establishment devolved on Mary Ann, who became a most exemplary housewife. But with all her work she was also prosecuting an active, intellectual life of her own. A master of languages from Coventry came over regularly and gave her lessons in Italian and German, and a Mr. McEwan continued her lessons in music. For a young girl such a life must have been very monotonous, no doubt this and the narrow field it presented for observation of society added immeasurably to the intensity of a naturally keen mental vision, and though the field of observation was narrow in one sense, it included every various grades of society. In 1838 she visited London with her brother, and was deeply affected at hearing the great bell of St. Paul's; as at this time she was deeply religious and ascetic. She would not even accompany her brother to the theatres, but stayed at home reading.

Her letters at this period are steeped in an intense piety: "O, that I might be made as useful in my lonely and obscure station as he

(Wilberforce) in the exalted one assigned to him! I feel myself to be a mere cumberer of the ground. May the Lord give me such an insight into what is truly good, that I may not rest contented with making Christianity a mere addendum to my pursuits, or with tacking it as a fringe to my garments! May I seek to be sanctified wholly!" And it is the spirit of all the letters of this period of her life.

In this same letter, referring to an oratorio at Coventry, she says she has no soul for music, and yet, two years later, at the Birmingham Festival, 1840, just previous to her brother's marriage, she was affected to hysterical sobbing, and in all her after years music was one of the chiefest delights to her, and especially oratorios.

In answer to a letter of Miss Lewis, she writes a curious letter on the bad effects of novels, stating that she had no time to spend on things that never existed.

In the next letter there is the first allusion to authorship, as follows:

"I send you some doggerel lines, the crude fruit of a lonely walk last evening, when the words of one of our martyrs occurred to me: 'Knowing that shortly I must put off this my tabernacle.'"—2 PETER, 1:14.

> " As o'er the fields by evening's light I stray,
>   I hear a still, small whisper, come away;
>   Thou must to this bright, lovely world soon say,
>   Farewell!
>
>   The mandate I'd obey, my lamp prepare,
>   Gird up my garments, give my soul to pray'r,
>   And say to earth, and all that breathe earth's air,
>   Farewell!
>
>   Thou sun, to whose parental beam I owe
>   All that has gladden'd me while here below,
>   Moon, stars, and covenant confirming bow
>   Farewell!
>
>   Ye verdant meads, fair blossoms, stately trees,
>   Sweet song of birds and soothing hum of bees,
>   Refreshing odors wafted on the breeze,
>   Farewell!
>
>   Ye patient servants of creation's Lord,
>   Whose mighty strength is govern'd by his word,
>   Who raiment, food and help in toil afford,
>   Farewell!

Books that have been to me as chests of gold,
Which, miser like, I secretly have told,
And for them love, health, friendship, peace have sold,
                              Farewell!

Blest volume! whose clear truth-writ page once known,
Fades not before heaven's sunshine, or hell's moan,
To thee I say, not of earth's gifts alone,
                              Farewell!

There shall my new-born senses find new joy,
New sounds, new sights, my eyes and ears employ,
Nor fear that word that here brings sad alloy,
                              Farewell!

In 1841 they removed from Griff to Foleshill, near Coventry. Here, with ample means and leisure, her real education began. She took lessons in Greek and Latin from the Rev. T. Sheepshanks, then head master of the Coventry Grammar School, and she acquired French, German and Italian from Signor Brezzi. An acquaintance with Hebrew was the result of her own unaided efforts. From Mr. Simms, the veteran organist of St. Michael's, Coventry, she received lessons in music, although it was her own fine musical sense which made her in after years an admirable piano player. Nothing once learned escaped her marvelous memory; and her keen sympathy with all human feelings, in which lay the secret of her power of discriminating character, caused a constant fund of knowledge to flow into her treasure house from the social world about her. Among the intimate friends whom she made in Coventry, were Mr. and Mrs. Charles Bray—both well-known in literary circles. In Mr. Bray's family she found sympathy with her ardent love of knowledge, and with the more enlightened views that had begun to supplant those under which (as she had described it) her spirit had been grievously burdened. Emerson, Froude, George Combe, Robert Mackay, and many other men of mark, were at various times guests at Rosehill while Miss Evans was there.

This was in 1844, when working at Strauss six hours a day, and her feelings at this period of her life will be best stated in a letter dated Sunday, May of that year, to Miss Sarah Hennel.

"To begin with business, I send you, on the other side, the translations you wished (Strauss), but they are perhaps no improvements on what you have done. I shall be very glad to learn from you the particulars as to the mode of publication—who are the parties that will find the funds, and whether the manuscripts are to be put into the hands of any one when complete, or whether they are to go directly from me to the publishers? I was very foolish not to imagine about these things in the first instance, but ways and means are always after thoughts with me.

" You will soon be settled and enjoying the blessed spring and summer time. I hope you are looking forward to it with as much delight as I. *One has to spend so many years in learning how to be happy.* I am just beginning to make some progress in the science, and I hope to disprove Young's theory that 'as soon as we have found the key of life it ope's the gates of death.' Every year strips us at least of one vain expectation, and teaches us to reckon some solid good in its stead. *I never will believe that our youngest days are our happiest.* What a miserable augury for the progress of the race and the destination of the individual in the more matured and enlightened state is the less happy one! Childhood is only the beautiful and happy time in contemplation and retrospect; to the child it is full of deep sorrows, the meaning of which is unknown. Witness colic and whooping-cough, and dread of ghosts, to say nothing of hell and Satan, and an offended Deity in the sky, who was angry when I wanted too much plum cake. Then the sorrows of older persons, which children see but cannot understand, are worse than all. All this to prove that we are happier than when we were seven years old, and that we shall be happier when we are forty than we are now, which I call a comfortable doctrine and one worth trying to believe!"

The labor of rendering Strauss' masterpiece into clear, idiomatic English was by no means light, yet she completed her task of translating the "Leben Jesu" in one year, and had the satisfaction of being complimented by Strauss upon the success that had attended her efforts. Such an undertaking by a young woman of twenty-five may certainly be ranked among the marvels of literature.

As characteristic of her life at this period read the following extracts from her letters. "Another little trip with the Brays to the Cumberland Lakes." "This lovely autumn! Have you enjoyed its *long shadows* and fresh breezes?" "I am quite happy, only sometimes feeling the weight of all this unintelligible world." Or her references to books she had been reading: "What an *exquisite* little thing that is of Harriet Martineau's, 'The Crofton Boys.' I have had some delightful crying over it." "I received 'Sybil' yesterday, quite safely. I am not utterly disgusted with D'Israeli. The man hath good veins, as Bacon would say, but there is not enough blood in them."

Her study deserves a passing mention. It was a little room on the first floor, with a charming view over the country, and an ivory image of the crucified Christ over the desk.

In August, 1846, we find her first allusion to Dr. Chapman in a letter written to Miss Hennel, asking if he would have any unusual facilities for obtaining cheap classics, as she wanted to complete Xenophon's Works. In the same letter she writes: "I have been reading the 'Fawn of Sertorius.' I think you would like it, though the many would not. It is pure, chaste and classic, beyond any attempt at fiction I ever read. If it be Bulwer's, he has been undergoing a gradual transfiguration, and is now ready to be exalted into the assembly of the saints.

"Many things, both outward and inward, have occurred to make this November far happier than the last. One's thoughts

'Are widened with the process of the suns;'

and if one is rather doubtful whether one is really wiser or better, it is some comfort to know that the desire to be so is more pure and dominant. I have been thinking of that most beautiful passage in Luke's Gospel—the appearance of Jesus to the disciples at Emmaus. How universal in its significance! The soul that has hopelessly followed its Jesus—its impersonation of the highest and the best—all in despondency; its thoughts all refuted, its dreams all dissipated. Then comes another Jesus—another, but the same—the same highest and best, only chastened—crucified, instead of triumphant—and the soul learns that this is the true way to conquest and glory. And then there is the burning of the heart, which assures that 'this was the Lord!'—that this is the inspiration from above, the true comforter that leads unto truth. But I am not become a Methodist, dear Sara; on the contrary, if I am pious one day, you may be sure I was very wicked the day before, and shall be so again the next."

In her letters there is noticeable a deep undercurrent, which every now and then reveals the gradual change of her opinions on religion.

As, for instance, in her first letter to Mr. John Sibree, she says: "I must write to you *more meo*, without taking pains or laboring to be *spirituelle* when Heaven never meant me to be so. I am glad you detest Mrs. Hannah More's letters. I like neither her letters, nor her books, nor her character. She was that most disagreeable of all monsters, a blue-stocking—a monster that can only exist in a miserably false state of society, in which a woman with but a smattering of learning or philosophy is classed along with singing mice and card-playing pigs." Or in this other, written shortly after to the same gentleman.

"It was impossible to think of your career with hope, while you tacitly subscribed to the miserable *etiquette* (it deserves no better or more spiritual name) of sectarianism. Only persevere; be true, firm, and loving; not too anxious about immediate usefulness to others—that can only be a result of justice to yourself. Study mental hygiene. Take large doses of *dolce far niente*, and be in no great hurry about anything in this vassal world! Do we not commit ourselves to sleep, and so resign all care for ourselves every night; lay ourselves gently on the bosom of nature or God? A beautiful reproach to the spirit of some religionists and ultra good people."

In May of 1848 Mr. Evans and his daughter went to St. Leonard's, and remained there until the end of June. His mortal illness had now taken hold of him, and this was a depressing time for both.

On her return to Coventry in July she met Emerson, who was on a visit to the Brays. All she says herself about it is, "I have seen Emerson—the first man I have ever seen." In a letter to Mr. Bray at this time we have her first hint as to her own views of marriage: "I have read 'Jane Eyre' and shall be glad to know what you admire in it. All self-sacrifice is good, but one would like it to be in a somewhat nobler cause than *that of a diabolical law which chains a man, soul and body, to a putrefying carcass.* However, the book is interesting; only I wish the characters would talk a little less like the heroes and heroines of police reports." In another letter she writes: "I can only bless you for those two notes, which have emanated from you like so much ambrosial scent from roses and lavender. Not less am I grateful for the Carlyle eulogium (on Emerson). I have shed some quite delicious tears over it. This is a world worth abiding in while one man can thus venerate and love another."

But, however pleasant this staying by the wayside reading of letters may, be I must hurry on. Her father's long illness and her constant attendance on him began to tell on her health, and we find her writing: "My life is a perpetual nightmare—dear father very uneasy, and his moans distract me." On the last day of May, 1849, her father died, and in the summer of that year she accompanied her friends, the Brays, on a continental tour, they returning and leaving her behind at Geneva, where she stayed till the following spring. On her return to England she stayed with the Brays until 1851, when she was persuaded by Dr. Chapman to take up her residence in the Strand and assist him in the conduct of the *Westminster Review.* A new period now opens in George Eliot's life, and emphatically the most important period, for now she is to be thrown into contact with Mr. Lewes, who is to exercise so paramount an influence on all her future, and here, too, she met all the distinguished writers of the day: Mr. and Mrs. Geo. Combe, Mr. Herbert Spencer, Miss Frederica Bremer, Frederick Foxton, etc.

Mr. Lewes had already secured for himself a wide reputation in the literary world. Here is George Eliot's first notice of him in a letter to the Brays, October, 1851. "I was introduced to Lewes the other day in Jeff's shop—a sort of miniature Mirabeau in appearance." But it was not until later in the same year when Spencer took Lewes to call on her they were brought into close relations. As assistant editor of the *Westminster Review* she was now brought into connection with many distinguished men and women. Professors Newman and Owen, Tom Taylor, Chas. Knight, Sir David Brewster, George Cruickshank, Carlyle, J. S. Mill, W. R. Greg, Professor Forbes, Dickens, Florence Nightingale, Jas. Martineau, Mazzine, etc. Her letters are now joyous and full of life; with little stories and bits of fun. "I must tell you a bit of Louis Blanc's English, which Mr. Spencer was reciting the other night. *The petit homme* called on some one, and said "I come to tell you how you are. I was at you the other day but you were not."

"I had a pleasant talk with Greg and Foster, Greg was much pleased to have made my acquaintance. Foster, on the whole, appeared to think that people should be glad to make his acquaintance." Harriet Martineau is a trump—the only Englishwoman that possesses thoroughly the art of writing." This seems the happiest time of her life. Meeting all the best people—now at the opera with Spencer—next night at the theatre with Lewes—the third at a meeting of authors, with Dickens in the chair. On Monday evening they hold their receptions; on Thursday she hears "La Juive," and falls in love with Prince Albert,—next night she enjoys Grisi in "Norma." Everything seems bright and sunshiny. May, 1852, she writes: "My brightest spot, next to my love and *old* friends, is the deliciously calm, *new* friendship that Herbert Spencer gives me. We see each other every day, and have a delightful *camaraderie* in everything," and so, busy, let her speak for herself.

"I will just tell you how it was last Saturday, and that will give you an idea of my days. My task was to read an article of Greg's in the *North British*, on 'Taxation,' a heap of newspaper articles, and all that

J. S. Mill says on the same subject. When I had got some way into this *magnum mare*, in comes Mr. Chapman, with a thick German volume. 'Will you read enough of this to give me your opinion of it?' Then, of course, I must have a walk after lunch, and when I had sat down again, thinking I had two clear hours before dinner, rap at the door—Mr. Lewes, who, of course sits talking till the second bell rings. After dinner another visitor, and so behold me, at 11 p. m., still very far at sea on the subject of Taxation; but too tired to keep my eyes open. We had Bryant, the poet, last evening—a pleasant, quiet, elderly man." Her letters, at this time particularly interesting—with shrewd criticism of cotemporary literature of Mrs. Gaskell, Currer Bell, and others, telling how she fell in love with Helen Faucit, "the most poetic woman she had seen for a long time." How people were very good to her, especially Mr. Lewes, so kind and attentive, who had quite won her regard, being much better than he seemed,—a man of heart and conscience wearing a mask of flippancy.

As to her union with Mr. Lewes,—in forming a judgment we will take her own words. Writing to Mrs. Bray, six weeks after she and Mr. Lewes had gone to the continent, she says: "If there is any one action or relation of my life which is, and always has been, profoundly serious, it is my relation to Mr. Lewes. It is, however, natural enough that you should mistake me in many ways, for, not only are you unacquainted with Mr. Lewes's real character, but also it is several years since you and I were much together. * * * That any unworldly, unsuperstitious person who is sufficiently acquainted with the realities of life can pronounce my relation to Mr. Lewes immoral. I can only understand by remembering how subtile and complex are the influences that mould opinion. * * * We are leading no life of self-indulgence, except, indeed, that, being happy in each other, we find everything easy. * * * I should not care to vindicate myself if I did not love you and desire to relieve you of the pain which you say these conclusions have given you."

And thus Miss Evans found what had been awanting to her loving and generous nature since her father's death—some one "whose life would have been worse without her" In return we owe to Mr. Lewes the complete works of George Eliot, not one of which would have been written or even planned without the inspiriting influence of his constant encouragement, his obvious, unfeigned, unforced delight in her powers and success; his total freedom from the least inclination towards self-comparrison. And not only so, he was most careful to guard her mental independence, and for nearly a quarter of a century watched over her with a protecting love. He stood between her and the world; relieved her from all minor cares; wrote her letters, in a word he so smoothed the course of her outer life as to leave all her powers free to do what she alone could do for the world, and for the many who looked to her for help and guidance. It is, therefore, good to know that great as his reward was, it was no greater than was merited by the most faithful, perfect love that ever crowned a woman's life.

On November 28, 1878, Mr. Lewes died; for many weeks after George Eliot saw no one except Mr. Charles Lewes, and the very few persons she was obliged to receive on necessary business. She read no letters, and wrote none, but at once began to occupy herself busily with Mr. Lewes's unfinished MSS., assisted by Mr. Charles Lewes. The only entry in her diary on January 1, 1879, is, "Here I and sorrow sit." On May 6, she was married to Mr. Lewes's friend, Mr. J. W. Cross, from whose life of George Eliot I have made these few extracts. Her own death occurred on December 22, 1880. Her body rests in Highgate Cemetery, in the grave next to Mr. Lewes, where it was placed during a storm of sleet and snow, which did not deter many whom she did not know from coming with their tributes of affection.

The chief characteristics of George Eliot's writings as a novelist seem to me to be these:

1. Perfect intelligence.
2. Immense flexibility of sympathy.
3. Perfect power of reproducing the surfaces of things.
4. A wonderful power of writing effective dialogue.
5. A quiet undercurrent of half sympathetic, half contemptuous humor; and lastly,
6. Great accuracy and beauty of style.

As to this last, however, I prefer the style of her early works which have a lyrical freedom wanting in her later. They have, too, less of the subacid note, though they lack that rapid clinching and unfaltering vigor of dialogue so strong in "Felix Holt" and "Middlemarch;" where every word is a blow, and is returned with interest. But in all of them we note that extreme sensitiveness of congruity between style and thought which characterizes the supreme artist who is also a poet. Most of her writings are, to a large extent, autobiographical. "Adam Bede" is, perhaps, the most purely objective of her works, the one in which it is least possible to recognize the writer's self in any part of either of her characters. But, if we look beyond the subtle analysis of character and passion, and the fascinating idealization of rustic humor, the same profound sympathy, the same tolerant knowledge, as inspires the rare sentences of reflection, will be found underlying every passage in the drama.   The interest of the work culminates in the remarkable page before the charming scene in which Lisbeth rouses Adam to the consciousness of his new love.

In the "Mill on the Floss" the action runs more easily upon lines which have had their parallel in the author's thought and feeling, but we ought not to exaggerate the parallelism.   Read by the light of the really autobiographical sonnets of "Brother and Sister," even the tragic passages in poor little Maggie's childhood appear less painful; one is apt to undervalue the compensations, the mere increment of happiness, that comes from the "sweet skill of loving much."   But in this book the moral problems, as to what so many readers desire to know, George Eliot's thoughts, are more nearly discussed, the writer's own judgments more nearly delivered in express terms, than in any of her other works. No didatic purpose is obtruded, but here, more than anywhere else, the crisis of the story turns on the question in one of the actor's minds: What *ought* I to do?   Every one, to whom the writer is a moralist, as well as a story-teller, knows the spirit of the answer given; that she believed the force of moral obligation to lie in the keen personal *feeling* of the claims and needs of others, while the influence of such general rules of conduct as are commonly accepted seems, in her mind, associated rather with a sort of reverential custom than with the categorical imperative of speculation.

No personal bent is accepted as virtuous unless in the human relations of life it brings forth the fruits of virtue; a passion that exists by natural bias, apart from justifying conditions, is the one form of passion for which she has little sympathy to show.

In the " Mill on the Floss," again, the most general conclusion is that almost every situation has a right of its own.   That there is no royal road even to the discernment of what is really right, but that the guiding intuition comes from an upright, unselfish life, which enables the determining motive—of consideration for the good of others—to act predominatingly at last on the inmost feelings, without whose co-operation even right action is little more than uncertain and labored affectation.

When Tom and Maggie sink in the hurrying Floss there is left an aching sense of abrupt incompleteness, and imperious suspension, and intolerable arrest; and with this a sense of utter helplessness of our extremest language. The musician's band has broken the movement in the midst, and it can never be taken up again. This is cruel to all our tender desires for joy. But there is something more dreadful. When the heavens break up over the head of Silas Marner, when the lot declares him, the innocent man, guilty in the midst of the congregation of Lantern Yard; when he goes out with despair in his soul, with shaken trust in God and man, to live for weary years a life of unsocial and godless isolation, accumulating his hoard of yellow pieces, the tragedy is deeper. When the beautiful Greek awakes from his swoon beside the Arno to find no pleasant solitary lair, but the vindictive eyes of Baldassare looking down at him, and the eager knuckles at his throat, the real piteousness and terror are not that a young man is about to die, but that now the visible seal of finality is to be set upon that death of soul which had already taken place. When the story concerns itself with the ruin or restoration of moral character, every other interest becomes subordinate. The nodes of the plot from which new developments spring are often invisible spiritual events. It is a crisis, and we feel it to be such, when there falls into Maggie's hands a copy of "De Imitatione Christi"; the incident is fraught, we are at once aware, with momentous consequences.

" Father, I have not been good to you; but I will be, I will be," said Esther, "laying her head on his knee." Slight words, but words which determine an epoch. As they were uttered, self-love was cast behind, and the little action of laying her head upon her father's knee, was endowed with sacramental efficacy.

The relations that human beings can form with one another which are most intimate, most full of fate, are with George Eliot not intellectual or merely social relations, but essentially moral. Effie toddles in through the weaver's open door, and does much more than console him for his lost treasure; she is to him the sunshine and spring breeze, thawing the arrested stream of his affections, delivering him from his state of unnatural isolation, and reuniting him with his fellow-men. Edgar Tryan brings happiness to Janet, but it is by saving her soul. Felix Holt is much more than a lover; painfully divested of coats and neckties, with his somewhat formulated nobility, and his *doctrinaire* delight in exposition of principles, he yet is a genuine moral nature, and approaching Esther Lyon as a conscience approaches a conscience, and with an almost rude insistency of moral force, he becomes the discoverer to her of heroisms which lay concealed in her own dainty feminine nature. To Romola, her early love is as a morning cloud,

growing momently fainter and more distant; the one profound attachment which she forms is to her spiritual father, the man "who had been
for her an incarnation of highest motives," who had forced her to submit to the painful supremacy of conscience. Tito sells the ring—his
father's ring—and with it closes the bargain by which he sells his soul.

And yet this nature in which conscience asserts itself so sternly—so
strongly, is a nature of passionate sensibility. The pure gleaming of
gems, the perfect moulding of a woman's arm, the face of youth that is
like a flower, and its aureole of bright hair; the strong voice of the
singer that urges and controls; the exquisite movement and excitement
of the dance,—not one of these fails to find an answer in the large joy-
embracing nature of George Eliot. We recall to mind Tito's presence
in the dark library of Bardi, "like a wreath of spring dropped suddenly
in Romola's young but wintry life;" and the fascination exercised over
Adam by the sweet, rounded, blossom-like, dark eyed Hetty; and Maggie
borne along by the wave of arrogant baritone music too strong for her;
and the wonder and worship of Rufus Lyon in presence of that miracle
of grace; the Frenchwoman found by the roadside; and Fedalma
circling to the booming and ringing tambourine, under the flushed
clouds and in the midst of the spectators of the Plaça:

> 'Ardently modest, sensuously pure,
> With young delight that wonders at itself,
> And throbs as innocent as opening flowers,
> Knowing not comment, soilless, beautiful.
> *   *   *   *   *   *
> All gathering influences culminate,
> And urge Fedalma. Earth and heaven seem one,
> Life a glad trembling on the outer edge
> Of unknown rapture."

Her sympathy indeed was so many-sided she had no patience with
those who thought life dull, and in her earliest works—in the "Scenes
of Clerical Life" especially, the interestingness of commonplace lives
is insisted on.

She had an intensely acute sensibility.

In her later works, most of all in "Middlemarch," she ventures to
give the largest space—while keeping within the bounds of probability
—to the power of one character over another,—a power, of which the
first condition is, the ability to put on one side the consciousness of any
personal hurt or slight, and join with the other soul in considering only
its present feelings and its present good.

Nor is her sympathy concentrated, as is the case with so many novelists, one or two characters, one or two chief figures, that move in an oppressive glare of consciousness, while towards the rest she shows herself almost indifferent. Her splendid capacities for loving, for sympathising, take in the world; she embraces humanity, from the highest to the lowest, in those warm, womanly arms of hers. With a powerful and even flow her vast sympathy goes out like Burns', in every direction. Hetty, with her little butterfly soul, is viewed with the sincerest sympathy. Tito is condemned to death, but he is understood far too truly to be an object of hatred. Tessa, the pretty pigeon. Hinda, with the soul of a squirrel, are lovable after their kind; and up from these through the hierarchy of human characters to Romola and Fedalma, to Zarca and Savonarolo, there is not one grade too low, not one too high for love to reach. Poverty and nature, and the stains and sin cannot alienate the passionate attachment of this great heart to all that is human. "See, Lord," prays Dinah in the prison, "I bring her, as they of old brought the sick and helpless, and thou didst heal them; I bear her on my arms, and carry her before thee."

As a humorist, her reputation will be chiefly preserved by her pictures of English rural life. The humors of the old generation which she could remember well, were the main sources of her inspiration in those earlier tales, by which she at once gained the public ear, and leaped into a foremost place among the imaginative writers of the age. Easy to see what she really delights in. She revels in her Hackits, and Lammeters, and Tullivers, and Dempsters; turns them round and round, and exhibits them in every possible aspect, determined that nothing should be lost. We may see, in fact, the motive spring of these enchanting fictions in the opening pages of "Amos Barton," not less than in the picture of Old Leisure, to be found in "Adam Bede."

Contrast in her's, as in Scott's, the pathetic and tragic with the humorous and eccentric, and in both, it is to the latter we turn again and again with the fresher delight and zest. Mr. Gilfil, in his long pipes and his short sermons, and his old brown setter, and his top-boots and spurs, which sometimes got entangled in his surplice, will always constitute the charm of the story which goes by his name. Janet's repentance, and Mr. Tryan's earnestness are overshadowed by the picture of the conservative and orthodox party in the "Blue Lion." Hetty Sorrel, and even Dinah, must give place to Mr. Irwine and Lisbeth, and the old squire, and the parish clerk. The "Uncles and

Aunts" tower high above every other element of interest in the "Mill on the Floss;" while in "Silas Marner," though that marvelous portraiture of man's inner life claims the homage of our intellect, it is that good and wholesome woman Mrs. Winthrop, Mr. Solomon Macey, the clerk; Mr. Snell, the landlord, and Mr. Dowlas, the farrier, who really possess our hearts.

George Eliot was the first who took the village community as it stood, a little world by itself, with its aristocracy, its clergy, its middle and its lower classes, and drew materials from it for a series of dramas which will only be forgotten with the English language.

In her poems the idea and the matter don't really interpenetrate; the idea stands above the matter as a master above a slave, and subdues the matter to its will.   In her prose it is different.

Her genius embraces us like the air, on every side.   No part of humanity is left out; no part seems to have been originally deficient or malformed.   Her nature is complete, and in this completeness lies the importance of any solution George Eliot may have wrought out for herself of the moral difficulties of life.   No part or problem is likely to have been ignored; and in this nature, complete in all its parts, and with every part strong, the granite-like foundation of the whole is conscience, the moral perceptions and the moral will.   Abstract the ethical interest from her—what some critics have called—prose work "Romolo," or from what all critics pronounce her chief poem "The Spanish Gypsy," and there is total collapse of design, characters and incidents. Other story-tellers center our hopes and fears in the happiness or unhappiness of their chief personages; a wedding or a funeral brings to an end at once our emotional disturbance and the last chapter of the volume; with George Eliot it is otherwise, and much otherwise, while, of course, she is profoundly moved by the spectacle of human joy and human sorrow; and death to her is always tragic, there is yet something more tragic than cessation of the breath and of the pulse; there is the slow letting go of life and the ultimate extinction of the soul; to her the marriage joys are dear, but there is something higher than the highest happiness of lovers. "What better thing," she muses, while Adam and Dinah stand with clasped hands and satisfied hearts. "What better thing is there for two human souls, than to feel that they are joined for life, to strengthen each other in all labor, to rest on each other in all sorrow, to minister to each other in all pain, to be with each other in silent, unspeakable memories at the moment of the last parting " She has shown us one thing better than the obedience of man and woman to a summons more authoritative than that of any personal emotion.

> We must walk
> Apart unto the end. Our marriage rite
> Is our resolve that we will each be true
> To high allegiance, higher than our love.

And it is the profound moral and spiritual suggestions and truths that underlie and give form and ripple to the current of her narrative that exalts her works far above the ordinary plane of fiction, not many understand. The sphere which George Eliot has made specially her own, is that quiet English country life which she knew in early youth. No one has approached her in the power of seizing its essential characteristics, and exhibiting its real charm. She has done for it what Scott did for the Scotch peasantry. If not a voluminous writer, according to the standard of recent novelists, she at least has left a greater quantity of work representing the highest level of the author's capacity—putting aside Scott—than any other writer I know of.

SYNOPSIS LECTURE XX.

Subject—SCOTT—1771–1832.

1.—BIOGRAPHY. Scott, the first imaginative writer of the nineteenth century; his natural position; fortunate in his advent; delicate health; closely identified with Edinburgh; Lockhart's Life of Scott; born August 15, 1771; his character as a child; six years at Sandy Knowe; entered Edinburgh High School at eight; not brilliant; fond of adventure and story-telling; a great observer; travels as a young man.

His first literary venture at the age of twenty-five; again publishes a translation in 1799; marries; settles in Edinburgh; "Border Minstrelsy," 1802; "Lay of the Last Minstrel," 1805; "Marmion," 1808; "Lady of the Lake," 1810; enthusiastic reception of these works; discovers the uncompleted MS. of Waverley; completes it; its great success; breadth of characters shown in other novels; every figure an individual study; never repeats himself; love for children and dogs; power of observation and interest in life; the "Great Unknown;" other works follow "Waverley" rapidly; "Heart of Mid-Lothian," perhaps his best; Jeannie Deans, the perfection of Scott's work.

Scott's business arrangements unfortunate; building Abbotsford; his open-handed hospitality; "Ivanhoe," 1817, took England by storm; constable steps in as publisher; threatenings of ruin in 1825; Scott toils hard, but in vain; fits of paralysis; last work of power, "The Fair Maid of Perth," 1828; fits of paralysis; dies in 1832.

2.— HIS CHARACTERISTICS. Imagination, conservative; anomalous characters; his poor people; ideas of political economy; admiration for women; his pictures of the past; charm of "Ivanhoe;" his Mary, Queen of Scots.

447

3.—PLOT AND STYLE.   Not much plot; style vivid, picturesque and intelligible.

4.—HIS TREATMENT OF A SUBJECT.   Drew on his own store of observations; preserved illusion at the expense of truth.

5.—HIS POETRY.   Intelligible to all; not an epic poet, but much epic spirit; definition of epic poetry; Scott's inspirations; lived in the past; criticism of the "Lay;" spontaneity, swing and fire; "Marmion" has many heroic passages; quotation from the last canto; Jeffrey's criticism; favorite passages from the "Lady of the Lake;" "Bruce," his last love poem; Wordsworth's criticism of Scott as a poet; not just; his poetry will last; holds up noble ideals; loved by old people and children; Scott's poetry gave character to what came after.

6.—HIS INFLUENCE.   Very great; created taste for wholesome literature; influence on youth; on Scotland, marvelous; populated it in two ways, poetically and romantically; inspired the people with loyalty and respect for the law.

7.—HIS CHARACTER.

WALTER SCOTT.

The most beloved name in English literature, after Shakespeare, is perhaps Scott. No writer, of whom we have any record, is, or seems to be, so superior to all the jealousies and all the weaknesses of the literary character as he. While his creative genius is at once so wide and so fine, that, after making all deductions on account of the cheap literary material with which he was sometimes content to work, the critic who should declare him to be the greatest genius that has appeared in the imaginative literature of the nineteenth century would find many to agree with him.

Scott was the first great natural writer,—except Burns,—since Dunbar and Douglas. Scotland, for many a long year had other things more stern and terrible to attend to than literature, and no novelist had appeared. The "land of the mountain and the flood" was still in the hands of tradition, of ballads, fairies and witches. Scott was fortunate in the circumstances of his advent. His delicacy of health and his lameness were also fortunate circumstances for the world. That he was so thoroughly identified with Edinburgh is almost, if not altogether essential to our having Scott, as he is to us. "The grey Metropolis of the North" was then intensely provincial, and therefore swarming with characters. It was intellectual and literary, a city of wits, historians, poets and publishersl.

For Scott's biography I must refer to Lockhart's life, which is so charming, and so impartial and fair. The man whose name is incomparably the greatest in Scottish literature, historian, antiquary, poet, novelist and critic, was born August 15, 1771. He was a genial, poetic, sweet-tempered child, in whose manful simplicity and true childhood, were all the germs of the future man. The Walter Scott of Sandy Knowe was identical with the Walter Scott of Abbotsford. He was brought up for the first six years of his life in the sheepskin, on account of his lameness, with his grandfather and mother, in the lonely house of Sandy Knowe, going a-riding on the shoulders of the ewe-milkers as they went to work.

This lameness did not injure his nature. Such afflictions generally do much good or harm. In the case of Byron it had a most disastrous effect, but with young Scott it had all the beneficial results which in the best circumstances might be hoped for.

He entered Edinburgh High School at the age of eight, and has often been quoted as an instance of a stupid schoolboy, who has turned out a man of genius. He, however, although not brilliant, was by no means a dunce or dolt. Fond of story-telling and of adventure, he was frequently to be found on Arthur's Seat with a chosen friend and a packet of books. All this time Scot was storing up incidents, thoughts, characters, words and phrases, for future use. Nothing escaped him.

As a young man he journeyed, north and south, over the unexplored hills of Liddesdale, Perthshire, etc.

Scott's first venture in publication was a translation of Bürger's "Lenore," which he gave to the world in 1796, when he was twenty-five years old, and the picturesque force and spirit of which, justified from the first, his apppearance before the public. He followed up with a translation in 1799, of Goethe's "Goetz von Berlichingen." He married shortly afterwards, and a curious circumstance in this connection is, that his wife or family never read his books—his eldest son, Colonel Scott, not a word. He settled in Edinburgh, and employed his spare time in collecting for the "Border Minstrelsy," which appeared in 1802. But the first delighted surprise which Scott was to give the reading public of all classes was to be by "The Lay of the Last Minstrel," published, 1805. "Marmion" followed in 1808, and aroused even greater enthusiasm, whilst the most popular poem for the time being proved to be "The Lady of the Lake," 1810.

Scott undoubtedly made the reading of poetry not only the fashion, but the rage. People everywhere took up his works because they were fascinated, and found actual, undeniable pleasure in their perusal. He had the world at his feet from the first, and his poems were sold by thousands. They were, however, merely a preface to his real work. He was a great poet, one of the greatest, but not in verse. Probably the true reason of Scott turning his attention in another direction was the celebrity which Byron obtained as a poet, and yet, the works of Scott have stood the test of time better than Byron's.

There was a tremendous setting in of the tide of immortal verse after Scott, which was due, in a considerable measure, to his influence. He and others had begun with a study of German poetry, but he speedily rose to a height of his own, through his strong nationality, and his acquaintance, begun so early, with romances of chivalry. Among the five great poets of what is called the romantic revival, Scott, Wordsworth, Coleridge, Shelley, and Keats, it is the last three in whom we see the subtlety of the romantic spirit. While Scott always, and Wordsworth often, adopted a diction that was common to prose and unideal verse. Coleridge, Shelley, and Keats worked in all the subtle colors of romance. While the aim of Scott and Wordsworth was to bring the poet *en rapport* with the reader by means of a style as lucid and direct as possible, to carry the reader away from the common earth, beyond "the glimpses of the moon," and talk to him in the tongue of fairyland was what Shelley and Coleridge desired as much as Keats. In this regard Scott was not a poet of the first order.

After the success of the "Lay of the Last Minstrel," Scott wrote the first chapters of Waverley, but he was discouraged by his friends and afraid to risk his fame. The manuscript lay in a drawer for eight years, when, searching for some fishing tackle, he discovered it. Reading it over he wrote the last two volumes in three weeks. Good James Ballantyne found Waverley Manor dull, and Tully Veolan vulgar. But the public judged differently. Such a flash of enthusiasm has rarely, in the world of literature, been seen. Lord Holland said, "None of us went to bed all night." The world was taken by storm. There were practically no novels then, and the novelist had the field to himself.

Scott pronounced Waverley a piece of imbecility; but what of other heroes, of the Claudius, Bertrams, Bassanius, Sebastians of Shakespeare? So, in Scott, it is always the subordinate characters that are most life-like and interesting. The courtly Vich Ian Vor shines through mists, so does the stately and beautiful Flora, even to Evan Dhu, Callum Beg, and the gallant Fergus Mac Ivor.

The curious breadth of Scott's character is shown to us in his other novels. He has given us every possible kind of man and woman. Almost all other writers are limited in this respect—Dickens, Thackeray, Lytton,—but Scott, like Shakespeare, carried the world under his belt. From Jenny Dennison to Rebecca, what a range! From Cœur-de-Lion to Dirk Hatteraick, and yet they are so vivid we could shake hands with them. Every figure is an individual study. There is no division into classes, as is the fashion with some novelists, who have one stock old man, one humorous character, and one grave, to vary at will.

Baron Bradwardine and Jonathan Oldbuck are as little like each other as either is unlike Waverley or Fergus Mac Ivor. Except in the thankless role of hero—generally a no-character part—he never repeats himself. Guy Mannering, Pleydell, and Dandie Dumont are not to be confounded with the other soldiers, lawyers, or honest fellows. Neither have we any counterpart or echo of Baillie, Nicol Jarvie, Dominie Sampson, Gingling Geordie or Andrew Fairservice. Yet Andrew Fairservice, Cuddie Headrigg, and Ritchie Monyplies are all serving men.

Compare these again with that wonderful picture of an old-world Major-domo, Caleb Balderstone. He is as distinct from them, and in some respects, as superior to them, as it is possible to conceive.

Even Scott's children are life-like. There is not one whom he passes at a cottar's door but becomes individual to him. His love for children and dogs is well known. He said about dogs that it was a good thing they did not live any longer than they do, else we could not bear to part with them. There is an amusing story even, of how a little black pig conceived a great affection for him, and, if not shut up, would persist in trotting after him everywhere. So, also, he could tell the ewes individually, whilst most of us think that sheep are mostly so alike as to be indistinguishable to any one, except, perhaps, a shepherd on the hills.

These things point to a power of accurate observation, and a deep interest in life which is as rare as it is valuable, and which explains, to a great extent, the secret of "The Great Unknown," who saw the world with eyes in the sunshiny daylight, not through spectacles colored with his own or other people's theories. He was soon found out, and became the "Great Known." The authorship of the Waverley novels was acknowledged at a public banquet in Edinburgh.

"Waverley" appeared in 1814, and in 1818 his genius had reached high-water mark in the "Heart of Mid-Lothian." Between these dates came "Guy Mannering," 1815; "The Antiquary," 1816; "Old Mortality," 1816; "The Black Dwarf," 1816; "Rob Roy" was published in 1818.

All these, except "The Black Dwarf," show the full fervor and power of his first and freshest inspiration. It is hard to say which is his best work, but, if pressed, I should give preference to the "Heart of Mid-Lothian." Here is the humblest and commonest tale of deception and betrayal, a story in its beginning, like one of those that abound in all literature, and yet sublimed by genius and raised into the then altitudes of the imperishable heart.

In a common hand Effie would have monopolized our sympathy, and

WALTER SCOTT. 453

her sister Jeannie secured only our cold approbation. But Jeannie is the cream and perfection of Scott's work, all the more so that, in all ordinary circumstances, she would be so much less interesting to us than a score of beautiful Ravennas,—than even Flora or Rebecca. She is a piece of actual fact, real as the gentle landscape in which she is first enclosed, true as her kine that browse upon the slope,—and yet she is the highest ideal that Scott ever attained. This humble Scottish maiden is a creature pure, absolutely truthful, yet of a tenderness, a forbearance, and long-suffering beyond the power of man, willing to die rather than lie, but resolute that the truth her nature has forced her to speak shall not be used for harm, if her very life can prevent it. And how this most perfect flower of human nature expands and blossoms out. Always the same simple, straight-forward, untiring, one idea'd woman; yet so strong in her simplicity, so firm in her gentleness, so sensible and persevering! As little daunted by Duke or Queen as by the villain and other difficulties.

Here is one of the truest examples of Scott's pathos, where we find the passion of hope prevailing over that of anguish. It is Jeannie Dean's plea to the Queen for her sister's life: "My sister, my poor sister Effie, still lives, though her days and hours are numbered. She still lives, and a word of the King's mouth might restore her to a broken-hearted auld man, that never, in his daily and nightly exercise forgot to pray that His Majesty might be blessed with a long and prosperous reign, and that his throne, and the throne of his posterity, might be established in righteousness. O madam! if ever ye kenn'd what it was to sorrow for and with a sinning and suffering creature, whose mind is sae tossed that she can neither be sa'd fit to live or die, have some compassion on our misery. Save an honest house from dishonor, and an unhappy girl not eighteen years of age from an early and dreadful death! Alas! it is not when we sleep soft and wake merrily ourselves that we think on other people's sufferings. Our hearts are waxed light within us then, and we are for righting our ain wrongs and fighting our ain battles. But when the hour of trouble comes to the mind as to the body,—and seldom may it visit your Leddyship,—and when the hour of Death comes, that comes to high and low,—long and late may it be yours,—O, my Leddy! then it isna what we hae dune for ourselves, but what we hae dune for others, that we think on maist pleasantly. And the thought that ye hae intervened to spare the puir thing's life will be sweeter in that hour, come when it may, than if a word of your mouth could hang the haill Porteous mob at the tail of ae tow."

The end of the story is very poor. What do we care for Effie and her abandoned child! The interest is over, and the close indeed huddled up. All this time Scott toiled to meet his publisher, Ballantyne's terrible notes of hand. His business engagements were very unfortunate. Then, further, his ambition to build Abbotsford, at an enormous cost, and his extravagant hospitality still further complicated matters.

In 1817 "Ivanhoe" appeared and took England by storm. Lockhart calls it a mere work of art, the first of all Scott's efforts in prose or verse. With this judgment I am not prepared to coincide, although it may be admitted to be the best story.

Constable now takes over Ballantyne's responsibilities, but he is too impetuous and exhibits signs of staggering. Meanwhile, poor Scott goes on building castles in the air, until, in 1825, the first threatenings of ruin came.

How hard the unfortunate author worked to redeem his debt is well known. He accomplished miracles of labor and paid over vast sums of money. But it was all of no avail. His creditors showed their sense of indebtedness to him by presenting him with his own library, plate and furniture. They also permitted him to live at Abbotsford. But the end was near. A cold shadow began to creep over the great life. He had two fits of paralysis. His last work of power was "The Fair Maid of Perth," published in 1828. His wife died, and only one child, Anne, was left to cheer him. He died in 1832, a year which also saw the death of Goethe, and which closed an epoch in European literature.

Sir Walter Scott's imagination was strictly conservative. He had no thesis to maintain; no gospel to preach. This has sometimes been made an accusation against him, as similarly it has been made against other great writers, but art does not undertake to teach morality as such. The end of all true art will be found to be consistent with the just and the true, but that is in a higher way than by merely inculcating moral lessons as the preacher might. His historical characters are interestingly drawn, and, whether or not they are entirely true to history, we have at least a vivid conception of the personages presented to us.

Regarding his anomalous characters it should be said that although monstrosity has no place in art, yet every one is familiar with characters in every-day life, which, if photographed in books, would be considered unnatural and impossible. Meg Merrilies, Edie Ochiltree, Radcliffe, the pretended mute in " Peveril of the Peak," are of this description, but the fundamental explanation of the phenominal success is the distinctness with which Scott saw how such a character as Meg Merrilies, for instance, arose, and was produced out of the peculiar circumstances and gipsy life in the localities in which he has placed his scene.

Scott's poor people are never coarse and never vulgar, although they are, as might be expected, often narrow. Alone almost among novelists, Scott has given a minute, life-like description of poverty, which is, at the same time, genial and pleasing. Hazlitt remarks that Crabbe described a poor man's cottage like one who had come to distrain it for rent, giving a minute catalogue of contents. Scott, on the other hand, gives such a description as that a cheerful and sensible landlord might of his own property in which he had a pleasure.

His ideas of political economy are characteristic of his strong sense and genial mind. Read, for instance, his description of how the Laird of Ellengowan managed his property. Or, again, in a very interesting introduction to "The Fortunes of Nigel" he goes at some length into his views on this subject.

No one can lay down one of Scott's works without being impressed with the fact the world is subject to laws of retribution, which, though not apparent on a superficial glance, are yet in steady and consistent operation, and will be quite sure to work their due effect if time is only given to them.

His admiration for women is also a pleasant and very noticeable feature in his works. There is a gentle tone of manly admiration exhibited towards his heroines, and he always approaches them uncovered. If it is asserted that they are sometimes namby-pamby, it may be admitted that some of them are, but they are often delightful and almost always pleasing. Most modern novelists do not like their heroines, and that atrocious species, the *plain* heroine, has even been invented. With Scott, in these respects, there is no fault to find.

The same touch of romance gives a delightful glamor to his pictures of the past. Take, for instance, the mediæval details in "Ivanhoe." Robin Hood and Richard are no doubt spurious, but they are drawn as we would have them be. The charm of "Ivanhoe" is addressed to a simple sort of imagination,—to the boyish fancy which idolizes mediæval society as the "fighting time." There are tournaments, treges, duels, the merry greenwood tree, and all the rest.

The same sort of historical romance characterizes his historical characters. His Richard I. is the traditional Richard, ennobled and idealized in conformity to the spirit of tradition. Take again his Puritans and cavaliers, he always dwells on the traits and incidents

most attractive to a general and spirited imagination. A most remarkable instance of the power which romantic illusion exercised on Scott
is his Mary, Queen of Scots. He believed her to be guilty, and yet he
does not present her in colors which would lead us to infer that she
was so. It is perhaps his best historical picture, but it is principally
her picture, as she lives in the fond tradition of his countrymen.

In regard to his plot and style. As to the first he very much let things
take their own way, not being able to adhere to any given plot, and
changing his plan constantly. His style gives a most vivid picture, but
has not a single quotable line. It is, however, alike appreciated by all
and intelligible to all. The rapidity with which he wrote has something
to do with this. He composed "Guy Mannering" in six weeks, and the
"Bride of Lammermoor" in two.

He drew on his own stores of observation for his characters, then
he transferred them bodily to his pages, costumed them, and supplied
them with language. So, too, having exhausted Scottish ground he
continued the same methods, pushing further back, preserving the illusion, but at the expense of truth. Thus, beginning with Waverley, we
have a cavalier of the Revolution; a courtier of James I.; a borderer
of Henry VIII.; an adventurer of Louis XI.; a preux chevalier of the
Crusades,—but the historical truth is not preserved. Scott bodily trans-
ported the men of the nineteenth century into the fifteenth century.
There is, however, always the appearance of fairness, as in the case of
Claverhouse or Leicester. We are seldom conscious of anything incon-
gruous or repulsive in the process.

To pass from Scott's prose to his poetry we recognize it as being
intelligible to all,—the meaning lies on the surface. Living amid
beautiful scenery we forget its beauty and similarly, Scott is too familiar
to be greatly admired. He is not an epic poet, but yet he possesses
more of the epic or Homeric spirit than of the lyric or dramatic. From
his more heroic passages a stranger to Greek literature would gain
a more accurate idea of Homer.

The subject of an epic poem must be some one, great, complex
action, and the principal characters must belong to the high places of
the world,—grand and elevated in their ideas and bearing. The action
must be carried on by a mixture of narrative, dialogue, and soliloquy,
and told in a grand style, and with fullness of detail. Few European
nations possess more than one real epic,—some none. The chief great
epics are the Iliad and Odyssey, the Æneid, Niebelungen Lied, Jerusa-
lem Delivered, and Paradise Lost.

Scott's inspirations came from traditions and ballads taught him by his grandmother and his aunt Janet; then from impressions of the scenery,with their associations; and, thirdly, from Percy's "Reliques", and afterwards his own "Border Minstrelsy." He lived in the past, he had born in him the heroic soul, and therefore it is that he has more of the true ballad spirit than any epic writer since Homer. The Æneid is a literary epic, Milton's is religio-classical.

His "Lay of the Last Minstrel" opens in the grand, heroic style, where he, describing the custom of Branksome Hall. The concentrated fire, and measured tread of those first noble stanzas is very striking. So are those others, in which is described Deloraine's nightly ride from Branksome to Melrose. Here at last he found a poetic setting for his .favorite localities. One of their grand beauties is the complete absence of artistic consciousness, their spontaneity, naturalness, absence of effort, swing and fire, and this is more prominent in the " Lay" than in any of the subsequent poems.

It is in "Marmion," however, that whatever was epic in Scott found fullest vent. He could hardly have chosen as the center and climax of the poem, a more national and truly heroic action than Flodden. The most heroic passages are the opening stanzas, describing Marmion's approach to Norham at sunset; the muster of the Scottish army on the Borough Muir on their march to Flodden; and, above all, the whole last canto, descriptive of the battle itself. Here he put out all his strength. I quote at some length:

> " Blount and Fitz-Eustace rested still
> With Lady Clare upon the hill;
> On which (for far the day was spent)
> The western sunbeams now were bent.
> The cry they heard, its meaning knew,
> Could plain there distant comrades view;
> Sadly to Blount did Eustace say,
> ' Unworthy office here to stay!
> No hope of gilded spurs to-day.—
> But see! look up, on Flodden bent
> The Scottish foe has fired his tent.'
> And sudden as he spoke
> From the sharp ridges of the hill,
> All downward to the banks of Till
> Was wreathed in sable smoke,
> Volumed and fast, and rolling far
> The cloud enveloped Scotland's war,

As down the hill they broke;
Nor martial sound, nor minstrel tone
Announced their march; their tread alone
At times one warning trumpet blown,
At times a stifled hum,
Told England, from his mountain home
King James did rushing come,—
Scarce could they hear or see their foes
Until at weapon point they close.
They close in clouds of smoke and dust,
With sword-sway, and with lances thrust;
    *   *   *   *
Far on the left, unseen the while,
Stanley broke Lennox and Argyle;
Though there the western mountaineer
Rushed with bare bosom on the spear,
And flung the feeble targe aside,
And with both hands the broadside plied.
'Twas vain:—but Fortune, on the right
With fickle smile cheered Scotland's fight;
Then fell that spotless banner white,
The Howard's lion fell;
Yet still Lord Marmion's falcon flew
With wavering flight, while fiercer grew
Around the battle yell.
The border slogan rent the sky!
A Home! a Gordon! was the cry:
Loud were the clanging blows;
Advanced,—forced back,—now low, now high
The pennon sunk and rose;
As bends the bark's mast in the gale,
When rent are rigging, shrouds and sail,
It wavered 'mid the foes.
No longer Blount the view could bear;
'By heaven, and all its saints!   I swear
I will not see it lost!
Fitz-Eustace, you with Lady Clare
May bid your beads, and patter prayer,—
I gallop to the host.
And to the fray he rose amain
Followed by all the archer train.
The fiery youth, with desperate charge
Made, for a space, an opening large,—
The rescued banner rose;—
But darkly closed the war around,
Like pine-tree, rooted from the ground,
It sunk among the foes.

Then Eustace mounted too, yet staid,
As loth to leave the helpless maid,
When fast as shaft can fly.
Bloodshot his eyes, his nostrils spread,
The loose rein dangling from his head,
Housing and saddle bloody red,
Lord Marmion's steed rushed by;
And Eustace, maddening at the sight,
A look and sign to Clara cast,
To mark he would return in haste
Then plunged into the fight
    *   *   *   *

The war that for a space did fail,
Now trebly thundering swelled the gale,
And Stanley! was the cry;—
A light on Marmion's visage spread,
And fired his glazing eye;
With dying hand, above his head
He shook the fragment of his blade
And shouted ' Victory !'
'Charge, Chester, charge!' On, Stanley, on!'
Were the last words of Marmion.

By this, though deep the evening fell,
Still rose the battle's deadly swell;
For still the Scots around their king,
Unbroken, fought in desperate ring.
    *   *   *   *
The stubborn spearman still made good
Their dark, impenetrable wood;
Each stepping where his comrade stood
The instant that he fell.
No thought was there of dastard flight:
Linked in the serried phalanx tight,
Groom fought like noble, squire like knight,
As fearlessly and well;
Till utter darkness closed her wing
O'er their thin host and wounded king,
Then skillful Surrey's sage commands
Led back from strife his shattered bands;
And from the charge they drew
As mountain waves from wasted lands
Sweep back to ocean blue.
Then did their loss the foeman know;
Their king, their lords, their mightiest low,
They melted from the field as snow,

When streams are swollen and south winds blow,
Dissolved in silent dew.

Tweed's echoes heard the ceaseless plash
While many a broken band,
Disordered through her currents dash
To gain the Scottish land;
To town and tower, to down and dale,
To tell red Flodden's dismal tale,
And raise the universal wail
Tradition, legend, tune and song
Shall many an age that wail prolong:
Still from the sire the son shall hear
Of the stern strife and carnage drear,
Of Flodden's fatal field,
Where shivered was fair Scotland's spear,
And broken was her shield.

Lord Jeffrey's criticism is that "of all the poetical battles which have been fought from the days of Homer; there is none comparable for interest and animation—for breadth of drawing and magnificence of effect—with this." The best parallel to be found is in the sixteenth book of the Iliad, where Patroclus dons the armor of Achilles and flies to the rescue of the Achaian host.

I should like to go through Scott's other poems and lay the finger on favorite passages, but I can only refer to one or two in "The Lady of the Lake"—the gathering, the combat between Roderick and Fitz James, the battle stare of the lord to the dying Roderick, with its noble couplet:

"''Twere worth ten years of peaceful life
One glance at their array!'"

In his last long poem he selects the wanderings of Bruce and Bannockburn, but though not without fine passages, it betrays the decay of the poetic fire, the growing disgust of the author at the trammels of verse, and the hastening on to his period of prose creation.

Wordsworth asserted that as a poet Scott could not live, as he had never written anything addressed to the immortal part of man. So, too, Carlyle says that he had no message to deliver, and wrote for money. But poetry and prose that appeal directly to innocent and child-like hearts must surely have their value and their abidingness. Again, it is old people who have kept their hearts green under the snow-white head, that most love Scott. His poetry describes man and outward nature broadly, freely, truly as they are. The object of poetry is to give high and enduring pleasure. Modern poetry is self-originated from within, and much of it is morbid, unhealthy, and introspective. We cannot, perhaps, find a better antidote than Homer, Shakespeare and Scott.

Again, he holds up noble ideals, the highest and most generous types of character, and, in a money-grabbing age, he dared to be romantic. "Scott's poetry impressed its own character upon all the poetry that was produced among us for many years after. It put an end to long works in verse of a didactic, or merely reflective character, and directed the current of all writing of that kind into the form of narrative. Even Wordsworth's 'Excursion' (1814), is, for the most part, a collection of tales."

His influence has been very great, and has been felt in many directions. He introduced, with Coleridge, Carlyle, Lewes, etc., the German influences which have been so much felt in literature and philosophy. He, too, created a taste for wholesome literature, and gave the death-blow to the absurdity and weird horrors of the "Castle of Otranto," the romance of Mrs. Radcliffe, and writers of that school. With Burns, Cowper, and Wordsworth he joined in a love of nature and a natural style. In history he substituted vivid portraiture, and clear description for philosophical comparison and analysis.

Michelet tried to write French history as Scott did his romances, and so De Barante did his History of Burgundy, and Thierry, in his History of the Norman Conquest, acknowledges the inspiration of "Ivanhoe."

As regards American literature, Scott may be said to have inspired Cooper.

His influence on youth has been great and wholesome. He has inspired the young with the love of history and with noble types of character, and has made *pure* literature popular. The modern novel when he appeared was unknown. Richardson, Smollett, and Fielding belonged to a bygone age. Like secondary moons around the planet of the greater magician rose Miss Edgeworth, Miss Austen and Miss Ferrier.

His influence on his own country has been marvelously great. He brought Catholic and Protestant, Saxon and Gael, Whig and Tory together, and healed the bitterness of centuries. He may be said to have discovered the Celtic Highlands, now so well known to countless tourists, and the subject so frequently of the painter and the novelist

From Schiehallion to Cuffel, from the soft caves and locks of the west, to the rugged grandeur of the eastern coast, something of him is on every hillside and glen. Scott was indeed patriotic to the backbone. Scotland had his whole heart, and he summed up in his writings the genius of the nation. He was the troubadour of its past glories, sounding his clarion out of the heart of ancient times; the sweet singer of the present, whose kindly, soft-beaming light and affectionate interest brightened the cottages of the entire Lowlands. He has populated Scotland in two ways, poetically and romantically. Arthur's Seat recalls David Dean's college; Sterling, Fitz James; the Ladies' Rock, Douglas, Loch Katrine, and her isles would be in darkness without the courageous Ellen. Once the only passenger to Scotland was Samuel Johnson, now it is the greatest resort of tourists in the world.

Scott inspired its people with loyalty and respect for law. He is not only the most perfect example of a national poet, but he is in himself a typical Scotsman, alike in his strength and weakness an example of the best and most characteristic qualities of his race.

Finally, a word or two as to his character.

He was an upright man, the soul of honor, affectionate, hospitable, genial, a hard worker, grandly brave and resolute in misfortune; a Tory, but liberal in politics and religion, a good husband, father, citizen and friend. His dying words to his son-in-law were, "I have but a short time to live, and my last advice is, to be a good man, virtuous, and a Christian." And so one of the truly great ones of the earth passed away.

SYNOPSIS LECTURE XXI.

SUBJECT—MRS. BROWNING—1809-1861.

EARLY LIFE. A delicate child; illness and affliction; precocious; wrote at ten; voracious reader; in print at fifteen; contributions to periodicals before twenty; studied Greek. Her first published volumes: 1833, "Prometheus Bound;" 1838, "Seraphim;" 1844, "Drama of Exile," "Portuguese Sonnets," "Aurora Leigh."

CHARACTER OF HER GENIUS. Died at Florence, 1861.

E. B. BROWNING.

Elizabeth Barrett Browning, the daughter of an English country gentleman, was born in London, in the year 1809. The first image we have presented to us is that of a young girl, piously brought up, the child of wealthy parents, living a secluded life in a large London house. Elizabeth Barrett was a precocious genius, beginning to write when she was not ten years of age; in print at fifteen, and contributing to periodicals when under twenty. She was always delicate, and when twenty-eight years old she burst a blood vessel. She had hardly recovered from her sickness when she had to witness with the keenest anguish the drowning of her favorite brother at Torquay. The catastrophe brought on an illness which kept her in a darkened room for seven years. In 1846, she married Robert Browning, who took her off to Italy. She died in Florence, in 1861, and was buried beside Keats and Shelley.

Poets, like nightingales, sing best in the dark. Eastern travelers tell us of a rare bird that only sings its best when stung by pain, and the song of the dying swan has long passed into tradition. And so it was with Mrs. Browning. Had she been strong and healthful, her genius would never have borne such unequally rich and refreshing food. In her the sweetness of the strain resulted from the tightening of the chords. The trouble is, the chords were kept tight too long; the tension was too great and long continued, and there was no let up. She, herself, in one of her most remarkable poems, "The Great God Pan," expresses in wonderful words the faith that man suffers in making the poem. It is one of her most perfect creations, but the doctrine is not always true. The pith of the poem is the heart of the poet. The poet is made out of the man, and is often a sadly self-conscious and spoilt creature. Some poets, only inferior ones though, are always posing.

Mrs. Browning's entire works are autobiographical, so much so that we can trace in them not only the spiritual and mental growth of the writer, but even her physical growth. I have more than once had occasion to remark on the influence of physical peculiarities on the development of character and genius. Dwarfs, and generally deformed

men, are malicious and satirical. What an unhappy influence Byron's
lameness had in forming his character. It was not so with Scott. So
from Pope, with his peevishness; from Cowper's melancholia; Heine's
life-long disease, and Hood's illness, a great deal might be learned.

She studied Greek and Latin with her favorite brother, and was an
omnivorous reader, a fact made evident enough by a perusal of "Aurora
Leigh." In these things her father encouraged her, and her first publication, in 1826, entitled "An Essay on Mind and other Poems," contains
some verses to him, in which she says:

> " For 'neath thy gentleness of praise
> My father! ran my early lays
> And when the lyre was scarce awake,
> I loved its strings for thy dear sake
> And the kind Muses; but the while
> Thought only how to win thy smile."

She continued her Greek studies under Hugh Stuart Boyd, and
dedicated to him her "Wine of Cyprus."

In 1833, "Prometheus Bound" of Æschylus was produced, and other
poems appeared in periodicals, till, at last, in 1838, "Seraphim and
other Poems" was given to the world under her own name.

About 1835, Miss Milford first saw Elizabeth Barrett, and found her
most interesting. She adds, that everyone said so; going on to describe
her young friend as of a slight delicate figure, with a shower of dark
curls falling on either side of a most expressive face,—large tender eyes,
richly fringed by dark eyelashes; a smile like a sunbeam, and such a
look of youthfulness, that Miss Milford had some difficulty in persuading a friend, that the translator of "Prometheus" was old enough to be
introduced into company.

There came, in 1837, that breaking of a blood vessel, and one year
spent in London. Another year was spent in Devonshire, when she
saw her brother and two companions drowned at Torquay. Not for a
year could she bear being removed, and then only by journeys of
twenty miles a day to London; there followed that long illness spent
in a dark room.

Before passing to general criticism of her genius, allow me a word
or two as to one special phase of it.

There is one form of composition, and that the most difficult and
elaborate, in which Mrs. Browning has been eminently successful. The
sonnet has not been a favorite with English poets, nor would the

collection of really good English sonnets be very large. With the exception of Wordsworth, no English poet has written many excellent sonnets. Here and there one may be found of surpassing merit—one by Shelley, one by Blanco White, two or three by Milton, and half a dozen by Longfellow and Rossette. Now, I will venture to say, that from no English writer, with the exception, perhaps, of Wordsworth, can you select six sonnets so excellent as you might extract from those of Elizabeth Barrett Browning. In saying this I do not forget that Shakespeare wrote sonnets; or at least that a huge collection of poems so called, stand attributed to Shakespeare. I have my own opinion as to those sonnets, both as to their merit and their authenticity; but let that pass—all I have to say is, let some one who *can*, read them through, select his half-dozen—I stand ready with mine.

Now, when it is considered what a good sonnet requires—how much skill and patience, as well as poetic thought—how a noble or tender sentiment has to be rendered in most lucid language, and in a most difficult scheme, both of rhyme and metre, it will be admitted that one who has succeeded in this style of composition must be a consummate artist. And, after such an admission, to hint at such faults as a defiant carelessness of all the artistic requisitions of poetry, to suggest that there breaks out occasionally a headstrong, violent, turbid and obscure strain, sounds contradictory. It surely is a mistake. It is not a mistake, however. A willful abandonment of the very music of poetry by one who can write most musically—a confused commingling of thought and metaphor by one who can elucidate a chosen thought till it stands out distinct and graceful as an image of Parian marble—nay, even a turbulence and violence in the sentiment itself—in one distinguished for tenderness, for power blended with sweetness—all these contradictions are what the critic has to deal with. Nor are such inconsistencies, as we very naturally but not very accurately call them, at all uncommon. So far from surprising us, they ought rather to be expected from a writer of vigorous genius, writing at different periods of life on different themes, and under various influences. It is plain that the only way to form a just estimate of such writers is to examine each poem individually; or, at least, to attempt some classification of their works according to the nature of the subject, or of the epoch of their career in which they were written. I cannot attempt a minute examination of Mrs. Browning's numerous poems; but a perusal of her works, aided by such knowledge of the biography of the writer as has been long open to all the world, will enable me, in some measure to classify her poems, and will give the ability to describe the several *manners* of this individually great and amiable artist.

This young and delicate girl was a Greek scholar, and had translated the "Prometheus" of Æschylus; in her poems, with the characteristic boldness of youth, seized upon the theme which Milton had made his own, singing the triumph of Satan and the expulsion of our first parents from Paradise. She had even ventured on a higher theme than any Milton had attempted,—that of the crucifixion of our Saviour. Was ever mortal,—especially a girl hardly out of her short clothes,—so daring? The "Drama of the Exile," and the "Seraphim," are poems in which angels, and the spirits of nature, and God himself are introduced, and where man is seen in relationship with the supernatural. Others and smaller poems were also published with these, expressive of great tenderness and a habit of reflection, but not without those defects which young poets of both sexes are apt to fall into. The picture presented to us is interesting in the extreme, and lends an additional zest to the poems. Here, in the dim retirement of a sick room, in one of those dreary London houses, into which the sunshine and the breeze never enter, a young girl lives out her *thought-life*, and pours forth, from the exuberance of her imagination, many a strain, not only of men, but of angels, and not only of our present times, but of antiquated forms of existence. How beautiful a compensation! You have taken health and pleasure, and left little of companionship, and shut up the young heart in a darkened chamber, where the roll of the carriage wheel on the paved street is almost the only sound that penetrates. You would think the life of the soul must go out, but it burns all the more brightly. The roll of the carriage wheel, suggestive of many a social pleasure, is very patiently heard by one who is riding with Milton in the chariot of God; by one who has had her heart moved to tenderness by the record of romance; or, better still, by the recorded distresses of her own contemporaries. The dim life has only made immortality a more vivid and palpable reality.

The poems of this epoch form in some measure a class by themselves. Knowing so much only of her biography as her writings disclose, I do not pretend to specify the circumstances under which each individual poem was written. But this time in her writings is sufficiently marked for the purposes of criticism. A transition takes place in the sonnets called "From the Portuguese." After this we hear of the invalid breaking like a butterfly from the chrysalis; breaking from her dim retirement, the bride of a poet, of one whose genius had won for him the admiration of his contemporaries. She went from the sick chamber, from the London house, from the fogs of England, opening her new wings under the sun of Italy. The proud and happy bride of a man of genius, she awoke to new interests, the world itself grew larger, and present, and vivid to her. Its manifold progress, its politics, its social hopes and activities, and especially the great political revolution she witnessed in Italy, took possession of her heart and impressed a new character on her poetry. She lived now in the present, who had lived only for immortality. The moral and social aspect of the living world arrests her attention. She is now in the open air, in the bright sunshine, and stands face to face with nature, society and God. The problems of this world engage and oppress her, and something also of the doubts and fears, and occasional clouds of terror and distrust that attend upon all the speculations of mere human reason. She is still the Christian poet, but on earth, beset by all its fears, earnest with all its hopes.

Her great poem of this epoch is "Aurora Leigh." Others of a quite political character, as "Casa Guide Windows" and "Poems Before Congress", are inferior, but must not be overlooked. The latter especially interesting, as significant of the manner in which her mind was developing. It can never add to her poetical celebrity.

There are thus two well-defined epochs in Mrs. Browning's literary life, with a sort of transition stage between them. To begin with the former, the "Drama of Exile" takes up the great, eventful history of our first parents at the point where Milton has closed it.

> "They, hand in hand, with melancholy step,
> Through Eden took their solitary way."

Milton's close is where the imagination would naturally leave the subject, and it would have been better had it been left there. Our young poets, however, have not been content to let well alone.

I shall not proceed to quote the soliloquy of Lucifer, nor do I feel tempted to enter analytically into Mrs. Browning's personification of the spirit of Evil. She makes him, in one fine burst of utter irrationality, choose evil and hate for their own sakes, and thus far, I suppose, she is faithful to the character she intends to delineate, but her Satan, in spite of all his terrific wickedness, leaves the impression of a very weak, miserable, remorseful, irrational creature. After Lucifer had delivered his soliloquy, the angel Gabriel descends, charged apparently with the mission of expelling the Evil One from the earth. Lucifer refuses to take his departure, and, much to our surprise, he holds his ground, and Gabriel commands in vain. In this dialogue between these two personages there is a passage which I must quote, because it shows that our young poetess had not neglected her metaphysics, and was quite capable of a subtle train of reasoning. Lucifer has been boasting of his revolt, and of his independence, as if, whatever desperation he might assume, he could possibly project himself out of the laws of God. Gabriel replies:

> "Spirit of scorn,
> I might say of unreason! I might say
> That who despairs, acts; that who acts, connives
> With God's relations set in time and space;
> That who elects, assumes a something good
> Which God made possible; that who lives obeys
> The law of the Life-maker."

When this dialogue is closed we hear "a chorus of Eden spirits, chanting from Paradise, while Adam and Eve fly across the sword-glare." The song with which the "Bird-Spirit" dismisses the late occupants of the happy garden is pretty. I cannot say much for the poetry of the other spirits. Throughout the drama there are many of these spirits, personifications of the earth, or animal and vegetable life, which hardly seem to harmonize with the presence of Gabriel and Satan. These, so far as they are creations of our epic poet, may indeed be described as mythological persons; but, even so, they belong to another scheme of mythology.

The redeeming point in the drama is the tenderness thrown over the dialogue between Adam and Eve, and the sweet heroism with which Eve, in the name of all womankind, takes upon herself especial office of minister to the sick and the distressed. It illustrates the difficulty inherent in the subject that this very representation of the virtues and affections of Adam and Eve irresistably suggests to us the idea that they seem now more worthy of Paradise than before their expulsion from it. Indeed they seem more happy in their exile than the poet could possibly have portrayed them in the uniform prosperity of Eden. These supernatural themes are unavoidably encumbered with difficulties of this description.

The other sacred drama of this period of her productive life is, "The Seraphim." The plan of this poem is commendable for its simplicity.

The signs of the zodiac are not made to do duty like so many spectres in a grand incantation scene, as they do in the "Drama of Exile." Two seraphims, Ador and Zarah, witness together the Crucifixion. The poem almost entirely consists of the dialogue between these two spirits. They watch together from the gate of heaven, or, in mid-air, above Judea. Here and there we meet with a thought or a line that might be willingly quoted; but one looks through the drama in vain for any lengthened passage calling for special admiration. What has to be noted here is the strain of thought which had taken possession of the young poet. Almost contemporary with these sacred dramas are some romances, or pieces framed from mediæval manners and ideas, such as the "Duchess of May," and the "Romaunt of Margaret;" but I have not time to pause upon them

The poems which made Elizabeth Barrett dear to all her countrymen, were those which appealed directly to the sympathies of her contemporaries,—poems of the affections, full of tenderness, pity, sadness and love; such as "Bertha in the Lane," "Caterina," and that marvelous poem, "The Cry of the Children." Speaking generally, of these charming lyrics, one has to regret a fault very common amongst young poets of both sexes, and,—I must be excused for saying it—which especially besets our female poets—they do not know when to stop. One verse suggests another, and that another; and as they all have some bearing on the theme in hand, there seems to be no reason why they should not all be admitted. If the same labor were bestowed in completing a few verses (expunging every weak, slovenly and awkward line), that is expended in producing a greater number of verses, how much better would the poem be? There is scarcely one of these lyrics which would not be greatly improved by the simple process of taking one-half, or one-third of them away. Amongst our poetesses there is a mode of composition that is revealed to us as plainly by the structure of the verses themselves, as if we were in the confidence of the writer, and stood at her elbow as she wrote. Some image, thought, or sentiment occurs, and a single verse is penned; then this verse is allowed to suggest some other, that other its successor; without any idea of a preconceived whole ever crossing the mind. The inevitable result is, that, if the poem is not long, it still wearies before we have come to the end. The same idea is, perhaps, repeated several times, with little variation. Look at the effusions of Letitia E. Landon and Felicia Hemans'. Scarcely one has the unity and completeness that a short poem should particularly be distinguished by. If there be but three verses, one, you

may be sure is superfluous. From this weakness of unrestrained fluency
Elizabeth Barrett was far from being exempt. Examine the best of
these early poems, and if you have a pencil in your hand, you almost
involuntarily draw it through many a line and verse. Here is one
beginning with a stanza often quoted with approbation. It is entitled
"The Cry of the Human."

> " 'There is no God,' the foolish saith
>   But none ' There is no sorrow,'
> And Nature oft the cry of faith
>   In bitter need will borrow.
> Eyes, which the preacher could not school
>   By wayside graves are raised
> And lips say, 'God be pitiful,'
>   Who ne'er said, 'God be praised.'
>   Be pitiful of God !''

With the exception that words ought to be pronounced in poetry as
we pronounce them in prose, and no one says raised and praised, I
have not the least objection to make against this stanza. But read on,
and you find no second stanza of the same completeness, but the same
idea repeated or illustrated; and nothing but some measurement of the
eye seems to have set any limit to the facile production of verses on so
fruitful a theme. Even that beautiful poem which made all hearts ache
with pity, "The Cry of the Children," would have been twice as beautiful had it been half as long. Here are a few of its verses:

> "Do you hear the children weeping, O, my brothers,
>   Ere the sorrow comes with years?
> They are leaning their young heads against their mothers
>   And that cannot stop their tears.
>
> The young lambs are bleating in the meadows;
>   The young birds are chirping in the nest;
> The young fawns are playing with the shadows;
>   The young flowers are blowing toward the west—
>
> But the young, young children, O my brothers,
>   They are weeping bitterly!
> They are weeping in the play time of the others,
>   In the country of the free.
>
>   *   *   *   *   *

' For oh!' say the children, 'we are weary,
    And we cannot run or leap—
If we cared for any meadows, it were merely
    To drop down in them and sleep,
Our knees tremble sorely in the stooping—
    We fall upon our faces trying to go;
And, underneath our heavy eyelids drooping,
    The reddest flower would look as pale as snow.
For all day long we drag our burden tiring,
    Through the coal-dark underground—
Or, all day, we drive the wheels of iron
    In the factories, round and round.'
     *   *   *   *   *
And well may the children weep before you
    They are weary ere they run;
They have never seen the sunshine, nor the glory
    Which is brighter than the sun:
They know the grief of man, without his wisdom;
    They sink in man's despair, without its calm—
Are slaves without the liberty of Christdom,
    Are martyrs by the pang without a palm."

One of the most beautiful things in the English language is "Cowper's Grave".

" O, poets, from a maniac's tongue was poured the deathless singing!
O, Christians, at your cross of hope, a hopeless hand was clinging!
Oh, men, this man in brotherhood your weary paths beguiling
Groaned inly while he taught you peace and died whilst you were smiling."

There is a pathos in many of these poems of so delicate a character that it hardly bears transplanting. You are stirred and touched, and can hardly justify the emotion you have felt by any limited quotation. One may say, generally, that whenever our poet yields to some natural sentiment of her own, she always succeeds, more or less, in interesting us. It is otherwise where the strain is evidently an imitation of some other poet; whether she attempts to transfer some graces of a Greek poet into her own Saxon tongue, or is misled by the mannerisms of some poet nearer home, as Keats or Tennyson. "Lady Geraldine's Courtship" wears the appearance of an imitation of "Locksley Hall," and of a very exaggerated imitation. The poem is called a romance of the age, but it is not the manners of the age to rail at a lady, and to scourge her with our tongues into loving us. One wonders that Mrs.

Browning, at all times a champion of her sex, instead of caricaturing "Locksley Hall," did not write the proper *pendant* to it. If frivolous women overlook our poetic youths, and choose some wealthy squire, descending to a "lower level" of thought and feeling, what, on the other hand, is the sort of woman your man of genius most frequently chooses for the "idol of his soul?"

As to the strain of sentiment generally expressed in Mrs. Browning's poems, it is impossible to overrate their purity and tenderness. Sometimes there is a magical pathos suffused over the whole piece, and, more rarely, a couplet or a verse stands out from the rest, and fastens itself forever on the memory.

> "Thou knowest, though Thy universe be broad,
> Two little tears suffice to cover all."

How perfect in every way! And other gems like this might be collected. A fault might be hinted at in the general strain of her sentiments at this epoch, and it is that her piety sometimes takes the hue of asceticism. Even this may be thought hyper-criticism. All that I mean by it is, that in the glorious hope of immortality there is an undervaluing of this terrestrial life. The sadness of the young poet I am not complaining of,—this must always be excused. As she writes herself

> " Poets sigh—and poet's sadness—
> Alas! they come together!"

And a mere sentiment of sadness is too vague a matter to deal with controversially. You cannot argue against a sigh, but there may be a systematic disparagement of human life open to grave objection. Immortality is the faith which renders a grand life possible on earth,—possible to those even who tread the most retired paths of existence. It grows up from that which is the highest, purest, and best in human life, and eternalizes what is noblest. It is not built on a destruction of human life, as if all must be swept away to make a foundation for it. Accordingly, it is the constant labor of every sane theologian to teach us to exalt our lives, not to despise them. He does not teach us ever to regard external nature with any other sentiment than that of gratitude for the admirable relationship which has been established between it and the human being. A painful poem, called "Isabel's Child," will illustrate this occasional tendency to an ascetic piety. A mother is nursing a sick child, who is, indeed, on the point of death. She prays earnestly for its recovery, and the prayer is heard and answered. The prayer of the mother is very touching. The babe wakens, but the infantine features are animated by the wisdom of mature years, and in grave and solemn voice it reproaches the mother for calling it back from the gates of heaven:

> " The babe has awakened from sleep
> And unto the gaze of its mother!—
> Bent over is lifted another,
> Not the baby-looks that go
> Unaimingly to and fro,
> But an earnest, gazing deep,
> Such as soul gives soul at length,
> *When by the work and wail of years,*
> *It winneth a solemn strength;*
> And mourneth as it wears,
> A strong man could not brook,
> With pulse unhurried by fears,
> To meet that baby's look
> O'erglazed by manhood's tears,
> The tears of a man full-grown,
> With a power to wring our own
> In the eyes all undefiled
> Of a little three months' child."

The image is unpleasing and preposterous. The wisdom "won by work and wail" in a child that has not lived. The hour had, however, come, when the sort of asceticism, excusable, perhaps, on the ground of ill-health and other circumstances, was to vanish from the song of Elizabeth Barrett. This transition cannot be better indicated than by quoting from those exquisite sonnets described as "From the Portuguese." A great change had come and our poetess was now Mrs. Browning.

> "And yet *because* thou overcomest so,
> Because thou *art* more noble and like a king,
> Thou canst prevail against my fears, and fling
> Thy purple round me, till my heart shall grow
> Too close against thine heart, henceforth to know
> How it shook when alone. Why, conquering
> May prove as lordly and complete a thing
> In lifting upward, as in crushing low,
> And as a vanquished soldier yields his sword
> To one who who lifts him from the bloody earth,—

> Even so, Beloved, I at least record,
> Here ends my strife. If thou invite me forth,
> I rise above abasement at thy word.
> Make thy love larger to *enlarge* my worth."

Or again:

> " Is it indeed so? If I lay here dead,
> Wouldst thou miss any life in losing mine?
> And would the sun for thee more coldly shine,
> Because of grave-damps falling round my head?
> I marvelled my Beloved, when I read
> Thy thoughts so in the letter, I am thine—
> But,—*so* much to thee! Can I pour thy wine
> While my hands tremble? Then, my soul, instead
> Of dreams of earth, resumes life's lower range,
> Then love me, love. Look on me—breathe on me!
> As brighter ladies do not count it strange
> For love to give up acres and degree,
> I yield the grave for thy sake, and exchange
> My near, sweet view of heaven, for earth with thee."

There is now a larger and happier spirit. Whether those who have all along loved and admired the poetry of Mrs. Browning would find so many of their favorite passages in this, the second epoch of her genius as in the first, may be doubtful. I think not. But that her mind henceforth takes a wider range is indisputable. I pass over the "Casa Guide Windows," a piece devoted to Italian politics, so that I may give more time to "Aurora Leigh," which touches on great social problems— the thoughts that vex mankind—and which, I think, must be considered the greatest effort of her genius. At the time of the appearance of the poem, there were two opinions expressed by leading critical organs. All admitted the power and pathos, and even depth of thought displayed in many an individual passage. All condemned the structure of the story. Some of the events imagined were deemed grossly improbable, others painfully revolting, and the character of Romney, the chief person in the book, was, or might have been, very justly described as an impossible compound, inasmuch as he is at one time a hardheaded, practical philanthropist, and at another, a fanatic, half mad about some dream of equality. A man of cultivated mind and tastes, arranging his marriage in St. James' Church, with the child of a tramp, that he might *symbolize* before all England the blending of the two classes of society, can only be described as a monomaniac. I entirely agree with the favorable and unfavorable portions of this criticism. With the exception of Aurora Leigh herself, the characters do not strike one as life-like, nor is the story well contrived, or the events well selected. But the individual passages, admirable in every respect, that might be extracted from it, are numerous; and one may say, in general, that wherever Aurora Leigh speaks of herself, the poetry rises to the highest excellence.

The great general idea which pervades the poem, and which is from time to time most ably expressed, is that in your anxiety to minister to the material wants of your fellow creatures, in your most rational desire that all shall be well fed, well clothed, well housed, you must not overlook or disparage that mental culture, without which you will find, when you have thoroughly mastered your problem, that even the material wants of society will never be satisfactorily supplied. Mrs. Browning has here struck a blow, and struck it ably, at one of the most flagrant errors of Socialism. There are men who would stop the cultivation of the refined classes till they had fed all the hungry. It is that very cultivation which has induced the desire to feed the hungry. If you put a stop to it you stop the philanthropic movement altogether. Again, the great thing is to get people to take care of themselves and of their own offspring, and this intelligent and prospective care of themselves will never be extracted out of ignorant people. And, again, if the industry and intelligence of society could be addressed.

Aurora Leigh was a genius, and fortunately, her early life had been such as would favor the growth of the poetic faculties. Her native place was Italy, and her mother died at her birth. Her father, a grave and learned man of books, a mere child in worldly affairs, finding her thus cast upon his hands, had brought her up as he best knew how. With what admirable humor he is depicted; so deeply loving and anxious to do well for his little daughter, and yet so completely ignorant of woman's ways with children. But while he made the girl a scholar, he wisely took her to learn of nature amid the silence of the mountains. Thus her genius was allowed space to develop. She grew large in mind and heart, though ignorant of all worldly forms and practices. With her father's death there came a change, and she was taken to live with an aunt in her distant English home. This lady did everything by rule and line, and was a pattern of order. Her idea of a young person's education was a constant supervision which restrained all animation and freedom, and compelled the unlucky subject of it to the action of a machine. In addition to this, the very atmosphere of England was chilly and repulsive to one who had gazed upon those clear Italian skies, whilst every one around seemed to repel her love, and to unite in a conspiracy against her freedom. In her studies she was compelled to load her memory with a farrago of dry facts. She ranged far and wide through the genealogies of Spanish kings, the laws of the Birman empire, and the heights of mountains. She studied popular expositions of Scripture, or rather of "inhuman doctrines never taught by John, and thence passed on to learn the duties and capacities of her sex, their power of teaching to think (though unable to think themselves), their tact and rapid insight, and finally, their mission as household slaves and stocking-menders, bound in all intellectual questions to yield to the opinion of their husbands. And so the story goes on, full at least, even at its weakest parts, of food for reflection. There is no want of ideas. Everywhere one is reminded of what Mrs. Browning said regarding her own work: "My poems, while full of faults, as I go forward to my critics and confess, *have my soul and life in them.*"

Mrs. Browning is undoubtedly the first of female poets. After all, Sappho is little better to us than a myth, and when we think of anyone else, however lovable and admirable she may be in her genius, we are not likely, even in the greatest partiality, to place her on a level with this sweet singer and noble thinker. There is a vexed question of the intellectual superiority of the sexes, but it is not a very profitable one. The difference is one of degree, and not of kind. It is curious to note, however, that all our great literary women have flourished within the last century, with the exceptions of Sappho and Colonna.

De Stael, Mary Somerville, Mary Wollstoncroft, Mrs. Gaskel, Felicia Hemans, Dora Greenwell, Mrs. Oliphant, Mrs. Stowe, Joanna Baillie, George Sand, Charlotte Brontè, George Eliot. These are a few of the names that suggest themselves. At an earlier period it was considered unlady-like to write. Even half a century ago the woman who wrote a book was pointed out as a celebrity. But Mrs. Browning is the greatest of all the poets of womankind. She touched the most delicate chords of human sympathy and affection, and her pathos is that which could only be possessed by a woman. She is a poet of the affections, and her poems were the children of travail and sorrow. As she herself says:

> "When I attain to utter forth in verse
> Some inward thought, my soul throbs audbly
> Along my pulses, yearning to be free
> And something farther, fuller, higher, rehearse
> To the individual, true, and the universe
> In consummation of right harmony.
>   *   *   *   *   *   *
> Wait, soul, until thine ashen garments fall."

It was on a June morning of 1861 that she died. She who had had such a close acquaintance with the thought of death, and had so often contemplated a speedy and early departure from this life, did not know that she was going away when at length she was gently taken. It is very charming that one should have such a lovely life to contemplate. She is buried in the English burying-ground, outside the gates of Florence, and on the Casa Gurdi is placed, in Italian, the following inscription:

Here wrote and died
ELIZABETH BARRETT BROWNING.
Who, in her woman's heart, united
The wisdom of a sage, and the eloquence of a poet;
With her golden verse she linked Italy to England.
Florence gratefully placed
This Memorial,
A. D., 1861.

SYNOPSIS LECTURE XXII

Subject—MADAME DE STAËL.—1766–1817.

In the first ranks of female writers; the daughter of the famous Necker; a clever girl, and passionately fond of her father; her mother Puritanical; herself fond of life; gets to composing in secret; early attracts the notice of able men; her worship of Rousseau. Marries at twenty; unhappily; her father's career; her difficulties in the Revolution, and afterwards under the Empire; her brilliant drawing-rooms; Napoleon hates and fears her.

HER GENIUS. "Delphine." "Corinne." Byron's tribute.

MADAME DE STAËL.

No more brilliant name than that of Madame de Staël is to be found among the female writers of any country. She stands in the first rank o all. As a brilliant writer of fiction she was unrivalled until George Eliot. No woman's novel ever attained a greater celebrity than "Corinne"; her "De l' Allemagne", her "Reflexions sur la Revolution Francaise", her "Dix Années d' Exil", and her works upon Literature, soar into regions, and successfully, to which female genius seldom ventures to aspire, whilst as a conversationalist, those who enjoyed the happiness of her society say that she even surpassed herself as a writer.

Anne Louise Germane Necker was born in the spring of 1766. She was the daughter of the Genevese banker, afterwards so famous as the Minister of Louis the Sixteenth. From her earliest years until his death, her love for her father was almost idolatrous; like the maternal love of Madame de Sévigné, it is almost unique in domestic annals. "I owe to the wonderful penetration of my father," she says, "whatever candor my character possesses. He unmasked all false pretences, and from him I acquired the habit of believing that people see straight into my heart." He was to her the model of all that was great and good; a man endued with all the virtues of an ideal Roman. So absorbing was her affection that she was jealous even of her mother, and her mother was jealous of her. A good story is told by Madame Necker Saussure, in her introduction to the collected works of Madame de Staël, which, as illustrating her filial love, and certain vain glorious traits of character, is worth repeating. On the occasion of a certain visit which the narrator paid to the Neckers, at Coppet, M. Neckers estate, near Geneva, the carraige which had been sent to covey her from Geneva was overturned. Upon hearing of this accident, Madame de Staël was agitated with the wildest terror, not, as may be imagined, on account of her guests narrow escape from injury, but from a possible contingency which the accident suggested to her mind. "Ah Heavens!" she exclaimed; "it might have been my father!" She ran to the bell, rang it furiously, and, in a voice trembling with agitation, ordered that the coachman should be instantly sent for. In a few moments the offender stood before her. "Have you heard that I am a woman of genius?" were the first words she spoke to him. Her question was so odd, and her manner so excited that he could not find a reply. "Have you heard that I am a woman of genius?" she repeated yet more angrily. The servant more confused than ever, was still silent. "Well, then, I *am* a woman of genius, of great genius, of prodigious genius! And I tell you that all the genius I possess shall be exerted to secure your rotting all your days in a dungeon, if ever you overturn my father." When her agitation was over, her friends rallied her upon this curious speech, but she failed to see the absurd side of it. "What had I to threaten him with, except her poor genius?" she said, naively.

The only injuries she could not forgive were those offered to her father. She could not endure to think that he was growing old, and a mere hint of such a thing would drive her into a fury. When he was dead, every old man she saw recalled him to her memory, and to watch over the comforts and alleviate the sufferings of age was her greatest · pleasure. She believed that her soul communicated with his in prayer, and, whatever piece of good fortune befell her, she would say, "My father has obtained it for me." "In Madame de Staël's case," says Saint-Beuve, "there is no difficulty in accounting for the enduring warmth of her filial devotion. Amid the misfortunes which, as she advanced in life, successively overtook all the illusions of her heart and thoughts, one single mortal, one only of her old loves, retained his exalted place in her memory, untouched, untainted, without the slightest stain or infidelity to the past; and the immortal and purified flames of her devotion still played about that august head."

Madame Necker was the daughter of a Swiss Calvinistic clergyman. She was a woman of talent, but cold, Puritanical, and severe. She wrote a little, and would have written more, but her husband was averse to such employment of her time; for which aversion he alleged a very strange excuse; he disliked when entering her apartment to feel that he had interrupted her in a serious occupation. So when madame did write it was by stealth. But she principally devoted herself to her daughter, of whom she desired to make a prodigy. The consequence of this ambition was that the child fell ill from overstudy, and was peremptorily ordered by the doctors to be sent into the country, and entirely exempted for some months frow all intellectual exertion.

Nevertheless, little mademoiselle was a prodigy—a wonderfully p ecocious child. Years before, there had been love passages between Madame Necker and Edward Gibbon, the historian, but his father had threatened him with disinheritance if he married her, so the affair was broken off, not, seemingly, with very much heart-aching on either side. After the lady's marriage the quondam lovers renewed their acquaintance. Gibbon, great enough to do without his christian name, was a frequent visitor at the Necker's, and was very fond of little Staël, and, whenever he came her seat was upon his knee. Seeing that both her parents took great delight in his society, she one day gravely proposed that she should marry him! In vain did the father and mother point out the impossibility of such a match, she being at that time ten years of age, and her proposed husband forty. She argued against all their objections, and could by no means be convinced that her idea was not perfectly feasible.

She was passionately fond of the theatre, and, after witnessing a play, always wrote down a plot, and the parts which struck her most. Like Goethe, she had a toy play-house, and cut out figures of kings and queens, making them act, whilst she declaimed their speeches. This, however, she had to do by stealth, owing to her mother's Puritanical ideas. In a like manner she had to enjoy her love for sentimental romances. She would pace up and down the room with a lesson or religious book in one hand, and a romance in the other, reading them alternately, as she advanced or receded from the paternal eye.

In the drawing-room she sat on a stool beside Madame Necker's chair, very upright, and looking very demure. Thither came Raynal, Grimm, Marmontel, and the celebrities of the day, and all would gather around the little stool, and converse with the girl of eleven, as though she had been a woman of their own age.

We have, very fortunately, a most amusing and interesting account of the childhood of Mademoiselle Necker, from the pen of Madame Rilliet, then Mademoiselle Huber, who became acquainted with her about the year 1777, and who ever after remained one of her intimate friends. Here are some characteristic extracts:

"She spoke to me with a warmth and an ease, which might already be called eloquence, and which produced on me the greatest impression. * * * We did not play like children; she asked me immediately what my lessons were; if I knew any foreign languages; if I often went to the theatre. Having told her that I had been there only two or three times, she expressed her astonishment, saying that we should often go together; 'at our return,' added she, 'we shall write down the subjects of the plays we see, and the passages which have struck us most. That is my habit. * * * Besides, we shall write to one another every morning.'

"We entered the drawing-room. By the side of Madame Necker's arm-chair was a small wooden stool, for her daughter, who was obliged to sit bolt upright. Scarcely had she taken her place, when three or four old gentlemen approached her, and addressed her with words of the liveliest sympathy. One of them who had a little round wig, took her hands in his, and began conversing with her as if she had been twenty-five years of age. That man was the Abbé Raynal.

"The company sat down to dinner. How Mademoiselle Necker did listen! Although she never opened her lips, it seemed as if she spoke, such was the expression of her animated features. Her eyes followed the looks and gesticulations of those who carried on the conversation; she seemed as if she met their ideas half way. She was *au fait* of everything, even of political subjects, which at that time already formed the staple topic of discourse.

"After dinner a large number of visitors came. * * * Each one, as he approached Madame Necker, had a word to say to her daughter—a compliment or a witticism. She answered all with ease and grace; people seemed to delight in provoking, in puzzling her, in exciting that young imagination which displayed already so much brilliancy. The men most eminent for their wit were those who particularly endeavored to draw her out. They asked her to give an account of her readings, recommended to her new books, and imparted to her a taste for study in conversing with her, both of what she knew, and of what she did not know."

At twelve, she wrote a little comedy, which was highly praised by Grimm, and at the representation of which Marmontel is said to have shed tears. At fifteen, she studied Montesquieu's "Esprit de Lois," made extracts from it, and written comments in the margins of her copy. She was about the same age when her father, having been dismissed from office, published his "Compte rendu," or account of moneys expended by him during his ministry. The then all-absorbing theme of conversation was politics. Anxious to exercise her mind upon it, she wrote to M. Necker an anonymous letter upon his publication. But her little secret was quickly discovered, as he immediately recognized the style. From that time a yet more close and intimate intercourse subsisted between father and daughter.

Anecdotes of the childhood of great minds are infinitely interesting and suggestive. One such will reveal more of real character than pages of mature conversation and opinions. The constituent elements of our nature never change; they may be modified or expanded by education and circumstances, suppressed by hypocrisy, or good or bad fortune, but they never undergo any radical change. In the tiniest bud is concealed every petal, pistil and stamen which shall hereafter form the flower; favorable or unfavorable influences may advance or retard its perfect development, but cannot change its component parts. So it is with the mind. An ignoble child never became a noble man or woman, and *vice versa*.

Mademoiselle Necker was an idolatrous worshipper of Rousseau, of whose genius her first work was a passionate eulogy, and upon that genius her own was modelled. Indeed, its influence is apparent in all her works of fiction, in their burning passion and their tender melancholy. All her works (some half-a-dozen at this time) were of the lachrymosely sentimental kind. They suggest the English novelist Sterne. They are filled with the words of deserted lovers, and in each there is the tomb of some beloved being half concealed by trees. Little promise so far of "Corinne" and "De l'Allemagne."

Madame Necker's cold and probably prudent nature was desirous of checking this precocious brilliancy in her daughter, who, in deference to these feelings would retire behind her father's chair. But it was of no use. One by one the company would gather round her, until she again became the center of attraction. She was not what is vulgarly called beautiful. The charm of her face was its wonderful expressiveness. A contemporary author thus describes her: "Her great black eyes speak with genius; her black hair falls back on her shoulders in wavy curls; her features are rather strongly marked than delicate; one discerns in her countenance a promise of something above the usual promise of her sex."

At twenty, her parents married her to the Baron de Staël—Holstein, the Swedish ambassador at Paris. It was what our French friends call a marriage of convenience, in which her heart was not consulted. The Baron was handsome, many years her senior, of no intellect, and in all other respects the opposite of what the husband of this passionate, brilliant young creature should have been. As might have been expected, it did not bring happiness to the wife. He was a man of gay and extravagant habits, utterly careless of money, and after a few years she was compelled to separate from him. This was in order to preserve the wreck of her fortune, her own dowry being $400,000. When, however, his health was broken down, he found at Coppet a home and the tenderest of nurses, until death terminated his sufferings. Three children (two sons and a daughter) were the fruits of this marriage.

Since her father's dismissal from the ministry, in 1781, she had resided with him at Coppet, where she mingled with some of the highest personages of France, all of whom entertained the highest respect for M. Necker. In 1787, the family returned to Paris, in consequence of his restoration to power. The restoration lasted but a short time, and he was again dismissed, to be again recalled. His opposition to the nullification of the decrees of the *Tiers État* procured him a third dismissal, and a command to quit the kingdom immediately. His popularity at this time was enormous; the news of his dismissal, revealed to the people by Camille Desmoulins, raised a terrible insurrection, which culminated in the destruction of the Bastille. Poor vacillating Louis was compelled to send a courier post-haste, to bring him back, long before he crossed the frontiers. His return was a triumph, every town and village he passed through greeting him with the warmest demonstrations of joy and sympathy. At Paris his reception was an ovation. Shouts, bonfires, illuminations heralded his approach. He was the mob-deity—for the hour.

How the heart of his daughter must have glowed at this triumph, this splendid acknowledgment of those talents which she regarded as superlative. Alas! both her triumph and her dreams were short lived. A few months after his triumphant re-entrance, he was compelled to resign amidst the hootings and revilings of the mob. In 1790 he retired to Coppet, where he passed the remainder of his days, and where, in 1804, he died.

Madame De Staël stayed in Paris all through the revolution, passing through many tragic scenes. Finally, making her escape, she joined her father for a short time, and then visited England. During her stay in Switzerland she published those early fictions which I have already mentioned. A year later, 1796, she published her work upon the Passions, the most striking and remarkable that had yet appeared from her pen. Order being restored, she returned once more to her beloved Paris.

France was now ruled by the Directory. The Reign of Terror had passed away, and its creators had expiated their crimes upon the scaffold, or were expiating them in distant exile under a tropical sun. The Jacobins had been swept into holes and corners, where they lurked wolf-like, waiting hopefully for the hour when they might again uprear

the standard of anarchy. No one could, however, recognize Paris.
Decay, ruin, disorder, were everywhere. Trade was stagnant, stores
closed—a dead level of impecuniosity was everywhere. Within certain
doors, nevertheless, there was luxury. Slowly and timidly the less
stiff-necked of the *emegries* returned to Paris.

The first five years of the revolution had been an interregnum in
literature. Even Madame de Staël, hundreds of miles away, could not
pen a line. "I should ever have reproached myself for a thought," she
says, writing of that time, "as something too independent of grief."
Such was the effect produced upon all intellectual minds by that awful
period. When, however, she returned to Paris, émigrés were daily
coming back, and more refined coteries were being formed. In 1799,
the Directory was overthrown by a *coup d'etat*, and the Consulate
established, with Napoleon for First Consul. From their first introduction Madame de Staël never liked Bonaparte. It was aversion
mutual at first sight. He inspired her with an instinctive dread—a
feeling which was not unique in her. Being an earnest lover of true
liberty, she early devined his ambitious projects, and foresaw the des-
potism that he was working to erect. "That which characterises Bonaparte's government," she says, "is a profound contempt for all the
intellectual riches of human nature, virtue, dignity of soul, religion, enthusiasm. He would desire to reduce men to mere force and cunning,
and to designate everything else as mere folly and silliness." On the
other hand, Napoleon remarked: "She pretends to speak neither of me
nor of politics, yet I do not know how it happens, but people love me
less who have been with me. She gives them fanciful notions, and of
the opposite kind to mine." At another time he said, "Madam de
Staël has shafts that would hit a man were he seated on a rainbow."

In the year 1800 he established himself in the Tuileries, where he
held a sovereign court, which in gorgeousness would have shamed
the *ancien regime*. In that same year French society had resumed
much of its brilliancy, and gathered around, as usual, different centers.
Madame Récamier was then in all the delicate flower of her youth and
exquisite grace; Madame de Visconti, in all the blossom of her majestic beauty; Madame Josephine Bonaparte gave splendid reunions; and
the Princess de Poix small and exclusive parties. In such salons gathered whatever of beauty, wit and birth the guillotine had spared. But
most notable and brilliant of all these gatherings were those of Madame
de Staël, whose genius and celebrity attracted the finest intellects of all
nations. Brilliant as are her works, her conversation is said to have

been infinitely more so.   Here is how Madame Necker Saussure writes of her.

"In *tete-a-tete* her conversation was a thing that could not be conceived by those who have not enjoyed the privilege of her intimacy. Her finest pages, her most eloquent discourses in society, are far from equalling in all absorbing power that which she spoke when, not being compelled to conform to the ideas of certain auditors, she gave free play to the daring and original thoughts that filled her soul.   Then her grand genius, spreading its wings, took flight; then, knowing not whither it might lead her, a witness rather than a mistress, of her own inspiration, she exercised a power more than natural, to which she herself seemed to submit,—a power good or bad, but over which she had no control; sometimes animated by a bitter and biting spirit, she would wither, as with the breath of death, all the flowers of life, and carry sword and fire into the depths of the heart; she would destroy all the illusions of sentiment; the charm of the most cherished relations.   Sometimes, delivering herself up to a singularly original gaiety, she had the ingenuous grace and confidence of a simple child, who is the dupe of everything; then, at length, soaring into higher regions, she would abandon herself to the sublime melancholy of a religious inspiration, which penetrates the nothingness of terrestrial existence.   But it was when in the society of friends in misfortune that she displayed her grandest powers. Hurried away by rapid and profound feelings, it seemed that she traversed heaven and earth to find solaces for their afflictions.   There was nothing good or ingenious that she did not invent to distract them, to lighten for a time the sombre images of their sadness.   She appeared to dispose of the future, and to create one expressly for them, in which, by the power of friendship, she made amends for everything."

The night before Benjamin Constant, her most intimate friend, made his speech in the Assembly against the growing power of the First Consul, he drew her aside.   "If I make this speech," he said, "to-morrow night your drawing-room will be deserted."   "I know it, but you must do what is right," she answered intrepidly.   Their prognostications were correct.   What could more eloquently describe the slavish adulation of the Parisians to their Moloch?   But Fouché waited on her, and told plainly that Napoleon suspected her of having composed that speech.   A short time after she was commanded to leave Paris, and not to reside within forty leagues of it.   In vain did Josephine Bonaparte, whom she frequently visited, and with whom she passed the last few days of her Parisian residence, intercede for her; the Consul was immovable.

"Delphine," the first of her great fictions, was now published, and created a sensation. This was followed by the celebrated "Discourse upon Literature." During the two following years (1803-4) she travelled through Italy and Germany, passing the greater part of the time at Berlin, Vienna, and Weimar, where she diligently pursued the study of the German language and literature, and contracted an intimacy with Goethe, Schiller, the two Schlegels, Wieland, and other of the finest spirits of Germany. In the last named year she was suddenly recalled to Switzerland by the death of her father. How terrible a blow this was to her may be imagined from what I have already said of her doting affection for him.

She now took up her residence at Coppet, and, as soon as her affliction would permit, gathered about her some of the greatest men of the age. Among them Sismondi, and Benjamin Constant. Nothing more delightful than the life of this intellectual circle can be imagined. Discussions on literary and scientific subjects commenced at eleven o'clock, the breakfast hour, after which the party drove out on some pleasant excursion in the neighborhood of the lake. Conversation was resumed at dinner and supper, and was often prolonged until midnight. Constant—whom she declared to be "the first of living minds"—and herself, de Staël, were the principal talkers. Nothing, if one may believe the testimony of those present, was ever more wonderful or daring than the canversation of those two, in the midst of that select circle. Her mode of composition was admirable. Each work was written three times. The first draft was by her own hand, and, after this had gone through emendations and additions, it was copied by her secretary; then passages were read to select friends; after which, adopting any hints of value that might be offered, it was again corrected and recopied. When composing her work on literature she employed herself as follows: Each morning she arranged a chapter; during the day she turned the conversation upon the subject she proposed to treat of; listened to and argued the various opinions; and, the following day, the chapter was written.

The greatest blow that fell upon her after her father's death was the suppression of her great work, "De l' Allemagne." The minister of police demanded to know why neither the Emperor nor the army had been mentioned in the work upon Germany. She replied that, the subject being purely literary, she did not know how such references could be introduced. "Have we then made war upon Germany for eighteen years in order that a person should print a book without speaking of us?" cried the Minister. "That book shall be destroyed, and the author ought to be sent to Vincennes." The book had been submitted to the censor of the Parisian press, and his alterations and excisions had been carfully observed; it was put in type and printed; then came the veto of the emperor, by whose order 10,000 copies were destroyed. This book had been the labor of years, and she looked forward to its publication with the utmost eagerness. Her mortification may be imagined.

In 1807 was published her greatest and best known fiction, "Corinne," which at once took, not only France, but Europe by storm. Every one read it, and every one, young and old, frivolous and grave, was carried away by its marvelous beauty. Even Scotch professors. stopped one another in the streets to comment on it, and to inquire how far each other had read. It will live forever as one of the most brilliant and passionate works that ever emanated from female pen. Jean Jacques's pupil, had equaled, if not surpassed, the master on his own ground. "Corinne" was the outpourings of the inward soul of its great authoress, or rather it was the embodiment of her soul incorporeally. "Delphine"—it was the reality of her youth, "Corinne" was what Madame de Staël would have been. I cannot forbear giving Saint Beuve's fine analysis of this work. The main idea of the book is the conflict between a noble, of sentimental ambition, and that desire for domestic happiness which was ever present with Madame de Staël. No wonder that Corinne shines by moments like a priestess of Apollo, while, in the daily intercourse of life, she is the simplest of women— gay, versatile, susceptible of a thousand fancies; capable of the most graceful and effortless *abandon*. But from her external or internal resources, she will never escape herself. From the moment when she feels herself seized by passion, by "that vulture grip to which happiness and freedom succumb," I admire her incapability of consolation, the sentiment which is stronger in her than genius; her frequent invocation of the sanctity and permanence of those ties which alone can prevent heart-rending separation. I love to hear her confess in the Swan Song, of her dying hour—"of all faculties that were born with me that of sorrow is the only one which I have exercised to the full." This. continuation of Delphine in Corinne is the most fascinating and endearing characteristic of the book to me. The noble framework, which everywhere surrounds the experiences of this ardent and irrepressible soul, enhances their effect by its severity. These names of lovers, no

longer graven upon beech stems, but inscribed on the walls of eternal
ruins, are associated with a solemn history and come to have a living
share in its immortality. This divine passion of a being, whom we cannot believe imaginary, introduces into the antique arena one more
victim, whom men will not forget. Genius, whose child she was, becomes the last and not the least, in the long list of illustrious victors."

In 1810 there came to the neighborhood of Coppet, a young French
officer of Bonaparte's army, invalided on account of his wounds. He
was twenty-five, Madame de Staël forty-four, and yet a mutual passion
sprang up between them, which resulted in a secret marriage. People
will smile at this, as the image of the average worldly and matter-of-
fact woman of that age rises before them. But it is great folly to compare ordinary humanity with exceptional genius; as the one differs
from the other intellectually, so it does in passion and sentiment.
There are souls that are ever youthful. The body grows old, and
beauty departs from it, or can only be discerned by the inward eyes;
but the soul is still juvenescent, lovely and passionate, as was Psyche
when the rays of her lamp fell upon the sleeping face of Eros.

So wearisome and unbearable became the constant espionage kept
upon her by Bonaparte, that she at length determined to quit Coppet,
and take shelter in England. All direct access was impossible. Escap-
ing out of Switzerland, she journeyed toward Russia, and succeeded in
reaching St. Petersburg, where she was well received by the Emperor,
and remained some time. The news of her enemy's invasion hastened
her departure. It was 1813, however, before she arrived in London.
Her reception was immense. All the fashion and all the celebrities of
the day crowded to visit her. Her residence was at 30 Argyle Place,
Regent Street. Accustomed to the freer society of Paris, and not
understanding English exclusiveness, her assemblies were more numerous than select. Lord Byron said that her table reminded him of the
grave, because there all distinctions are leveled. Peers, dandies, the
most eminent literati, and Grub street scribblers, were equally to be
found there.

It was at this time that "De l'Allemagne" was at length given to the
world. It is the finest of all her works, and, as in his earlier essays,
Carlyle first fully revealed the German genius to England, so did de
Staël perform the same office for France. The book, however, attained
a European perusal, and so anticipated the labors of the Scotch author.

Upon the restoration, Madame de Staël returned to Paris, for which
she was ever pining. Her salons were more brilliant than ever.

Wellington, Chateaubriand, Humboldt, Blucher, Sismondi, Constant, Lafayette, Guizot, Madame Récamier, and large numbers of old friends from England—among them Madame D'Arblay—were constantly to be seen there. The news of the escape from Elba scattered all these brilliant spirits to the four winds, and Madame De Staël once more retired to Coppet. But soon afterward M. Rocca's health obliged her to go to Italy. There she remained until 1816, in which year she returned to Switzerland. About this time Byron hired a house near Geneva, and was her constant guest. Writing of her after her death, the great poet says: "Her loss will be mourned the most where she was known the best, and to the sorrows of very many friends, and more dependent may be offered the disinterested regret of a stranger, who, amidst the sublime scenes of Lake Leman, secured his chief satisfaction from contemplating the engaging qualities of the incomparable "Corinne."

Her last literary productions were among the finest—her "Reflexions sur la Revolution Francaise," and her "Dix Années d'Exil." In the latter she gives some striking pictures of Russia, Poland, and the different countries through which she passed on her way to England.

In 1817 she was seized with a violent fever, to which she ultimately succumbed. The day before her death she read a portion of Byron's "Manfred," and marked some of the finest passages. Upon her sickbed none of her good qualities abandoned her. To the last she was patient and devout, and her intellect undimmed. "I have always been the same," she said, when dying, "lively and sad. I have loved God, my father, and liberty."

And she spoke truly. What better epitaph can one desire than this!

SYNOPSIS LECTURE XXIII.

SUBJECT—CHARLOTTE, EMILY AND ANNE BRONTÉ.

Their lonely upbringing; Haworth parish; their father and mother; sent early to school; ambition to write; Charlotte's account of it.

"Jane Eyre."
"Wuthering Heights."
"Agnes Grey."

THE BRONTÉS.

Genius has often taken up its abode in unpromising soil. Where nature has been most stern and sterile, bleak and bare, thence have sprung some of the choicest spirits, whose lives were fragrant, and whose memories still

"Smell sweet and blossom in the dust.'

Perhaps no example could be cited which more clearly demonstrates the inexpressibility of genius than that of the remarkable trio of sisters, who were known originally as Currer, Ellis and Acton Bell. The truly surprising vigor of their mental constitutions can only be accurately gauged by a consideration of the natural and other disadvantageous circumstances which they successfully overcame.

The village of Haworth lies among the Yorkshire uplands, the parsonage looks down upon the village. There are no trees, and little vegetation of any kind, save a few stunted bushes and shrubs in front of the houses, whilst behind and right up to the kitchen door, is a wild expanse of bleak and melancholy moor. For weeks together the inhabitants are blockaded by the snow, which the north wind brings down from the hills. In addition to the dull, monotonous stretch of moorland, with here and there a "beck" or craig, as the sole variation to the weary eye; there was a population to be met with which, in some respects, exhibited no advance whatever over that of the Middle Ages. There were living individuals who never had beheld a railway. Great natural shrewdness was undoubtedly a characteristic of the inhabitants of the Riding, and, in many cases, a rough sort of *bonhomie* was added, which, however, were frequently rendered more offensive than positive rudeness. The people were hard-fisted, but kindly; good friends and good haters.

Many years ago now, the Rev. Patrick Bronté (the name is Irish, extremely ancient, and an abbreviation of Bronterre), then living in

Penzance, Cornwall, married, against the wishes of his friends, a very
delicate and impressionable young lady, on whose frame it would appear,
consumption had already set the seal of doom, and bore her to this
village in Yorkshire, of which he had been made perpetual curate. Her
family ceased to have any communication with her, and her husband
was of a studious, unworldly and almost unintelligible character; a
character in which a natural tendency to reserve, and self-suppression
was extremely strong. It is one of the mysteries which perpetually
haunt us, in observation of life, that this stern secretiveness can and
does exist in association with strong affections and fine integrity. The
young wife, perhaps conscious that she carried the seeds of an early
death in her bosom, now spent her days in a seclusion which must have
affected her as might a residence on a little island in the sea. In the
quietest of parsonages, whose windows opened upon the graves of the
church yard, what a life this woman must have lived! Of a mother leading this strange existence were born Charlotte, Emily and Anne
Bronté

The early training of the children, especially that of Charlotte,
could scarcely have been happy. At an early age, Charlotte induced
her father to send her and her sisters to the Clergy-School at Cowan-
bridge, which is the "Lowood" of Jane Eyre. The account of the
school was only too true. The "Helen" of that tale is,—not precisely
the eldest sister, who died there—but more like her than any other real
person. Another sister died at home, soon after leaving the school,
and in consequence of its hardships; and "Currer Bell," (Charlotte
Bronté) was never free while there—for a year and a half—from the
gnawing of sensation, or consequent feebleness, of downright hunger;
and she never grew an inch from that time. She was the smallest of
women and it was that school which stunted her growth. Such experiences as those of these girls at Lowood were excellently adapted to
give a premature insight into the recesses of human motive, the varie-
ties of human character, and to strengthen a natural tendency to surround the ordinary and the real with a preturnaturally tragic atmosphere.
That they would deepen that morbid *taste* for self-communion and self-
suppression which so evidently existed in all three of these remarkable
beings, most of all of Emily, is obvious. After Lowood, came for all
three, the life of a governess. Charlotte went to the Continent as is
plain from "Villette."

The literary history of those three sisters is given by Charlotte
herself, in the biographical notice of her sisters prefixed to the edition

of "Wuthering Heights" and "Agnes Grey," published after their death, and dated 19th September, 1850; she says:—

"About five years ago, my two sisters and myself, after a somewhat prolonged period of separation, found ourselves reunited and at home. Resident in a remote district, where education had made little progress and where, consequently, there was no inducement to seek social intercourse beyond our own domestic circle, we were wholly dependent on ourselves, and each other, on books and study, for the enjoyments and occupations of life. The highest stimulant, as well as the liveliest pleasure we had known, from childhood upwards, lay in attempts at literary composition. Formerly we used to show each other what we wrote, but of late years this habit of communication and consultation had been discontinued; hence it ensued that we were mutually ignorant of the progress we might respectively have made.

One day, in the autumn of 1845, I accidently lighted on a MS. volume of verse in my sister Emily's handwriting. Of course I was not surprised, knowing that she could and did write verses; I looked it over, and something more than surprise seized me—a deep conviction that these were not common effusions, nor at all like the poetry women ordinarily write. I thought them condensed and terse, vigorous and genuine. To my ear they had also a peculiar music—wild, melancholy and elevating. * * * Meantime my younger sister produced some of her own compositions, intimating that since Emily's had given me pleasure, I might like to look at hers. I could not but be a partial judge, yet I thought that these verses too had a sweet sincere pathos of their own.

We had very early cherished the dream of one day becoming authors. This dream, never relinquished, even when distance divided, and absorbing tasks occupied us, now suddenly acquired strength and consistency; it took the character of a resolve. We agreed to arrange a small selection of our poems, and, if possible, get them printed. Averse to personal publicity we veiled our own names under those of Currer, Ellis and Acton Bell, the ambiguous choice being dictated by a sort of conscientious scruple at assuming Christian names positively masculine, while we did not like to declare ourselves women, because, without at that time suspecting that our mode of writing and thinking was what is called "feminine"— we had a vague impression that authoresses are liable to be looked on with prejudice. We had noticed how critics sometimes use for their chastisement the weapon of personality, and for their reward a flattery, which is but true praise.

The bringing out of our little book was hard work. As was to be expected neither we nor our poems were at all wanted; but for this we had been prepared at the market; though inexperienced ourselves, we had read the experience of others. The great puzzle lay in getting answers from the publishers, to whom we applied. Being greatly harassed by this obstacle, I ventured to apply to the Messrs. Chambers, of Edinburg, for a word of advice; *they* may have forgotten the circumstance, but *I* have not, for from them I received a brief and business-like, but civil and sensible reply, on which we acted and at last made way.

The book was printed; it is scarcely known, and all of it that merits to be known are the poems of Ellis Bell. The fixed conviction that I held, and hold, of the merits of these poems has not indeed received the confirmation of much favorable criticism; but I must retain it notwithstanding.

Ill success failed to crush us; the mere effort to succeed had given a wonderful zest to existence; it must be pursued. We each set to work on a prose tale; Ellis Bell produced "Wuthering Heights," Acton Bell "Agnes Grey," and Currier Bell also wrote a narrative in volume. MSS. were perseveringly obtruded upon various publishers for the space of a year and a half; usually their fate was an ignominious dismissal.

At last "Wuthering Heights" and "Agnes Grey" were accepted on terms somewhat impoverishing to the two authors; Currier Bell's book found acceptance nowhere, nor any acknowledgement of merit, so that something like the chill of despair began to invade his heart. As a forlorn hope he tried one publishing house more—Messrs. Smith & Elder. Ere long—in a much shorter space than that on which experience had led him to calculate—there came a letter which he opened in the dreary expectation of finding two hard hopeless lines, intimating that Messrs. Smith & Elder were not disposed to publish the MS., and instead, he took out a letter of two pages. He read it trembling. It declined, indeed, to publish the tale for business reasons, but it discussed its merits and demerits so courteously, so considerately, in a spirit so rational, with a discrimination so enlightened, that this very refusal cheered the author better than a vulgarly-expressed acceptance would have done. It was added that a work in three volumes would meet with careful attention.

I was then just completing " Jane Eyre," at which I had been working while the one volume tale was plodding its weary round in London;

in three weeks I sent it off; friendly and skillful hands took it in. This was in the commencement of 1847; it came out before the close of October following, while "Wuthering Heights" and "Agnes Grey," my sisters' works, which had already been in the press for months, still lingered under different management. They appeared at last. Critics failed to do them justice.

"Jane Eyre" was an immense success. It was one of those books which take the world by storm. The author was universally supposed to be her own heroine, but she altogether denied it. She declared that there was no more ground for the assertion than this: She once told her sisters that they were wrong, morally wrong, in making their heroines beautiful, as a matter of course. They replied that it was impossible to make a heroine interesting on other terms. Her answer was: "I will prove to you that you are wrong. I will show you a heroine as small and plain as myself, who shall be as interesting as any of yours. Hence ' Jane Eyre,' " said she, in telling the anecdote, "but she is not myself, any farther than that."

The melancholy story of the only brother, Branwell, a young man of once brilliant promise which was early blighted, is well-known. Charlotte loved him deeply in spite of his numberless errors, and terrible slavery to one master-passion. To his end succeeded that of Emily, the sister whom Charlotte loved best. These were heavy trials. "Shirley" was conceived and written in the midst of terrible griefs. Her remaining sister died the same year. "There was something inexpressibly affecting" says one who knew her, "in the aspect of the frail little creature who had done such wonderful things, and who was able to bear up with so bright an eye and so composed a countenance, under such a weight of sorrow, and such a prospect of solitude. In her deep mourning dress (neat as a Quaker's), with her beautiful hair smooth and brown, her fine eyes blazing with meaning, and her sensible face indicating a habit of self-control, if not of silence—she seemed a perfect household image,—irresistably recalling Wordsworth's description of that treasure. And she was this. She was as able at the needle as the pen. The household knew of the excellence of her cookery before they heard of that of her books.

The novels of Charlotte Bronté were of a different kind to what the world had been previously accustomed to, nor were they such as to create immediate interest. Masculine in their strength, and very largely so in the cast of thought, there could be no wonder that the public should assume that Currer Bell was a man and even persist in the delusion after the most express assurance to the contrary. Certainly, one can sympathize with the feeling of astonishment that "Jane Eyre" should have been written by a woman. But, at the same time, it may be said that shortly after the book appeared, and it was published in 1847, the opinion of more than one critic, not in the secret, was that it was from the pen of a lady, and a clever one too. The reality of many of the scenes and personages, was also recognized, the characters being too life-like to be the creatures of mere fancy; and, sketchy as some are, they are yet so wondrous telling, some of them persuading us that we have met them in real life. The Rev. Mr. Brocklehurst, with his "straight, narrow, sable-clad shape, standing erect on the rug; the grim face at the top being like a carved mask, placed above the shaft by way of capital;" the lady-like Miss Temple; sweet Helen Burns, whose death scene is so touchingly related; the neat and prim little Mrs. Fairfax, and the eccentric Mr. Rochester, whom with all his faults and eccentricities, one cannot help getting to like; are but a few of the characters in the drama, though essential ones.

I cannot do better than give a few extracts, to give some idea of this, the most striking and famous of Charlotte Brontë's works. It is called an autobiography, which to a great extent it is, and the fact explains the style. The following is Jane's position in life at the beginning of the narrative:

"I learned for the first, from Miss Abbot's communication to Bessie, that my father had been a poor clergyman; that my mother had married him against the wishes of her friends, who considered the match beneath her; that my grandfather, Reed, was so irritated at her disobedience, that he cut her off without a shilling; that after my mother and father had been married a year, the latter caught the typhus fever, while visiting among the poor in a large manufacturing town, where his curacy was situated and where that disease was then prevalent; that my mother took the infection from him and both died within a month of each other."

Her mother's brother, not participating in the feelings of his father, took the orphan into his own house, with the intention of bringing her up with, and as one of, his own children; but he, too, died, and left poor Jane to the tender mercies of her purse-proud aunt and cousins; how these mercies were displayed may be guessed.

Jane's first remove was from the Hall to Lowood Institution—in some respects a second edition of Dotheboy's Hall—where for the payment of $75 per annum, young female orphans were boarded and educated to enable them to act as governesses. The treasurer and sole manager of this semi-charitable establishment is the Rev. Mr. Brockle-hurst, before mentioned. The reverend gentleman has been lecturing Miss Temple, the superintendent, on the enormity of the hose being allowed to go too long unmended, and other little household matters of a like description, but more especially for pampering the appetites of the scholars with a lunch of bread and cheese, when their porridge had been spoiled at breakfast time so that they could not eat it.

"Meantime Mr. Brocklehurst, standing on the hearth with his hands behind his back, majestically surveyed the whole school. Suddenly his eye gave a blink, as if it had met something that either dazzled or shocked its pupil; turning, he said in more rapid accents than he had hitherto used:

"'Miss Temple, Miss Temple! what—*what* is that girl with red hair? Red hair, ma'am, curled—curled all over?' and extending his cane he pointed to the awful object, his hand shaking as he did so.

"'It is Julia Severn,' replied Miss Temple, very quietly.

"'Julia Severn, ma'am! And why has she, or any other, curled hair? Why, in defiance of every precept and principle of this house, does she conform to the world so openly—here, in an evangelical, charitable establishment, as to wear her hair a mass of curls?'

"'Julia's hair curls naturally,' replied Miss Temple, still more quietly.

"'Naturally! Yes, but we are not to conform to nature; I wish these girls to be the children of Grace; and why that abundance?'"

How bewildered, yet how hearty and infectious, is Jane's delight at the unexpected discovery of relatives of whose existence she had pre-viously no suspicion! The information has just been imparted by her cousin.

"'I surveyed him. It seemed that I had found a brother; one that I could be proud of; one that I could love; and two sisters whose quali-ties were such that, when I knew them but as mere strangers, they had inspired me with genuine affection and admiration. The two girls on whom I, kneeling down on the wet ground, and looking through the low latticed window of Moor House kitchen, were my near kinswoman; and the young and stately gentleman who had found me almost dying at the threshold was my blood relation! Glorious news to a lonely wretch! This was wealth indeed!—wealth to the heart!—a mine of pure affection. This was a blessing, bright, vivid, exhilarating! Not like the ponderous gift of gold, rich and welcome enough in its way, but

sobering from its weight. I now clapped my hands with sudden joy—
my pulse bounded, my veins thrilled.' "

There are many other passages which I would gladly quote, some
perhaps of a more telling description than those now given; but they
cannot be properly separated from the context.

The morality of "Jane Eyre" has frequently been condemned, but
there is really no foundation for such a charge as is implied. What has
been laid hold of chiefly is the sudden confidence between the heroine
and Rochester. There is no doubt truth in the criticism that there is too
little attractiveness in her to account for the excessive passion in such a
man, but passion has its caprices, and I am not inclined even to put down
to slender or feminine knowledge of the world, the author's portraiture
in this respect. Charlotte Bronté herself was sorely grieved and hurt
by the charge of immorality in her work. It is one continually raised
by a certain class of persons. So it was made against Sir Walter Scott
and his Effie Deans—and so it was made against Mrs. Browning and
her Marian Earle in "Aurora Leigh." I prefer to quote Mrs. Gaskell's
words on the subject, remarking in passing that her "Life of Charlotte
Bronté" is a charming book, which those who have hitherto passed
it over, would give themselves great pleasure to read. She says:

"Who is he that should say of an unknown woman, 'She must be
one who, for some sufficient reason, has long forfeited the society of
her sex?' Is he one who has led a wild, struggling and isolated life,—
seeing few but wild and outspoken Northerns, unskilled in the euphu-
isms, which assist the polite world to skim over the mention of vice?
Has he striven through long weeping years to find excuses for the lapse
of an only brother, and through daily contact with a poor lost profligate,
been compelled into a certain familiarity with the vices that his soul
abhors? Has he through trials close following in dread march through
his household, sweeping the hearth-stone bare of life and love, still
striven hard for strength to say, 'It is the Lord! Let Him do what
seemeth to Him good'—and sometimes striven in vain until the kindly
light returned? If through all these dark waters the scornful reviewer
has passed clear, refined, free from stain, with a soul that has never in
all its agonies cried *Lama Sabachthani!*—still, even then, let him pray
with the Publican rather than judge with the Pharisee."

Let us pass to "Shirley," however, in which we see our authoress in
a different phase of her character. Let us call to mind the agony of
sorrow through which she had passed and was still passing, in order to
realize how she has artistically developed. She is no longer held down

by the oppressions of life. She rises above mere hardship and the overwhelmingness of the griefs and ills of life to higher things. There is even humor here previously unsuspected. It is a good book all round, and has well worked and delightful portraits,—delightful for we feel that without exaggeration they are real and yet interesting. Because a character may be very real and yet very stupid. The three curates, the Yerkes, and Mrs. Prior are all portraits. Then there is the description of the revival in the New Wesleyan Chapel at Briarfield, when "Doad o' Bill's" announced that he had "*fun* (found) liberty," and the excitement amongst the brethren was intense. "The roof of the chapel did not fly off, which speaks volumes in praise of its solid slating." And here is a female character, "Nature made her in a mood in which she makes her briars and thorns;" whereas for the creation of some women she reserves the May morning hours, when with the light and dew she woes the primrose from the turf, and the lily from the woodmoss." "Shirley" is a "Holiday of the Heart." The imagination is liberated and revels in its liberty. It is the pleasant summer time, and the worker is idling among the hills; the burn foams and sparkles through the glen; there is sunshine among the purple harebells; and the leaves in the birken glade dance merrily in the summer wind.

I remember very well this fact that the "The Professor" lay a long time aside. The works of many authors—that is, their first writings, have lain aside till more ambitious efforts have been accepted. It is the old story of the world; you do a thousand things well, and nobody thinks much about it—indeed nobody knows—you do one thing well, and immediately all else you have done becomes of value. "The Professor" which was the first work written by Charlotte Bronté, ostensibly for publication, though not by any means her first work in fiction, exhibits a great amount of conscious power, but also an inability on the part of the writer to let herself away. A comparison between this and succeeding works will show how she was cramped in its composition. It went as the story has been told, through the hands of many publishers,—wandering about, an untold story. And yet it found its market, and has for all lovers of the Brontés, not only an historical, but an essential interest. Her idea is that the hero of the book was to succeed by the sheer force of his genius. "As Adam's son he should share Adam's doom, and drink throughout life a mixed and moderate cup of enjoyment." It was a picture drawn by one who had looked on the stern realities of life. That is Charlotte Bronté all over. She looked at things with her own eyes, and if, in a certain way,

you wish to know her, you must catch the light of her eyes,—or if you
can borrow them, look through them.   For it will not do to say for you
and me, that to take up a book from Boccacio's "Decameron" through
say Shakespeare, afterwards Smollett and Fielding; and latest on say
George Eliot and Mrs. Browning, and remark—"this won't do for me."
After all the eyes, even in reading, bring with them only what
they have the power of seeing.   Just as in walking along a street,
one person may observe many things and the next person nothing.   So
is it with books.   You must be there, and it is an impossible thing to
teach.   It is like growing older, your parents leaving you or dying, and
your having to walk alone.   There is much in "The Professor" which
is characteristic of the author in her later works.   Some of the materials
we are told were afterwards used in "Villette," but if so, they were
carefully disguised, and the world could very well afford to welcome
the two.   Passages occur in "The Professor" which are almost startling
in their strength of passion and eloquence.   All the toil, by which the
person who gives the title to the volume is led to her conclusions, is
marked by the intensest sympathy on the part of the author, and
although the reader may not be able to feel much personal enthusiasm
in the various characters, he must at once yield the point that he is
perusing the thoughts of no common mind.   The knowledge which
Charlotte Brontë acquired abroad is used with no inconsiderable skill.
Of course she is at home in describing the family life of the Crimsworths.
If she was at home anywhere, why should she not be in Yorkshire.
Most novelists are after all narrators.   They tell you with a little
imagination, and more or less skill, just what they have seen with their
own eyes.   It is not given to every man to write "Don Quixote."   "I
am no Oriental," says the Professor, "white necks, carmine lips and
cheeks, clusters of bright curls do not suffice me, without that Prome-
thean Spark, which will live after the roses and lilies are faded, the
burnished hair grown gray.   In sunshine, in prosperity, the flowers are
very well, but how many dark days are there in this life—November
season of disaster—when a man's hearth and home would be cold
indeed, without the cheering gleam of intellect."   There you see our
authoress at home again, in that lonely parish in Yorkshire.   The
Professor and the Oriental are now here.   It is her own idea and her
own longing for something different.   "Love without the union of souls
is nothing; the sheen of a summer's day, and quite as fleeting."   There
again you see the lonely heart in Yorkshire, cut off meantime from
what she aspired to, and with that premonition of death common to all

people, especially perhaps poets, who are not intended by the gods to live long.

It is most certain that those girls who wrote so well, and so admirably, were the creation, if we are to analyze things which cannot be easily analyzed, greatly, of the circumstances in which they were placed. It is a subject for the materialist, or phsychologist, or any wise person, just as you please; but it is too long for me to discuss in my limits. I may hint that hereditary ability stuck up in a corner, generally, if it lives, shows itself in some way. What could those girls, bound to think, because they were bound, do but write first poems and then books! That is the Brontés. People in the city mostly exhaust themselves with what they have to see and do. It is quite enough for them. Authorship of this kind comes, I should fancy, almost invariably from a knowledge or imagination of the world—*and seclusion*. Books brought the world home most certainly, as now newspapers do; but they never will replace the real thing. The world is the great thing for the most, if not all, of us. The city, its reality, its memory, or, if you choose, its imagination, is what inspires our genius—if we have any. People are what we want. Even father and mother wont do; they are not enough. And want of bread does not enable people to write. From Ovid to Cervantes you will find this so.

But to pass from this let us turn to Emily Bronte. She was perhaps the most remarkable of those sisters. Read about her; that facing of a fierce dog; that saying of hers that if her brother would not do right she would have him whipped; think of her altogether, she is a woman that most men would like to know. Strong and gentle, as I have known many girls, with city traditions and severely country life. With all, if you choose, of two or three generations of thought in their mind, and the loneliness of the prairie cast around them. They, those people, get to know everything and see everything. They are not necessarily gossips, unless they have weak or common minds, but not a plant they do not get acquainted with, not a foolish person passes them but they could tell you all about him, predict what he will do, and tell you what he has done. Not a dog but is their friend. It is Piccioln and the prison flower *transplanted*.

Emily Jane Bronté died before she was thirty. She, to my mind, must have been a singularly loveable woman. I have described her in what I have said. She wanted an outlet and only partly got it. We know about her, and care for her "Wuthering Heights", and if we are not altogether city bred, and know something of limits of country life which do not resolve themselves in utter stupidity, we can understand and sympathize with her genius. Otherwise I could not safely predict who would care to have her realistic pictures. She depicted characters about whom most persons know nothing and care less. There is that imagination in her work, however, which comes of that isolation of which I have spoken. Heathcliffe, "as dark almost as if he came from the devil," is purely her own invention; and this,—"Cathy! Oh my heart's darling, hear me this once! Catharine at last!"—smacks a little like of a dime novel. The book is well worth reading, however. Although one may suggest that it is a little like the production that a clever sister might send to her brother who has lived many years in the city.

Anne Bronté was different from her two sisters. The youngest of the three, she most likely learned early to lean, and to do what she was told. "Agnes Grey" is interesting, but not worthy of any special remarks. "The Tenant of Wildfell Hall" is an interesting story to those who wish to make a study of human nature in many places, and presents, no doubt, a faithful picture of what Anne saw with her own eyes.

Altogether, however, to me the Brontés are interesting, in a world full of difficulties, for their noble courage, their self-denial, and their devotion to what they deemed the highest. Their verses at the best are but the echo of what one has read before. But still those sisters are of those whose memory the world will not willingly let die, and I confess that, notwithstanding the eldest sister's fame, I do not know whether I like personally Charlotte or Emily the better. As I said before, Mrs. Gaskell's "Life" is simply charming, and should be read by all lovers of literature.

SYNOPSIS LECTURE XXIV.

MARGARET FULLER OSSOLI adds another to the list of great men and women whose genius literally triumphed over ungenial and unfavorable surroundings.

No kind, well meaning friend dare take from or add to her life—mark here, without injuring, aye marring this most singular, deeply pathetic being that soared so much above the commonality. She was the eldest child of Timothy Fuller and Margaret Crane, of Cambridge Port, Massachusetts, and was born on the 3d of May, 1810. When barely six years old she began to read Latin.— Placed, much against her will, in a school in Groton, Mass. At fifteen she had said, "I am determined on distinction;" at twenty she had attained it. She founded a "Ladies' Conversazione," which the force of her eloquence and influence managed to keep alive for six years, at weekly meetings, at which were constellated, from time to time, all the ladies most distinguished for talent, worth and beauty in the place. During her short stay in England, saw many characters well known in the literary world, and describes them in her letters to friends. Her portraiture of Carlyle. Finds another self, dearer to her than her own, in the gentle and amiable Marquis Ossoli, whom she first met by accident at St. Peters. Her secret marriage. "O Father, give me a bud on my tree of life, so scathed by the lightning and bowed by the frost." A peaceful winter of the purest domestic happiness in Florence, followed by the months of anguish. Margaret, with her husband and child, sailed from Leghorn for New York, on May 17, 1850. Many gloomy presentiments. The ship was driven, by the combined force of currents and tempest on to the sand-bars at Long

Island.   At last the final moment came and the prayer was granted—Ossoli, Angelo and herself went down together, and "the
anguish was brief."   Her early trials were loneliness of heart, and
obstacles to the development of her genius; her later ones, that
chill penury that represses noble rage, doubly trying to a disposition munificent as hers, and the depressing uncertainty as to the
power of turning her abilities to the account her circumstances
required.

MARGARET FULLER OSSOLI.

Margaret Fuller Ossoli adds another to the list of great men and women whose genius literally triumphed over ungenial and unfavorable surroundings. You remember how Madame de Staël wrote standing, so that she might not be disturbed when her autocratic father entered her apartment. Nor can you have forgotten that other picture of one of the most gifted Englishwomen of all time, who spent three years of her youth copying mercantile letters,—the only curb her merchant father could find for an ideality he could not comprehend. For all such natures God provides such discipline. To us it may look harsh. But the experience of all the ages warns us that we can trust Him that it shall prove wise. To the study of the character of Margaret Fuller Ossoli I come with mixed feelings. In the first place it is many years since I first became acquainted with her life and works, and since I have renewed that acquaintance within the last three weeks, circumstances have made it impossible for me to refresh my memory in such a way that I can rely implicitly on the facts, or enter at the detail I should like into the particulars of her wonderfully sad, sublime and touching story. I have, therefore, to some extent, to ask your indulgence in advance, and attribute my shortcomings to the slips of a memory, always treacherous, which I have found it impossible adequately to refresh, and which it finds hard to recall with precision the impressions of thirty years ago. Besides, we English boys were not taught at school anything about Margaret Fuller, largely because she was a foreigner, and partly because her achievements are not of the kind that bulk most largely in the popular history of the world.

Again, there were certain traits in her character, like flaws in Carrara marble, with which I have always been unable to sympathize— certain angularities and a spirit of self-satisfaction and exaggeration which to a certain extent repel a student brought up in the narrower atmosphere of an island, where you live in hourly fear of toppling over the edge into the German or Atlantic ocean. But all the same, my impressions of her are extraordinarily vivid, for she was so full of love and sympathy herself with every living creature—man, bird and beast; was in such intimate communion with the good and true, and the sublimity of her ideals and life-long efforts were so pathetically emphasized by the tragic nature of her end, that I can honestly say the life of no other woman ever made on my plastic mind as a student so intense and wholesome an impression as that of Margaret Fuller. And the admiration and respect thus excited it was, that led me to sympathize with the extraordinary warmth with which men like Emerson and Channing wrote of her. To those, indeed, who knew her, these memoirs of theirs are fraught with a melancholy, even painful interest, and when I consider her vast, conversational powers—almost equal to those of Carlyle or Coleridge—with a more useful application of them; her deep and multifarious reading, and the energy with which she employed her acquirements and abilities for all whom she could either benefit or serve, calling forth at the same moment all the sweetest and most feminine attributes; all the tender sympathies and holy charities of life, by which her memory is embalmed in the hearts of the Old as well as the New World. I feel that to fully understand Margaret Fuller one must take her simply as she stands. No kind, well-meaning friend dare take from or add to her life—mark here, without injuring, aye marring this most singular, deeply pathetic being that soared so much above the commonalty.

Margaret Fuller was the eldest child of Timothy Fuller and Margaret Crane, of Cambridge Port, Massachusetts, and was born on the 3d of May, 1810. Her father was a lawyer and a politician, a fair scholar, though hardly perhaps a ripe and good one, but well acquainted with general literature. To be an honored citizen and to have a home on earth were, from her account of him, the great aims of his existence; and very praiseworthy aims they would appear, according to the estimate of most rational persons; but they were not lofty enough to satisfy the early intellectual ambition of his daughter, who had, even at the time she thus describes him, little respect for what she terms "the common places of a mere bread-winning, bread-bestowing existence." Bread and butter is all very well, she thought, but bread and butter, or the aquisition of them, is not the be-all and the end-all of life. "To open the deeper fountains of the soul," said she, "to regard life here as the prophetic entrance to immortality, to develop his spirit to perfection,—motives like these had never been suggested to him, either by fellow beings, or by outward circumstances. The result was a

character, in its social aspect, of quite the common sort. A good son
and brother, a kind neighbor, an active man of business,—in all these
outward relations of life he was but one of a class which surrounding
conditions have made the majority in all respectable and god-fearing
communities. In the more delicate and individual relations, he never
approached but two mortals, my mother and myself." This mother
appears to have been a creature of angelic temperament, breathing
love, and inspiring it in every living thing that came within her gentle
influence. Mr. Fuller, proud of the capabilities of his daughter,
developed even in her childhood, undertook himself to be her instructor;
but by imposing on her tasks beyond her strength, on subjects beyond
her years,—requiring her, moreover, to repeat them to him on his
return from his office late in the evening, under all the terror of incurring
his displeasure if she were not letter-perfect, even while nature was
calling for sleep, he did her the double injury of making her fancy
herself "a youthful prodigy" by day, and rendering her at night
the victim of spectral illusions, of nightmare, and somnambulism;
which at a later period changed their forms into headaches, weakness,
and every description of nervous affections. When barely six years
old, she began to read Latin, and in translating it was expected to give
the thoughts in as few words as possible, clearly arranged, and without
breaks or hesitation. Of Greek she seems to have acquired but little
knowledge; although her youthful studies were divided between the
mythologic fables of that poetic country and the sterner realities of
Roman history; and day after day the enchanting visions of the one
and the heroic deeds of the other, were mused over by her, in a little
garden behind the house, full of choice flowers, and commanding
through its gate, a view of the glories of the setting sun. "Here,"
says she, "the best hours of my lonely childhood were spent;" and
this childhood she describes with an analytical minuteness that appears
much more the effect of mature reflection than of childish recollections;
particularly when she informs us that Shakespeare, Cervantes and Mo-
liere were her favorite authors at eight years of age! At the time I speak
of, her absorbing love of books was wholesomely interrupted for a
season, by a passionate attachment she formed for an English lady,
whom she first saw at church. This lady from her captivating manner,
beautiful sweet face, and elegant dress—pardon the use of the word
"elegant," it was a slip—burst upon the poor lonely overworked child
like some glorious meteor, and so captivated the youthful scholar, that
on the lady's return to the old world, Margaret's heart seemed to die

within her, and she fell into such an alarming state of despondency and languor, that her father, beginning to fear that he had too highly worked upon her nervous system, wisely resolved to correct his error by sending her to school; where she would have the advantage of companionship, and be tempted to relieve sedentary occupation by bodily exercise. She was accordingly placed, much against her will, in a school in Groton, Mass. Passing at once from the monotony and, to her, loneliness of her own home, to a little world of youth and vivacity, she felt all her powers called forth, and resolved on the subjugation of her schoolfellows, by gaining their admiration and their love,—like George Eliot she hungered for love all life through—for while her head claimed the one, her heart equally claimed the other. At first, she succeeded in her endeavor; gradually, however, her peculiarities and caprice undid the spell her mental superiority had cast around; she as often teazed as pleased; and at last finding her empire totter, she began, in revenge for a joke played upon, (which she magnified into an insult) to act upon the well known despotic maxim "divide et impera," and descended to sow discord among her schoolfellows. On account of her quick perception of character she was able to bear upon the weak point of each, until distrust and dissatisfaction separated even those who had before been bosom friends. On being found out, the grief and horror she felt on being made sensible of the enormity of her fault, so overpowered her that for many days she lay motionless and speechless, and only showed consciousness by waving her hand in token of refusal, when food or medicine were offered to her lips.

Nobly and truthfully does Margaret Fuller tell this part of her story. Most impressive and encouraging is the lesson it holds out, that no single fault, however heinous, once seen, acknowledged, and sincerely repented of, can mar the whole course of life. Slowly recovering from her shock, under the judicious treatment and tender sympathy of one of her teachers, whose friendship she ever afterwards retained, Margaret took the first step towards the restoration of her bosom's peace, by discharging it of the weight of remorse that loaded it, in a full confession of her fault, and an humble petition for forgiveness. Many years after, when speaking of this period to the wise and kind friend who had supported her through it, she says: "You need not fear to revive painful recollections. I often think of those sad experiences. True, they agitate me deeply. But it was best so. They have had a most powerful effect on my character. I tremble at whatever looks like dissimulation. The remembrance subdues every proud, passicnate impulse. * * * Can I ever forget that to your treatment in that crisis of youth, I owe the true life—the love of Truth and Honor?" Shortly after this Margaret Fuller returned to the parental roof, and betook herself again to her studies. Rising a little before five she took an hour's walk, then practiced on the piano till seven, when breakfast took place, after which she read French till eight, then two or three lectures in Brown's "Philosophy." About half-past nine she went to a Mr. Perkin's school and studied Greek till twelve, when, the school being dismissed, she recited, went home and practiced again till dinner, at two; after dinner read Italian for two hours; at six took a walk or drive; before going to bed she always played or sang for half an hour, and about eleven wrote a little while in her journal—exercises on what she had read. She was then fifteen. Two years later she says: "I am engrossed in reading the elder Italian poets, beginning with Berni, from whom I shall proceed to Pulci and Pelition. I read very critically Miss Francis, and I think of reading Locke, as introductory to a course of English metaphysics, and then De Staël on Locke's system." In Spanish literature she likewise made great progress, but her chief attainment was in German. Goethe became her idol, and her criticism on his writings, Emerson says, is, in his opinion, the best that has ever been written. Five more years were given to incessant reading, and to deep contemplation of the human character. At fifteen she had said, "I am determined on distinction;" at twenty she had attained it.

In 1835 she was introduced to Harriet Martineau, with whom she rapidly passed "the barrier that separates acquaintanceship from friendship." In this same year Margaret was attacked by a severe fever. When her father came to her bedside in the course of it, he said; "My dear, you have defects, of course, as all mortals have, but I do not know that you have a single fault." These words from one who, upon principle, had always abstained from praising her, or, indeed, any of his children in their presence, and the deep thankfulness he evinced on her recovery, were treasured up in her heart, and she had soon need of the consolation afforded by their recollection, for very shortly after, the revered parent, to whom she owed so much of her mental culture, was attacked with cholera, and expired under it on the second day of his suffering.

Her first thought, after the first shock of her grief had passed, was how far she could supply his place. "I have prayed to God," said she, "that duty may now be the first object, and self set aside. May I have light and strength to do what is right, in the highest sense, for my

mother, brothers, and sister." And now it is that Margaret Fuller's
real excellence of character appears. For the fulfilment of the duties
she had solemnly taken upon herself she relinquished the object which
had formed the vision of her life, and that was to visit Europe, "its
scholars, libraries, lectures, galleries of art, museums of science, antiq-
uties, and historic scenes." The opportunity of going with her warmest and best friends, Mr. and Mrs. Farrar, was now presented to her,
with the pleasure, in addition of Miss Martineau's society. Yet this
long-anticipated delight she unrepiningly renounced, because she feared
the sum required would be more than her family, as then situated,
could spare; yet she had been promised it by her father especially for
that very purpose, and had, indeed, justly earned it, in devoting her
time to the instruction of her brothers, in order to share the expense of
other tuition for them. Ten years later she accomplished the object
she had so passionately desired, and which, alas! terminated in her
finding her grave beneath the billows that were to have borne her
back, exultant, a happy wife and mother, to her native shore.

The intervening period was passed by her in exemplary exertions
for the honorable maintenance of her family and herself. She resided
chiefly in Boston, where she gave lessons in Latin and French in Mr.
Alcot's then flouishing school, and had classes of young ladies in
French, German, and Italian. She also, during these years, published
her "Summer on the Lakes," "Woman in the Nineteenth Century,"
besides several translations from the German, and contributed largely
to the *Dial* and *Tribune*, two publications, as you all know, of no little
note in their day. The Atheneum Library and Musuem, of Boston, were
a fund of intellectual wealth to her, and she deeply felt the exalting
influence of the study of the Greek art, and the Italian masters, though
only through the imperfect medium of casts and engravings. There too
she, founded a "Ladies' Conversazione," which the force of her eloquence
and influence managed to keep alive for six years, in weekly meetings, at
which were constellated, from time to time, all the ladies most distinguished for talent, worth and beauty in the place. The first day's topic,
we are told, was the genealogy of heaven and earth; the Will (Jupiter);
the Understanding (Mercury); the second day's was the celestial inspiration of genius, perception and transmission of divine law (Appollo),
then (Bacchus), etc., etc. To these succeeded a debate on "What is
Life?" and other mysterious themes, which more than likely were
attended with the usual results of negation. However, they served to
spread the name and fame of Margaret Fuller far and wide, a fact of

which she herself was perhaps too conscious, as we find her saying at this time: "I know all the people worth knowing in America," this in a letter to one of her friends, "and I find no intellect comparable to my own."

The same opinion is repeated by her in various ways, and, to my thinking, is a weakness such as few real women would care to intrude so openly, and I might add so coarsely, to the detriment of all the literary stars with whom she had ever come in contact. And now let us bear her away, in the zenith of her fame, to London, "the grave of so many celebrities," and thence to the classic land of which she had nursed such waking dreams of inspiration, and where she was destined to find all the warmest affections of her heart called forth and satisfied.

Margaret Fuller, during her short stay in England, saw many characters well known in the literary world, and describes them in her letters to her friends with her usual discernment and felicity of expression. Her portraiture of Carlyle, one of her almost idolized writers before she wearied of him, is excellent. She complains, however, that his habit and power of haranguing were such, that the unfortunate listener whom he once got hold of, became a perfect prisoner.

"To interrupt him," she says, "is a physical impossibility. If you get a chance to remonstrate for a moment, he raises his voice and bears you down." To this I would add, "Well done, old seer of Chelsea, if you managed to silence Margaret Fuller, you richly deserved a crown of laurels."

At Paris she sees Fourier, George Sand, LaMennais and others; her accounts of whom I regret that want of time will not allow me to give. Her remarks from Rome are remarkably scanty and barren, considering the exciting period in which she arrived there,--the spring of 1847. In Italy it is evident that her character underwent a great change, as did that of Elizabeth Barrett Browning in somewhat similar circumstances. Arriving there at a most stirring and eventful period, the politics and ambition of minor scenes in America lost their interest to her; in the contemplation of the noble characters around her, she ceased so continually to analyze her own. She saw and acknowledged it with her accustomed candor. There she met many Italian ladies, intellectually her equals, and far surpassing her in the acquired graces of society; every day, moreover, brought with it some event to interest her attention or excite her sympathies,—everything conspired to divert her from herself, but most of all the circumstance of her finding another self, much dearer to her than her own, in the gentle and amiable Marquis Ossoli, whom she first met by accident in St. Peters. She at first refused him on account of the disparity of their ages, she being ten years

older than the Marquis, but like all Italian Romeos, he was not discouraged; so he renewed his suit and was accepted. The marriage,
which took place in December, 1847, was kept secret, from political and
economic motives; and their son, the fruit of it, was born at Rieti in
the September following. Never were holy hope, sweet love and patient heroism more beautifully set forth than in Margaret and her husband, under circumstances that must inevitably have chilled the selfish
and appalled the timid; never were feelings of wife and mother more
touchingly described.

Little was it thought when admiring the courage with which she
spoke of the thick coming dangers, in which the base attack of the
French upon Rome threatened to involve all who had advocated its noble
struggle for freedom; when paying homage to the exquisite tenderness
and unwearied attention she showed night and day to the wounded
and the sick in the hospital "Fate Bene Fratelli", to which she was
appointed by the Princess Belgioso; that her poor heart was torn
by the dread of finding, among those wounded her own husband.
All that Margaret says of herself, at this period, is so interesting, that I
much regret my limits do not allow me to give it in full.

It is beautiful to see the haranguer, the transcendentalist, the fervid,
eloquent stickler for her sex's rights, to see all this ferment of an un-
quiet, though lofty soul, subsiding into holy gratitude for domestic
peace, and affectionate appreciation of her husband's love, and of his
unassuming merits.

To her friend, the Marchioness Visconti Arconati, she writes thus
of him : "He has very little ot what is called intellectual development, but unspoiled instincts, affections pure and constant, and a quiet
sense of duty, which to me (who have seen much of the great faults in
characters of enthusiasm and genius), seems of highest value.'

But it is in speaking of her child that all the passionate emotions of
her heart burst forth. Years before, she had written in her journal:
"O Father, give me a bud on my tree of life, so scathed by the lightning and bowed by the frost   *   *   *   always before I have wanted
a superior or equal, but now it seems that only the feeling of a parent
for a child could exhaust the richness of one's soul." This treasure
now secured to her, she says to her mother:—"What shall I say of my
child! All might seem hyperbole, even to my dearest mother. In him
I find satisfaction, for the first time, to the deep wants of my heart."

A peaceful winter of the purest domestic happiness in Florence,
followed the months of anguish which she had endured in Rome during

its last noble struggles. But the time drew near for her return, when she hoped to publish her work on Italy.

Margaret with her husband and child sailed from Leghorn for New York, on May 17, 1850, in the bark Elizabeth, commanded by Capt. Hasty. Many gloomy presentiments had haunted her mind for some weeks before. Ossoli had been told when a boy, by a fortune teller, to "beware of the sea," and it happened that, till then, he had never set his foot on board a vessel. "I am absurdly fearful," says she, "and various omens have continued to give me a dark feeling. *   *   * In case of mishap, however, I shall perish with my husband and my child;" again, "It seems to me that my future upon earth will soon close. I have a vague expectation of some crisis, I know not what." The first few days all went well, then the captain, who was exceedingly attentive to them, died, off Gibraltar. The baby caught the disease. On Thursday, 15th, at noon, the Elizabeth was off the Jersey coast, between Cape May and Barnegat, when the commanding officer promised his passengers an early landing at New York. That morning the ship was driven, by the combined force of currents and tempest, on to the sand bars at Long Island, and at four o'clock struck on the beach of Fire Island.

Margaret refused to the last to be separated from her husband and child. Twelve hours were passed by them in communion, face to face with each other and death. At last the final moment came and the prayer was granted—Ossoli, Angelo and herself went down together, and "the anguish was brief."

Thus perished a woman who, by her strength and intellect, and rectitude, and principle, combined with her wonderful insight into character, and the warmth and sympathy of her great nature, obtained a wider range and personal influence than perhaps ever fell to the share of any other of her sex, devoid, like her, of beauty, wealth or influential connections. Her early trials were loneliness of heart, and obstacles to the development of her genius; her later ones, that chill penury that represses noble rage, doubly trying to a disposition munificent as hers, and the depressing uncertainty as to the power of turning her abilities to the account her circumstances required. But He who bestowed on her the gold, granted her also the strength to bear the purifying process which was to separate it from its dross; and there can be little doubt, that, had her life been spared, she would have afforded a still brighter example of female virtues, than she had given even in her most brilliant days, of female talent.

SYNOPSIS LECTURE XXV.

SUBJECT—MRS. H. B. STOWE AND THE MODERN NOVEL.

HISTORY OF THE NOVEL.—Objections to it, a thing of the past. Used moderately its influence beneficial. Definition — a fictitious story. Historically the oldest form of literature. Its growth regular and well defined. First came song and epic, then drama, and lastly prose fiction. In Jewish literature made its appearance toward the close of their national existence. In the Third Century among the Greeks, and a century earlier among the Romans.

In modern times its growth very similar to that just noticed. Before the Twelfth Century very little literature worthy of the name. Almost the only specimen left is that of the "Thousand and One Nights," if we except the religious fictions which are utterly unworthy of notice. On the revival of literature verse passed rapidly into prose writing, knight-errantry being the one theme until Cervantes exploded the subject by writing "Don Quixote". French fiction more advanced, as in the works of Rabelais a century earlier it reached a degree of perfection almost unattainable.

Anglo-Norman Literature the source from which was drawn most of the literature of the next two centuries. Effect of Sir Thomas More's "Utopia" on the writers of that age, including those of Bacon, Barclay, Sidney, and even Bunyan and Milton. After which, for half a century fiction disappears until the advent of Swift and Defoe, in the beginning of the Eighteenth Century, when a revival occured, and a distinct form and character was given to English literature, noted more especially by its naturalness which made a marked line of distinction between romance and the modern novel, removing it entirely from the ground it occupied in common with poetry.

Sir Walter Scott's appearance; his writings breathe a spirit of chivalry, generosity and benovolence with no direct teaching. His influence marked by the number of writers that entered the field of fiction, among them some of our most powerful and finished writers.

New phase of character of the modern novel compared with that immediately preceeding it. Writers no longer confine themselves to the office of mere ministers of pleasure, but write with a definite purpose; illustrations given in Dickens, Thackeray, and Mrs. H. B. Stowe.

INFLUENCE OF DICKENS, THACKERAY, AND MRS. H. B. STOWE.—The first drew men towards suffering, and pointed out the shame of neglecting it. Thackeray, by satire, showed up the frivolities, vanities, petty jealousies and miserable aims and ends, heart-burnings and frauds of fashionable life.

Mrs. Stowe reminded the world of the crying evils all around, wrongs to be redressed, great corruptions to be removed; and opened the eyes of Europe to American society, scenery, life and thought, and thus she must always be reckoned a most potential factor in the development of the modern novel.

MRS. STOWE'S LITERARY CHARACTERISTICS.—Strength and faithfulness of her descriptive power standing without a compeer in this country. Her pathos pure and deep. Her humor and satire genuine and racy, but quiet. Compared with Dickens she is every whit as true and tender, her sympathies are as keen and subtle, her spirit as generous and her perception as quick and vivid as his own.

HER LIFE.—Born in Litchfield, 1812. Educated in Boston. At an early age assisted her sister in the management of a school. Removed to Cincinnati with her father, who was appointed President of the "Lane Seminary." There she was married to the Rev. Calvin E. Stowe. Blessed with a large family, her married life was a happy and busy one, attending to her children and contributing articles to magazines and newspapers.

But in the midst of all her joy her future life for the next seventeen years was darkened by the baleful shadow of slavery, at the end of which time "Lane Seminary" had to be abandoned and she went east with her husband, where, out of the very agony of all these years of suffering and anxiety, together with her hatred of the system of slavery, she penned her greatest work, "Uncle Tom's Cabin."

MRS. STOWE AND THE MODERN NOVEL.

Excuse my reversing the order of my title, and as I hurriedly glance over the history of the English novel, and the many phases it has passed through, try for yourselves to solve my reasons for thus connecting the two subjects together.

Objections to novels and novel reading in the present day will not abate one iota the production. As long as the wish for them exists so long will they continue to be published, and when I consider the vast and varied kinds of pleasure—the tens of thousands of homes brightened, the wearisome hours soothed, the great minds that have been refreshed by them, and even the litte minds that have been lifted out of the rut of lowly thoughts—the memory of all this gives to the subject a certain interest and power of a very touching kind.

A man who by temperate indulgence in the pleasure keeps his love of story-reading fresh and pure—tasting discreetly, and never going in for a debauch—has done well for himself; no pleasure is so cheap, none so independent of weather or friends, none so easily linked with home happiness, few more natural, few more pure. Even where faults in design or workmanship may be acknowledged yet there is still a mysterious natural gift in story telling difficult to analyze, which the most unliterary and inartistic writers sometimes possess, and which will live in the literature of the language long after the more polished and artistic works have passed into oblivion. A novel is a fictitious story—the literature of imagination—designed primarily to please. This is the governing object, to which everything should be made subservient. It is accordingly one of the first requisites of a novel that the readers should become acquainted with and concerned for the chief actors in the plot. And since one seldom becomes much concerned for those whose affairs glide along quietly, it is usually required that the hero or heroine should be led through a maze of perplexities, the changing phases of which, and his struggles and conflicts, hopes and despondencies in them, make up the tale. Still further, since some degree of passionate emotion is a condition of pleasing excitement, the story must be conducted in such a way as to move and excite the desired passions in the reader.

Historically fiction is among the oldest forms of the literature of every nation and people. In nearly all cases it has entered largely into the matter of the heroic songs and stories that universally distinguish the early literature of all nations. In the unformed states of society the common mind is highly imaginative, and impatient of the rigid restraints of historic reality, and therefore it demands the more gorgeous creations of fiction.

In the earlier stages of the prose fiction their growth among the ancients was regular and well defined. First came their heroic songs and epics, and after these more artificial dramas, indicating an advanced stage of culture, and not until the national character had passed the culminating point did the prose fiction appear. In the literature of the Jews it belonged to the latter days of the local national existence of that people. Among the Greeks it did not appear till as late as the third Christian century; while with the Romans, whose culture never equaled that of the Greeks, it showed itself a century before. Of these later Greek and Latin novels Mr. Masson, M. A., author of the "History of Prose Fiction", aptly remarks: "When we look into the works themselves we can see that, by their nature, they belong to an age when the polytheistic system of society was in its decrepitude. They are most of them stories of the adventures of lovers, carried away by pirates, or otherwise separated by fate, thrown from city to city of the Mediterranean coast, in each of which they see strange sights of sorcery and witchcraft; are present at religious processions, private festivals, crucifixions, and the like; become entangled in crimes and intrigues, and have hair-breadth escapes from horrible dens of infamy; sometimes were changed by magic into beasts; but at last reunited and made happy by some sudden and extraordinary series of coincidences.

There is a force of genius in some of them, and they are interesting historically, as illustrating the state of society toward the close of the Roman empire; but the general impression which they leave is stifling, and even appalling, as of a world shattered into fragments, the air over each inhabited fragment stagnant and pestilential, and healthy motion nowhere, save in some inland spots of grassy solitude, and in the breezes that blow over the separating bits of sea. One of the most curious features of them, as compared with the earlier classic poetry, is the more important social influence they assign to the passion of love, and consequently the more minute attention they bestow on the psychology of that passion, and the increased liberty of speech and action they give to women.　Another particular in which they differ from the earlier Greek and Latin works of fiction is the more minute, and as we might say, more modern style in which they describe physical objects, and especially scenery.　This is most observable in the Greek romances. It is as if the sense of the picturesque in scenery then began to appear more strongly than before in literature.　In the Daphnis and Chloe of Longus, which is the sweet pastoral romance of the single Island of Lesbos, there are descriptions of the varying aspects and the rural labors of the seasons, such as we find in the modern pastoral poems."

With the moderns, after the revival of learning, the course of things was similar to that just noticed, but distinguished by characteristic differences.　The ancients had to invent their own modes and processes. Before the twelfth century, there was very little literature in any of the modern European tongues.　The only robust form of fiction which remains a living specimen and enduring monument of the Eastern nations is that of the famous "Thousand and One Nights."　A kind of fiction may be found in the religious forgeries of the middle ages, but whether considered as histories or literary compositions, they are alike deserving of no respect.　At its first revival modern European literature took the form of verse, but passed rapidly into prose writings.　Knight-errantry was their all-pervading theme, of which the national mind seemed incapable of wearying, till the whole subject culminated and exploded in Cervantes' "Don Quixote."　During the same period in France, the prose fiction, though apparently less favored by circumstances, had steadily advanced, and a hundred years earlier, in the works of Rabelais, it reached a degree of perfection that it has scarcely surpassed to the present day.　English history, literary as well as political, dates from the Norman conquest, traces of which remain in the old chronicles, and especially the *Mort d'Arthur*, itself the monument and storehouse of the older Anglo-Norman literature, and the fountain from which was drawn most of the literature of England during the next two hundred years.

Toward the close of this period, when English literature had been somewhat modified as well as enriched by English translations of Boccaccio and Cervantes, an original type of pure fiction appeared in England, led on by Sir Thomas More's "Utopia."　In that work, under the guise of a description of the imaginary island of Utopia, given in conversation by one Raphael Hythoday, a seafaring man to whom More

is supposed to be introduced in the city of Antwerp, we have a philosophical exposition of More's own views respecting the constitution and
economy of a state, and of his opinions on education, marriage, the
military system, and the like.

The effect of that work upon the popular mind of England was immediate and strongly marked, and most evidently along with Bacon's
"Atlantis," Barclay's "Argenis," and Sidney's "Arcadia,"—prose fictions
of rare excellence as to both matter and style—prepared the way for
Bunyan's great religious allegories. Of this there could be no doubt,
were it not for the prevalent notion that Bunyan was almost wholly
illiterate.

Bunyan and Milton mark a transition stage in the literature of their
country, but their works were not at once appreciated. Prose fictions
almost wholly disappeared for half a century, and it was not until the
appearance of Swift and Defoe in the beginning of the eighteenth century that a revival of fiction occurred. After them, extending over the
greater part of the century, came a large and varied class of writers in
every department of letters. Its prose writers, both religious and sec-
ular, are those who have given form and character to the literature of
the English tongue, among whom we find such names as Addison,
Steele, Johnson and Goldsmith, who occasionally wrote fictions, and
Richardson, Fielding, Smollett and Sterne, who are distinguished *par
excellence*, as novelists. This school of fiction was especially distinguished from all that has preceded it by its naturalness. The new novel
presented as its characters simply men and women endowed with only
the common traits of our every-day humanity; thus making a broad
line of distinction between the older *romances* and the modern *novel*,
and removing it beyond the ground it formerly occupied in common
with poetry, though some of the most esteemed modern poems are only
novels in verse.

But the cycle of that school of fiction terminated before the end of
the century, and extending over the first decade of the present, prepared things for the incoming of a new form of the novel which soon
after occured.

Sir Walter Scott's first appearance in prose romance as a writer without a name made a new epoch in the literature of fiction, and before his
light, when it shone out in its first intensity, all others paled. He knew
how to combine the ideal and the actual as no man had done before.
His eye traveled over far space and distant ages. He touched the past,
and it woke to life after the slumber of centuries. He called up long

processions of glory and beauty; he opened the gates of the palace thronged with gay retinues—crowned monarchs, proud scarlet cardinals, women rich in beauty and attire, stately queens and timid maidens. He opened the door of the peasant's hut, where the fugal meal was shared with the stranger, where the children played in rough sport, and the dogs barked a welcome or growled an alarm; with kindly truth he showed the best affections of poetry. He relieved the sorrows of his fiction with breezes from the mountain, the forest, and the sea; he alternated his dark scenes of passion with glimpses of pleasant humor; his extensive reading, shaped by his brilliant fancy, gave him the life of history; his long country rambles, his pauses at way-side inns, his love of field sports, his wanderings over heather and moor with the shepherd and his dog, added to his other varied sources of knowledge the most precious of all, the knowledge of humanity.

There was no direct teaching to be found in his pages; but a spirit of loyalty, of chivalry, of generosity, and of benevolence breathe through them all.

Like all great artists, he closely followed nature and availed himself to the utmost of the wide range of his personal observations. But the winning man of the world and indefatigable student of manners was a poet before anything; his genius refused to be fettered, and notwithstanding his fidelity to nature he occasionally departed from inartistic realities and took bold liberties for the sake of his art. It was not that he did it of deliberate purpose. The man who threw off page after page of his great fictions with the swift regularity of an office drudge, probably seldom paused to reflect, never hesitated as to how he should express himself. He wrote from inspiration, and such is the glamour he throws over his works that criticism is charmed into silence, or forgets to carp at details. He was the idol of his time; no work, however paramount its excellence, can excite so passionate an enthusiasm as that which greeted the first appearance of "Waverley." Hot disputes arose as to its authorship, and every succeeding volume by the new magician's hand was hailed with still increasing delight. Sir Walter's reign was long, and his popularity was undiminished till his death.

The impulse which Scott's works gave to literature was vivid; the interest they awakened excited all thinking minds to new energy, and prose fiction became so abundant that it is difficult even to name his contemporaries and successors.

Of the numerous race of novelists (they can scarcely be called a class) who lived and wrote during the second quarter of the present century, I have not space to write at length. Among them some of our most powerful and finished writers may be found, including such names as Theodore Hook, Disraeli, Sir Bulwer Lytton, Samuel Warren, Douglas Jerrold, Wilson, Dickens, Thackeray, Mrs. Trollope, Mrs. S. C. Hall, Mrs. Gore, and Lady Blessington. The themes upon which they exercised their powers were almost universal. English, Irish, and Scottish life and manners, fashionable, domestic, and criminal life; continental, oriental, and American society and manners; military and naval life; phantasy, history, and education. The whole world of thought was seized and appropriated by them; but, beyond the purpose to write novels, no definite common aim appears to have directed their movements.

That the novel of the present day has passed into a new phase of character as compared with that immediately preceding it, is quite evident. Our cotemporary novelists no longer confine themselves to the office of mere ministers of pleasure, the characteristic earnestness of the age effects them, and ulterior purposes crop out from a large share of the novels of the last decade.

For nearly every pending or recently disposed of question or doctrine some novel has been written, to forward its interests or effect its defeat.

Illustrations of the successful use of the novel as a reformer may be seen in several of the novels of Dickens and Thackeray, but more especially in Mrs. Stowe's "Uncle Tom's Cabin." Since the date of the publication of "Waverley," in 1814, no work of fiction so suddenly roused and rivetted the attention of the English public as "Pickwick," by Charles Dickens, which appeared in 1836. Its novelty of subject, the originality with which it represented the humors of its own time, its new phases of character, its genial irresistible fun, its touches of genuine pathos, and the wide range of sympathies which it embraced, made it the wonder and the delight of every English human being who could read in every class of life.

Dickens' humor, and the popularity of his work, became a public frenzy, and other literature was sunk for the time in the excitement it produced. He had little to do with drawing-rooms; with almost every other sphere he had active sympathies. Old London inhabitants seemed to know London for the first time through his descriptions; and for the first time, perhaps, they knew the actual sorrows and struggles of those who lived below the surface of its society.

They also saw the good gleaming out of the dark abode, the flashes of fine feeling rising up through the weight of grimy misery or enforced sin; the pen, which at every stroke could win a smile, could bring a tear, too—a productive sympathic tear.

The author of "Pickwick" never lost sight of one motive (which runs through all his books). He continually and forcibly challenged the attention of the opulent to the toiling, suffering, neglected classes of society. He used his picturesque power to exhibit the better nature in contrast with the evil circumstances. But, while he thus worked for the welfare of humanity, he also consistently abhorred the cant of philanthropy and mock religionism.

The immortal glory of Dickens is not told by the immediate popularity of his novels, but by their action upon the minds of men in drawing them towards suffering and pointing out the shame which attaches to the neglect of it. Many reforms, much educational progress, much care for the weak and poor, have been due to the stir made by his genius; and should it ever happen that his works be relegated to the past, the effect of what he has done will still remain and continue to win from the future new seeds of good.

The writings of Thackeray are more satirical, they deal chiefly with the frivolities, the vanities, the petty jealousies, and miserable aims and ends, heart-burnings and frauds of fashionable life. His "Vanity Fair" is a painful exposure of such a mode of existence. He has the strength of Le Sage. His style is easy and finished, and he has the true art which looks like simplicity. He has occasional touches of generosity and tenderness, which relieve the bitterness of his sarcasm; and in some of his novels, especially in "Esmond" and in "The Virginians," he leaves the stifling atmosphere of London drawing-rooms for freer air and more imaginative regions. All the good that satire can do must have been done by his works. As a satirist he has not been surpassed, and, as a writer of English, he should be read as a perfect model. Unhappily, like Charles Dickens, he too was cut off in the fullness of his power.

But in none of the writings of these two great novelists can we find anything at all approaching, in direct result, the wonderful effects of the first publication of "Uncle Tom's Cabin." Its unprecedented popularity has no doubt rendered it familiar to all classes of our countrymen. And yet I cannot refrain from a consideration of its merits. "Uncle Tom's Cabin" is a remarkable book, unquestionably; and, upon the whole, I am not surprised at its prodigious success, even as a mere literary performance. I am quite aware that we have critics now-a-days who can see no dramatic power, and no literary ability in its composition, and whose one cry is that it had nothing whatever to do with the abolishing of slavery; but in presence of so many facts and testimonies to the contrary I need not take up your time answering such.

Of one thing I am persuaded—that its author has displayed in this one work genius of the very highest order, in some respects of a higher order than any American predecessor or contemporary.

The great characteristic of Mrs. Stowe, in a literary point of view, is her descriptive power. In this she stands without a superior in this country, and without equal, unless it be Washington Irving. In the description of scenes in "Yankee land" Mrs. Stowe seems to be emphatically "at home," and treads the soil of her native hills with a step as free as that with which Sir Walter Scott brushed the dew drops from the heather of his own dear Scotland. In delineating the character of slaves and the "slave-trader, kidnapper, negro-catcher, negro-whipper," as she herself groups them, she handles her pencil with the confident ease of a master. To her sadly-familiar eye there are some things about these slaves which cannot lie; "those deep lines of patient sorrow upon the face—that attitude of crouching and humble subjection—that sad habitual expression of hope deferred in the eye—would tell their story if the slave never spoke."

While the pathos of Mrs. Stowe is deep and pure, her humor and satire are genuine and racy, but quiet. Gloomy as is the prevalent tone of her work, her reader's feelings are discreetly relieved by many touches of quaint drollery, which even Dickens himself cannot surpass, and from many passages in her book it is self-evident that Dickens' works have had a good deal of influence on Mrs. Stowe's writings, yet all the same there are passages in Uncle Tom which he can never surpass. She probes human nature every whit as tenderly and truly as he, her sympathies are as keen and subtle, her spirit is as generous as his; her perception of the humorous as quick and vivid as his own. She shows also his—so to speak—structural faults; which, in a general way, we may indicate by saying, that condensation and directness of course would greatly improve the compositions of both. But the book had a purpose entirely transcending artistic purpose, and accordingly encounters, at the hands of the public, demands not usually made on fictitious works, that it was so entirely successful proves beyond doubt that the writer's aim to say only what was true carried more weight, than any amount of exaggeration, however artistically used, could have done.

A few remarks on the importance given to America in European fiction will not be out of place, and I think may be of service in the way of showing the wide-spread influence of American literature on the present novelists.

For years after the Declaration of Independence the United States was not recognized in European literature, and perhaps the first thing to call the attention of their writers to this country was the works of Washington Irving and J. Fenimore Cooper. The first English novelist of distinction—we omit such writers as Trollope and others—to weave American and so-called American characters and incidents into their story was Charles Dickens, and, we may add, almost the poorest passages in the work of that great humorist are those relating to America.

The publication and popularity in England of Cooper's novels and and Mrs. Stowe's "Uncle Tom's Cabin" with the works of Hawthorne, Bryant, Longfellow and Bret Harte, further deepened the impression. America now begins to be looked upon, not only as a vast expanse of prairie and hunting ground, covered by picturesque Indians and unpicturesque buffaloes, or as a Golconda, out of whose gold and petroleum mines untold of fortunes might be made, but as a country that in many respects offered an unequaled, inviting and hitherto unbroken tract of ground for novelists. One of the first to take up the trail was not an Englishman—although I am not unmindful of Capt. Marryatt's novels "Osceola" and others, founded on life in the Southern States—but a German, Gerstacker, who wrote what in boyhood I thought immensely thrilling stories of American life, or what was then supposed to be American life. One of these novels I remember was called "The Pirates of the Mississippi," and gave me nearly as much delight in the reading as the pirates in question undoubtedly gave pain and terror to their victims.

Then you know Thackeray crossed the ocean and wrote his "Virginians" and "Esmond." These are among the more distinguished names among European novelists who have selected American soil as the scene of their fictitious adventures. I have said "novelists" because poets—the poetic imagination spurning the limits of geography, and sometimes of grammar and sense—like the French Beranger and Hugo, and the Scotch poet Thomas Campbell (in his "Gertrude of Wyoming"), laid the scene of some of their most popular poems in America.

And for that part of it, is not one of the best known of the late Charles Kingsley's novels called "Westward Ho?"—a title, by the way, taken from one of Sir Walter Raleigh's essays descriptive of one of that great man's many adventures in search of the golden Hesperides of the

West, and giving epigrammatic expression to the sentiment that in-spired so many in the "Spacious times of great Elizabeth" to sacrifice fortune and life in the attempt to found new empires across the seas.

Since the publication of the works of Irving, Cooper and Hawthorne deepened European interest in America, although in the works of some writers, notably in the "Martin Chuzzlewit" and "American Notes" of Dickens that interest found somewhat strange expression.

Coming down to our own day, the novels of Henry James, Jr., Wm. Howells, Julian Hawthorne, Mrs. Mary Mapes Dodge, and others, have again directed the attention of English writers of "fiction" to America as a fertile soil for the production not only of bananas, stock yards and politicians, but of scenery, incident and character, to be turned into good account in the deft hands of the novelist.   But before proceeding to speak of recent English fiction, in which America has been given a prominent place, a word in passing may be allowed to one or two French and German novelists, who have enlivened their pages by so-called transcriptions of American life, such as Gerston and Mons. Claretie, the author of "Prince Zilah."   But more significant far is the attitude toward the country of the most popular living writers of English fiction—William Black and R. D. Blackmore, the most English since Trollope of all novelists, and of Black, since Scott, the most Scotch of writers of fiction, is it not strange that both Black and Blackmore, who in this respect may be thought to be more than Black, had to cross the Atlantic for fresh inspiration of their genius?

And now that I have thus hurriedly brought down the development of the novel to our own day, permit me a few words as to Mrs. Harriet Beecher Stowe, and indeed many words regarding a woman so distin-guished would be an insult to any cultivated audience, not only in Chicago, but in London, Paris, or Berlin,—for the fame of herself and her great work is limited only by the horizon.   And indeed few families that I can call to mind have been more distinguished than that of Dr. Lyman Beecher.   In number they were the apostolic twelve, of whom no fewer than nine were or are authors.

The father, of course, was that grand, good, old man and hero, the Rev. Dr. Lyman Beecher, born away back in 1794, the son of a New England blacksmith, and brought up to that trade himself.   When of mature age, however, Lyman went to Yale College to study for the ministry, and, ten years later, he entered the pulpit of a small country church, where his sterling qualities brought him into notice, from which place he was called to Boston, where he remained until 1832, when he was induced to start the Lane Theological and Literary Seminary in the immediate neighborhood of Cincinnati, where he remained until 1850. Well do I remember the first time I heard him preach, thirteen years ago, one Sunday morning, in New York, and though I have heard many sermons since, none has served to efface the profound impression caused by that one.

The more immediate object of our study.

Harriet Beecher was born in Litchfield, about the year 1812. After the removal of the family to Boston, she enjoyed the best educational advantages of that city. With the view of preparing herself for the business of instruction, she acquired all the ordinary accomplishments of ladies, and much of the learning usually reserved for the stronger sex. At an early age she began to aid her elder sister, Catharine, in the management of a flourishing female school which had been built up by the latter. When their father went west, the sisters accompanied him, and opened a similar school in Cincinnati.

For several years after her removal to this place, Harriet Beecher continued to teach in connection with her sister. She did so until her marriage with the Rev. Colvin E. Stowe, professor of biblical literature in the seminary of which her father was president. This gentleman was already one of the most distinguished ecclesiastical scholars in America. Mrs. Stowe's married life was a happy one, blessed with a large family, of whom four are still living, she has known the fatigues of watching over the sick bed, and her heart has felt that grief which elipses all others—that of a bereaved mother. Much of her time has been devoted to the education of her children, while the ordinary household cares have devolved on a friend or distant relation who has always resided with her. She employed her leisure in contributing occasional pieces, tales and novelettes, to the magazines and newspapers.

Her writings were of a high moral tone, and deservedly popular. Only a small portion of them are comprised in the "Mayflower." This part of Mrs. Stowe's life, spent in literary pursuits, family joys and cares, and the society of the pious and intelligent, would have been of as un-alloyed happiness as mortals can expect, had it not been darkened at every instant by the baleful shadow of slavery.

The "peculiar institution" was destined to thwart the grand project in life of Mrs. Stowe's father and husband. When they relinquished their excellent positions in the east in order to build up the great Presbyterian seminary for the Ohio and Mississippi Valley, they did so with every prospect of success. Never did a literary institution start under finer auspices. The number and reputation of the professors had drawn together several hundred students from all parts of the United States, most of whom, fired by the ambition of converting the world to Christ, were winning their way, through privations and toil, to education and ministerial orders.

They were the stuff out of which foreign missionaries and revival preachers are made. Some of them were already known to the public as lecturers; Theodore D. Weld was a historical celebrity. For a year all went well. Lane Seminary was the pride and hope of the church. Alas for the hopes of Messrs. Beecher & Stowe! this prosperity was of short duration.

The French Revolution of 1830; the agitation in England for reform and against colonial slavery; the fine and imprisonment by American courts of justice of citizens who had dared to attack the slave trade carried on under the federal flag, had begun to direct the attention of a few American philanthropists to the evils of slavery. In 1833, an Abolition Convention which met at Philadelphia, set on foot the anti-slave agitation, which only ended after many years, in the total abolition of slavery, costing hundreds of thousands of lives and millions of money. The president of that convention was one of the most liberal donors of Lane Seminary. He forwarded its address to the students; and a few weeks afterwards the whole subject was up for discussion amongst them. At first there was little interest, but soon the fire began to burn. Many of the students had travelled or taught school in the Slave States; a goodly number were sons of slaveholders; and some were owners of slaves. They had seen slavery and had facts to relate, many of which made the blood run chill with horror. Those spread out on the pages of "Uncle Tom's Cabin" are cold in comparison.

The discussion was soon ended, for all were of one accord; but the meetings for the relation of facts were continued night after night and week after week. What was at first sensibility, grew into enthusiasm; the feeble flame had become a conflagration. The slave owners among the students gave liberty to their slaves; the idea of going on foreign missions was scouted at, because there were heathen at home; some left their studies and collected the colored population of Cincinnati into churches, and preached to them, and others, again, left all to aid fugitive slaves on their way to Canada, or to lecture on the evils of slavery. The fanaticism was sublime; every student felt himself a Peter the Hermit, and acted as if the abolition of slavery depended on his own individual exertions.

At first, the discussion had been encouraged by the president and professors; but when they saw it swallowing up everything like regular study, they thought it time to desist. It was too late; as well talk of damming up Niagara. The commercial interests of Cincinnati took the alarm; manufacturers feared the loss of their southern trade. Public sentiment exacted the suppression of the discussion and excitement. Slaveholders came over from Kentucky and urged the mob on to violence. For several weeks there was imminent danger that Lane Seminary, and the houses of Dr. Beecher and Professor Stowe, would be burned or pulled down by a drunken rabble. These must have been weeks of mortal anxiety for Harriet Beecher.

The Board of Trustees now interfered, and allayed the excitement of the mob by forbidding all further discussion of slavery in the seminary. To this the students responded by withdrawing *en masse.* Where hundreds had been there was left a mere handful. Lane Seminary was deserted. For seventeen years after this, Dr. Beecher and Professor Stowe remained there, endeavoring in vain to revive its prosperity. In 1850, they returned to the eastern states, the great project of their ife defeated. After a short stay at Bowdoin College, Maine, Professor Stowe accepted an appointment to the Chair of Biblical Literature in the Theological Seminary at Andover, Massachusetts,—an institution which stands, to say the least, as high as any in the United States.

These events caused a painful reaction in the feelings of the Beechers. Repulsed alike by the fanaticism they had witnessed among the foes, and the brutal violence among the friends of slavery, they thought their time for action had not yet come, and so gave no public expression of their abhorrence of slavery. It is to this period Mrs. Stowe alludes when she says in the closing chapter of her book : "For many years of her life, the author avoided all reading upon, or allusion to the subject of slavery, considering it as too painful to be enquired into, and one which advancing light and civilization would live down."

The terrible and dramatic scenes which occured in Cincinnati between 1835 and 1847 were calculated to increase the repugnance of a lady to mingling actively in the *mele.* That city was the chief battle-ground of freedom and slavery. Every month there was some event to attract attention to the strife; either a press destroyed, or a house mobbed, or a free negro kidnapped, or a trial for freedom before the courts, or the confectionary of an English abolitionist riddled, or a public discussion, or an escape of slaves, or an armed attack on the negro quarter, or a negro school-house razed to the ground, or a slave in prison and killing

his wife and children to prevent their being sold to the south.   On one
occasion the Mayor dismissed, at midnight, the rioters, who had pulled
down the houses of some colored people, with the following filthy
speech: "Well, boys, let's go home; we've done enough."   One of
these mobs deserve particular notice, as its victims enlisted deeply the
sympathies of Mrs. Stowe.   In 1840 the slave-catchers, backed by the
riff-raff of the population, and urged on by certain politicians and merchants, attacked the quarters in which the negroes resided.   Some of
the houses were battered down by cannon.   For several days the city
was abandoned to violence and crime.   The negro quarter was pillaged
and sacked; negroes who attempted to defend their property were
killed, and their mutilated bodies cast into the streets; women were
violated by ruffians, some of them dying of the injuries received; houses
were burnt, and men, women, and children were abducted in the confusion, and hurried into slavery.   From the brow of the hill on which
she lived Mrs. Stowe could hear the cries of the victims, the shouts of
the mob, and the reports of the guns and cannon, and could see the
flames of conflagration.   To more than one of the trembling fugitives
she gave shelter, and wept bitter tears with them.

After the fury of the mob was spent, many of the colored people
gathered together the little left them of their worldly goods, and started
for Canada.   Hundreds passed in front of Mrs. Stowe's house.   Some
of them were in little wagons; some were trudging along on foot after
their household stuff; some led their children by the hand; and there
were even mothers who walked on, suckling their infants, and weeping
for the dead or kidnapped husbands they had left behind.   This road,
which ran through Walnut Hills, and within a few feet of Mrs. Stowe's
door, was one of the favorite routes of the "underground railroad", so
often alluded to in "Uncle Tom's Cabin."   This name was given to a
line of Quakers and other Abolitionists, who, living at intervals of ten,
fifteen or twenty miles between the Ohio river and the northern lakes,
had formed themselves into a sort of association to aid fugitive slaves
in their escape to Canada.   Any fugitive was taken by night on horse-
back or in covered wagons from station to station, until he stood on
free soil, and found the folds of the lion banner floating over him, and
the artillery of the British Empire between him and slavery.

The first station north of Cincinnati was a few miles up at Mill
creek, at the house of the pious and lion-hearted John Vanzandt, who
figures in Chapter IX. of "Uncle Tom's Cabin" as John Van Trompe.—
Mrs. Stowe must often have heard the quick rattle of the covered wagons,

and the confused galloping of the horses of constables and slave catchers in hot pursuit. "Honest John" was always ready to turn out with his team, and the hunters of men were not often adroit enough to come up with him. He sleeps now in the obscure grave of a martyr. The "gigantic frame" of which the novelist speaks, was worn down at last by want of sleep, exposure, and anxiety, and his spirits were depressed by the persecutions which were accumulated on him. Several slave-owners who had lost their property by his means sued him in the courts for damages, and judgment after judgment stripped him of his farm and all his property.

During her long residence on the frontier of the slave states Mrs. Stowe made several visits into them. It was then, no doubt, she made the observations which have enabled her to paint the noble, generous, and humane slave-holders, in the characters of Wilson, the manufacturer, Mrs. Shelby and her son George, St. Clare and his daughther Eva, the benevolent purchaser at the New Orleans auction sale, the mistress of Susan and Emmeline, and Symes, who helped Eliza and her boy up the river bank. Mrs. Stowe has observed slavery in every phase; she has seen masters and slaves at home, New Orleans markets, fugitives, politicians and priests, abolitionists and colonizationists. She and her family suffered long from it; seventeen years of her life have been clouded by it. For that long period she stifled the strongest emotions of her heart. No one but her most intimate friends knew their strength. She has given them expression at last. "Uncle Tom's Cabin" is the agonizing cry of feelings pent up for years in the heart of a true woman.

Finally, the most potent cause in originating and deepening this mutual and reflex influence of English and American fiction, in opening the eyes of Europe to American society, scenery, life, and thought, was, beyond all doubt, Mrs. Harriet Beecher Stowe. I can just remember the excitement caused in Scotland by her "Uncle Tom's Cabin". Our minister, I recall so well the good old man, was, like too many members of the same sect in the Old World, extremely narrow. The mere name of novel he detested. He went so far as to refuse to read the "Pilgrim's Progress" because it was fiction. You will, therefore, understand why I cite his conduct as a striking illustration of the excitement caused by Mrs. Stowe's great work, when I say that the man who would not read Bunyan allowed himself to be persuaded into reading "Uncle Tom's Cabin." Then when Mrs. Stowe visited England, what an uproar there was of enthusiam and hallelujahs all over the kingdom, for it must never be forgotten that with many prejudices and not a few faults, the heart of the'great English public has always, to use a common expression, been in the right place, and it was the spectacle of the little American lady, fighting so nobly on behalf of liberty and a down-trodden, enslaved race, that appealed irresistibly to that love of fair play, that chivalrous sentiment, that feeling of sympathy with the oppressed and with woman, which, say what you will, is at the core of all great nationalities. But of that visit what need I speak. Is not her triumphal progress recorded in her own "Sunny Memories of Foreign Lands"?

I cannot help thinking that justice has never yet been done to Mrs. Harriet Beecher Stowe. "Uncle Tom's Cabin", of course, was received with enthusiasm all the world over on the occasion of its first publication, but the excitement and conditions of the stirring days of which it was a conspicuous outcome have passed away, and although still popular, it has been, I fear, relegated by the masses to the dusty shelves wherein the so-called classics are preserved. All the same, Mrs. Stowe's great novel must always be reckoned a most potential factor in the development of modern poetry and fiction. Up to the time of its publication the influence of Scott and the romantic school reigned supreme, and the novelists and poets had recourse to the musty records of gray antiquity for the materials out of which to weave stories and poems with which to interest the public. By "Uncle Tom's Cabin", however, Mrs. Stowe reminded the world that he who would most deeply move the heart of humanity has no need to rumage amid mediæval relics and the musty legends of a forgotton past, but has around him, at his very door, beneath his very eyes, abundance, and more than abundance of material, by the artistic manipulation of which he can touch popular sympathies. On every side of us, Mrs. Stowe reminded the world, are wrongs to be redressed, great corruptions to be removed, dramatic incidents of the most moving kind transpiring before our eyes in every lane and hovel, and, catching the inspiration, there immediately issued from the European press a vast number of what I might call poems and novels of humanity. Tom Hood wrote his "Bridge of Sighs", "Song of the Shirt", and "Laborer's Lay"; Mrs. Browning, her "Cry of the Children"; Charles Kingsley, his "Alton Locke"; Charles Dickens and Charles Reade, those novels in which they have emphasized certain great grievances which were chrushing the life and brightness out of society; and Victor Hugo wrote the greatest fiction of modern times, "Les Miserables". This is the great work which this noble woman, to my poor thinking, has accomplished in literature. She struck off the fetters from the slave, and from imagi-native art, and redirected the imagination and creative powers and sympathies of the novelist and the poet into fresh, wholesome, pure and lofty channels. And, *apropos* of "Uncle Tom's Cabin", we can't help feeling at times that in fiction we have fallen upon evil times, though there is hope in the conviction that the novel is merely in pro-cess of evolution to a purer, stronger, and nobler form of imaginative narrative art. Contrast with the sublime and unselfish motives of "Uncle Tom's Cabin", and, in a less degree, of "Dred", the petty aims, the dilettante ideals, the finical style of most contemporary novels. One writer spends his force in photographing little tricks of speech and sentiment as illustrative of differences of character and manner between European and American girls; another exhausts his genius and his subject in painting Scotch sunsets and the dying agonies of salmon on Scotch heather; a third builds up ingenious trifles like houses of Chinese cards to develop impossible plots; a fourth descends into the gutters and the shambles, and dignifies his degrading and demoralizing efforts by the name of realism; where is the great work, inspired and sublimed by a noble love of humanity, and honest, whole-souled desire to elevate the race, and do something to hasten the coming of that divine event to which the whole creation moves—and what of eternal interest and veracity and moment is there in your "Madcap Violets", or "Lorna Doones", or "Washington Squares", to be for a moment compared with "Jean Valjean" or "Uncle Tom"? When Time, that only impartial critic, delivers up her verdict, it is not your creators of feudal cut-throats or maurading barons, red haired monsters or della-cruscan beauties that will loom up most grandly out of the mists and smoke of the Nineteenth century, but the men and women who have exerted their great genius towards the amelioration and progress of the race; and among them all I do not think a single figure will show more distinctly—more grandly—a holy rapture inspiring and making beautiful her homely face—pure, white, and stainless—her memory embalmed in the hearts of untold thousands—her labors and life occu-pying one of the noblest pages of humanity—than the figure of that great novelist, and greater woman, Harriet Beecher Stowe.

SYNOPSIS LECTURE XXVI.

Subject—MY LORD TENNYSON.

Alfred Tennyson—The curled darling of fortune. Born of affluent parents, nurtured amid the loveliest scenery in England, becoming poet laureate ere he had reached his prime; happy in his married life, with a large family, a comfortable competence, loved and admired by warm and noble friends, it is difficult to imagine a more ideally happy or enviable life or one more unfavorable to the development of the highest quality of poetic genius.

Defects and Limitations of his Genius.—*First*—Narrowness of sympathy. With the suffering, sorrowing, sinning, heavy-laden sons of toil Tennyson has nothing in common.

Second—Much of his work has in it an element of smallness,—let us call it feminine,—which not only displays itself in the form, but in the thought; notably in his replies to his critics. Even in the most powerful of his productions his passion is not so much the passion of a man as the hysterical explosions of a woman.

This tendency, though in a different form shows itself in the pernicious moral with which "Maud" closes. A moral that is more than once obtruded by Tennyson and which, spite of all his culture and genius, stamps him as the great poetic apostle of Jingoism.

National and War Songs.—Among the poorest of his productions. Comparison between them and those of Campbell, in which is shown the difference between the writings of one whose art has been crushed by over-refinement, and one of nature's bards.

LACK OF DEEP, SPONTANEOUS, NATURAL EMOTION.—Result of Tennyson's monotonously peaceful and luxurious life, or of a natural
coldness of temperament. Even his "In Memoriam" is, after
all, cold and heartless; it speaks to the understanding, not to the
heart; and this want of sympathy with the toiling masses detracts
from the effectiveness of some of his greater passages, as for
instance, in the famous interview between "Arthur and Guinevere."

WANT OF A MESSAGE.—Tennyson has no gospel, and this is his greatest
fault. If he has, should like to know what it is?

Even his "Idylls of the King" teach no great lesson; voice
the sentiments and character of no great age. "Arthur and
Launcelot" and "Gawain and Galahad," are monstrous anachronisms, and the hero, Arthur, lacks a healthy, muscular vitality; in a word, backbone. And so does Tennyson.

As to his other works they are of a kind that can never appeal to any wide range of feeling or passion. From his minor
pieces what lesson can we glean? What comfort? None.

HIS MANY AND UNDENIABLE EXCELLENCIES.—

First. The beauty and accuracy of his descriptions of scenery
and plants; uniting the scientific accuracy of the botanist with
the delicate fancy and romantic glamour of the poet.

In his larger efforts at descriptive painting, he unites a boldness of treatment and a suggestive breadth of effect that is distinctly and grandly Homeric.

Second. In his exceeding conscientiousness and care he affords a splendid example to all young writers. Of all poets,
Tennyson is the most artistic. Akin to which is the classical
repose of his best work, which, to a large extent, gives so satisfying a charm to his poetry. Closely allied to the eclectic nature
of his genius is its flexibility. He is indeed an English Virgil
with all the grace and more than Virgil's variety and strength.

Finally, and greatest excellence of all, there is the noble seriousness of Tennyson's verse. This alone entitles it to a high
place, and will, if anything can, hand it down to posterity.

Striking comparison between Tennyson and Burns. With no
desire to underrate the former, who stands without a rival in
literature as far as sweetness, finish, purity of sentiment, noble

repose and perfection go.   Would rather go down to posterity as the author of "A Man's a Man for a' That," "Scots Wha Hae," and "Tam O'Shanter," than of the "Idylls of a King" and "In Memoriam."

LORD TENNYSON.

Shelley, voicing the bitter experience of his own storm-tossed soul, has sung:

> "Most wretched men
> Are cradled into poetry by wrong;
> They learn in suffering what they teach in song."

And the lines have a pregnant bearing on the genius of Alfred Tennyson. All experience goes to show that great achievements are usually the outcome of great incentives; that to do a preëminently heroic deed, or write a preëminently great poem, requires the spur of some great intent, some mental shock, or all-absorbing, all-dominant conviction or passion. Homer, old and blind, singing his way from town to town; Æschylus and Sophocles, roused into impassioned expression of heroic thought by the sight of their country's ruin; Horace, reduced to a clerkship, and Vigil, stripped of his Mantuan farm, both compelled to seek in verse the only solace for their misfortunes; Dante, roaming Ulysses-like, with hungry heart, and snatching from the flames of his own "Inferno" the fruitage and flowers of Paradise; Petrarch, slain by his great love for Laura; Tasso, immured for a madman in a padded cell; Schiller and Goethe, extracting the sweets of most divine philosophy from the tumultuous experiences of a tempestuous youth; Cervantes, begging his way for bread, and enlivening the gloom of his dungeon by the company of "Don Quixote" and Sancho Panza; Spenser, heavy-hearted with long sueing in vain at royalty; William Shakespeare, holding horses' heads and acting as super of a London theatre; Marlowe, and Jonson, uncertain where to get a dinner or a bed; Greene, famous for his lives, as he was infamous for his life, dying of a surfeit of Rhenish wine and pickled herring; Chatterton, the marvellous boy, who perished in his pride; Milton, old, blind, ruined and forsaken; Bunyan, the sublime dreamer, making shoe-laces or tags in Bedford jail; Goldsmith, pawning his peach-colored coat for a meal; Dr. Johnson, writing his

"Rasselas" on his mother's coffin to procure money with which to defray the expenses of her funeral; Fielding, Burns, Scott, Hood, Byron, Shelley, Poe, Blake, DeBalzac, DeMusset, Heine, Beranger, Eliot and Carlye are among the host of names that crowd on the memory in confirmation of the truth of the aphorism, "They learn in suffering what they teach in song."

Now, Alfred Tennyson's life has flowed in one broad, easy and unruffled stream. From the cradle he has been the curled darling of fortune. Born of affluent parents; distinguished at school and at the university ; the possessor, through no self-effort, of a comfortable competence ; marrying early, and happy in his marriage ; successful from the outset of life ; blessed with a large and happy family; loved and admired by warm and noble friends ; surrounded by the luxuries of life ; living in a costly mansion, amid the lovliest scenery in what has been called the Garden of England ; succeeding, ere yet he had reached his prime, to the laureate wreath—

> The "laurel greener from the brows
> Of him who uttered nothing base;"

it is difficult to imagine a more ideally happy and enviable life. And just because it has been thus rounded and happy—thus unbroken by great storms—has it been unfavorable to the development of the highest quality of poetic genius.

Physicians will tell you, if indeed you need to be reminded of a fact which stares you in the face in every-day life, that poor people are the most prolific. Your double-chinned squire of acres broad, or your nervous, over-wrought, over-fed millionaire, groans for the want of an heir to whom to leave his vast possessions, while the tinker by the roadside—I am speaking now of another hemisphere than this—with hardly rags sufficient to cover him, is burdened with a regiment of swarthy, hungry, squalling, muscular little savages. And as in physiology so in art. Continuous prosperity is destructive to poetic fire. The poet needs some keener and more exacting incentive than the mere desire for fame in order to produce work that will touch the hearts of humanity, and move to finest issues the impulses and emotions of the ages. And this incentive has been denied to Alfred Tennyson, and hence at least one reason of his failure to secure a loftier place in the ranks of English classics, and a greater assurance than his works yet offer of abiding fame.

And here I may be allowed to interpolate a word by way of explanation; not as trying to disarm criticism by anticipatory meeting of possible objections, but merely to set myself right with such of my audience as may share the excessively high admiration in which Tennyson is popularly held. In attempting to criticise a living writer of eminence, I am hampered—as no honest student can help being—by the consciousness of the comparative futility of the task. Environed as we are by the same traditions, surroundings and sentiments, as those which gave birth to " Enoch Arden" and "In Memoriam"; breathing the very atmosphere that has nourished the genius of Tennyson; sharing to a large extent the prejudices, prepossessions and spirit that form an essential element of nineteenth century life; it is impossible to judge his productions with that approximate justice and impartiality which are the prerogative of time alone.

To study aright a painting, a statue, a landscape, a cathedral,—we must invoke the aid of that distance which proverbially lends enchantment. With our cheeks all but touching the pillars of Hercules, we can judge of the few inches only of work that immediately front us; to arrive at a fair impression of the majestic whole, we must stand back, and the larger and loftier the work, the further back must we stand. When, therefore, I presume to criticise Tennyson, I make no pretense to passing definite or final or even satisfactory judgements. I cannot even hope that my criticisms will be always just ; but this I do know, they are always honest ; and however much some of them may conflict with popular preconceptions and estimates, I can only ask you to give me credit for sincerity. The results of patient, independent study, however unpopular, cannot help but prove suggestive of thought, and in that hope I venture to lay before you these fragments of criticism.

And, first, merely premising that Tennyson is a true poet, if hardly a great one, let us consider the defects and limitations of his genius; after which we shall be the better prepared, if only by contrast, to appreciate his many and undeniable excellences.

And the first defect I would point out is the narrowness of his sympathies. Study literature attentively, and you will find that only those works have attained lasting fame which have voiced the characteristic sentiments and thoughts of the ages which respectively produced them. In the "Canterbury Tales" the England of the 13th century lives again, in all its minutest circumstance and detail. Every class here finds a representative : every popular aspiration a tongue. And so it is with most other great classical works. Dante reflects the growing seriousness of an age that was just emerging from the intellectual barbarism of 600 years; in the works of the Elizabethan writers all the splendid credulity, the fierce passions, the magnificent daring, the sweeping imagination of that great age, find large expression. Dryden and Pope, again, epigramatize the ethical and artistic predilections of a critical age in which creative genius having spent its force had been followed by a careful adherence to forms, and expression was more studied than thought. In DeMussett, Beranger, and Burns the natural passions and aspirations of suffering, loving, toiling humanity, found impassioned utterance, and Byron and Shelley are the winged seers and mouthpieces of the new spirit of revolt against conventionality and tradition, which is now being formulated into articles and creeds.

But Tennyson represents not the classes but *a* class; the spirit of caste, rather than that of universal brotherhood. He is a fine gentleman singing for fine gentlemen; the windows of whose study are always closed to keep out the smell of the people. Milton's art recalls the organ; Tennyson's the flute; as Tom Moore's does a musical snuff-box. Of the many thousands of the laboring and middle classes whose lives have been sweetened by song; to whom a ballad is a delight and Shakespeare a revelation; how many are there who can appreciate Tennyson! Put "In Memoriam" or "The Princess" or the "Two Voices" or the "Palace of Art" into the hands of an ordinarily intelligent and fairly educated laboring man, whose life from the cradle has been one continuous struggle for existence, and what will he make of it? Suppose, for example, I took the following verses, which I have taken at purest random, and read them to a mixed company, gathed promiscuously from any popular meeting :

"Thy voice is on the rolling air ,
  I hear thee where the waters run ;
Thou standest in the rising sun,
  And in the setting thou art fair.

What art thou then ? I cannot guess;
  But tho' I seem in star and flower
To feel the same delusive power,
  I do not, therefore, love thee less :

My love involves the love before ;
  My love is vaster passion now ;
Tho' mixed with God and Nature thou,
  I seem to love thee more and more.

> Far off thou art, but ever nigh ;
>   I have thee still, and I rejoice ;
>   I prosper, circled with thy voice ;
>   I shall not lose thee tho' I die."

What meaning, I ask you, would my audience extract from that ?
What comfort ? What definite impression or idea of any kind ? Not,
mark you, that it is not poetry ; for it is : but of a kind that is, and ever
must be, *caviare* to all but a select and cultured few ; out of the natures
of many of whom over-refinement, and the continuous self-repression
imposed by the necessities of social etiquette, have sucked the sap and
marrow of naked and intense humanity.

Nor is this narrowness of sympathy merely negative, as, while it generally manifests itself in a fine under-current of cultured indifference, it
not infrequently finds a positive expression which the author's better
poetic nature finds it impossible always to repress.   Take, for instance,
his frequent sneers at shop-keepers, with their cotton-spinning choruses,
his thinly veiled contempt for trade, his glowing eulogiums on the glory
and delights of war; his ridicule of cotton-made lords, Manchester mill-
ionaires :

> "Sick," he cries, "am I sick of a jealous dread ?
>   Was not one of the two at her side—
>   This new-made lord, whose splendor plucks
>   The slavish hat from the villager's head ?"

Not that the unbonneting was in itself an act to be censured, but
only because it was a new-made lord to whom the courtesy was paid ;
for, was not this parvenu one :

> "Whose old grandfather has lately died,
>   Gone to a blacker pit, for whom
>   Grimy nakedness dragging his trucks
>   And laying his trams in a poison'd gloom
>   Wrought till he crept from a gutted mine
>   Master of half a servile shire,
>   And left his coal all turned into gold
>   To a grandson, FIRST of his NOBLE line ?"

And again :

> "Sir Walter Vivian, all a Summer's day,
>   Gave his broad lawns until the set of sun
>   Up to the people."

There it is! *The people!* Do you detect the fine flavor of aristocratic contempt in the expression? Perhaps not. It is foreign to this free and more democratic atmosphere of ours; but to an Englishman it is eminently suggestive—"the people!" Faugh!

With the suffering, sorrowing, sinning, heavy-laden sons of toil, Tennyson has nothing in common. He moves in an entirely different world; breathes an entirely foreign atmosphere. The company of Burns' "Jolly Beggars" would have turned his stomach; from Hood's poor needle-woman, in her wretched garret, with her shabby clothes and haggard face, he would turn, shuddering away. Not *there* would Alfred Tennyson find inspiration. Rather in some "Palace of Art," or "Audley Court:"

> "Where on a slope of orchard, Francis laid
>   A damask napkin, wrought with horse and hound,
> Brought out a dusky loaf that smelt of home,
>   And, half cut down, a pastry costly made,
> Where quail and pigeon, lark and leveret lay,
>   Like fossils of the rock, with golden yolks
> Imbedded and injellied."

How nice it all is! How gentlemanly! How correct! And Tennyson is always that. If only he would be a little less perfect at times; a little less gracious and sweet and pleasing; one would like him the better. But his fine airs, his scented handkerchiefs, his nice manners, his oiled locks and his dainty compliments, put our ruder speech, and homespun clothes, and natural earnestness, to shame, and we never breath freely until he has left the room.

Secondly, much of his work has in it an element of smallness; which, with no intention to reflect on women, I call "feminine." Indeed, contemporary satirists, following the example of the late Lord Lytton, have more than once drawn Tennyson as a young lady, with affected airs and mincing gait; and he has certainly written some poems a perusal of which almost tempts the reader to exclaim,—Miss Alfred. You are doubtless familiar with the Lady Principal—(I dare not call so fine a personage by the simple title of school-mistress or school-teacher) —who tried to educate her pupils to enunciate elegantly by making them repeat over and over again "Prunes and prims, prisms and prunes." Now, there are many poems of Tennyson which I find it impossible to read aloud without thinking of "prunes and prisms." Listen to this: "The Sea Fairies."

"Slow sail'd the weary mariners and saw
  Betwixt the green brink and the running foam,
Sweet faces, rounded arms. and bosoms prest
  To little harps of gold ; and while they mused
Whispering to each other half in fear,
  Shrill music reach'd them on the middle sea."

Whither away, whither away, whither away ?"
    Fly no more.
Whither away from the high green field,
    And the happy blossoming shore ?

Day and night to the billow the fountain calls ;
  Down shower the gambolling water falls
From wandering over the lea :
  Out of the live-green heart of the dells
They freshen the silvery, crimson shells,
  And thick with white bells the clover hill swell
High over the full-toned sea."

And so on, and so on ; to all of which we cry, "Prunes and prisms :
prisms and prunes ; or take "The Merman":

              Who would be
              A merman bold,
            Sitting alone,
              Singing alone
            Under the sea,
              With a crown of gold,
            On a throne?

          I would be a merman bold ;
          I would sit and sing the whole of the day ;
          I would fill the sea-halls with a voice of power.
          But at night I would roam abroad and play
          With the mermaids in and out of the rocks,
          Dressing their hair with the white sea-flower,
          And holding them back by their flowing locks
          I would kiss them often under the sea,
          And kiss them again till they kissed me
              Laughingly, laughingly ;
          And then we would wander away, away,
          To the pale-green sea groves straight and high
              Chasing each other merrily."

To which, again, as to the equally amorous mermaid who follows,
we say "Prunes and prisms, prisms and prunes."

Of course this is from his earlier poems, and it would not be fair to cite such pieces as this, and the "Skipping Rope," the "Kraken," and similar puerilities, as specimens of his mature powers. I only refer to them as illustrating a certain element in his genius; a pettiness of method; a littleness of sentiment; which the production within recent years of such puerile verses as those on a "Spiteful Letter," "I stood on a Tower in the Wet," and his latest drama, "The Promise of May," shows to be constitutional, and not merely an excresence of inexperience and youth.

But not only does this feminine element display itself in the form, but in the thought; notably in those occasional verses in which the poet, in petty resentment of some criticism on his works, vents his irritation in small and biting verses. A somewhat contemptuous yet not ungenerous criticism of Tennyson's first volume, by Christopher North in *Blackwood's Magazine*, called forth this undignified and not very original retort:

TO CHRISTOPHER NORTH.

You did late review my lays,
    Crusty Christopher:
You did mingle blame with praise
    Rusty Christopher.
When I learnt from whom it came,
I forgave you all the blame,
    Musty Christopher.
I could not forgive the praise,
    Fusty Christopher.

Then there are the stanzas "On a Spiteful Letter," beginning:

Here, it is here—the close of the year,
And with it a spiteful letter.
ſy fame in song has done him much wrong,
For himself has done much better.

With the other, entitled "Literary Squabbles," and published in *Punch* in 1846:

Ah, God! the petty fools of rhyme,
    That shriek and sweat in pigmy wars
Before the stony face of time,
    And look'd at by the silent stars.

A piece that had evident reference to the brief but bitter war of epigram then being waged between the young poet and Lord Lytton, at that time in the height of his fame as a novelist. The latter, in his poetical satire entitled "The New Timon" had ridiculed Tennyson's pretentions to poetic distinction, whereupon the poet, stung into rage, vented himself in the pages of *Punch* in the caustic and femininely spiteful lines entitled

"THE NEW TIMON AND THE POETS."

We know him, out of Shakespeare's art,
  And those fine curses which he spoke ;
The old Tymon, with his noble heart
  That strongly loathing, greatly broke.

So did the Old : here comes the New.
  Regard him ; a familiar face :
I thought we knew him ; what, it's you,
  The padded man that wears the stays.

Who killed the girls and thrilled the boys
  With dandy pathos when you wrote !
A lion you, that made a noise,
  And shook a mane *en papillotes.*

And once you tried the muses too ;
  You failed sir ; therefore now you turn,
To fall on those who are to you
  As Captain is to Subaltern.

But men of long enduring hopes,
  And careless what this hour may bring,
Can pardon little would-be Popes,
  And Brummels, when they try to sting.

An Artist, Sir, should rest in Art,
  And waive a little of his claim ;
To have the deep poetic heart
  Is more than all poetic fame.

But you, Sir, you are hard to please :
  You never look but half content ;
Nor like a gentleman at ease,
  With moral breadth of temperament.

And what with spites and what with fears,
  You cannot let a body be :
It's always ringing in your ears,
  "They call this man as good as *me.*"

What profits now to understand
   The merits of a spotless shirt—
A dapper boot—a little hand—
   If half the little soul is dirt ?

You talk of tinsel ! Why, we see
   The old mark of rouge upon your cheeks.
You prate of Nature ? You are he
   That split his life about the cliques.

A Timon you ! Nay, nay, for shame !
   It looks too arrogant a jest—
The fierce old man—to take his name,
   You bandbox. Off, and let him rest.

This is bitter as aqua fortis, but it is hardly the sort of criticism we should expect from a largely masculine mind. *Apropos* of the verses, it is pleasant to think that both men subsequently repented of their littleness, and in dedicating his drama of "Harold" to his old antagonist's son, the ex-Governor General of India, now Lord Lytton, but better known as Owen Meredith, Tennyson made most graceful and flattering amends.

Even his passion, at the rare moments when he allows himself to rise out of his normal self-possession and repose, is not so much the passion of a man as the hysterical explosion of a woman. Take the two poems, in some respects the most powerful of his productions, in which he gives his natural self fullest play : take "Locksley Hall" and "Maud." Rhetorically, they contain some of the finest passages in English poetry, and there are times in a young man's life,—particularly a very young man's life—where the fierce scorn and defiant passion of the verse fairly echo his inmost emotions, experiences and despair. But it is not the expression of a strong man's disappointment and grief, but of a somewhat effeminate, nervous, sentimental, highly cultured and more highly conceited youth. With all their intensity one is conscious, if he but listen attentively, of an undertone of insincerity. The intense passion of a strong soul does not spend itself in gorgeous tropes, splendid rhetoric and small revilings of the woman one has lost, and the world in which one lives ; and it is with a feeling almost of relief that we watch the departure for war, of the historical hero of "Maud," not much caring even if he finds his death at the hands of some wild Cossack.

And while on the subject of "Maud," let me call your attention to the pernicious moral with which that poem closes : a moral that is more than once obtruded by Tennyson, who again and again gives artistic expression to that intensely insular and English jealousy of foreigners, and especially Frenchmen, and that wild, intermittant desire for war which every now and then seizes the English people, to which their own journals have given the name of "Jingoism." And Tennyson, spite of all his culture and genius, is the great poetic apostle of Jingoism. You find it cropping up everywhere throughout his works, and nowhere more so than in the stanzas of "Maud."

"And it was but a dream, he cries," yet it lighten'd my despair,
When I thought that a war would arise in defence of the right,
That an iron tyranny now should bend or cease,
The glory of manhood stand on his ancient height,
Nor Britain's one sole God be the millionaire ;
No more shall Commerce be all in all, and Peace
Pipe on her pastoral hillock a languid note,
And watch her harvest ripen, her herd increase,
Nor the cannon-bullet rust on a slothful shore,
And the cobweb woven across the cannon's throat
Shall shake its threaded tears in the wind no more.

And as months ran on and rumor of battle grew,
"It is time, it is time, O passionate heart," said I,
(For I cleaved to a cause that I felt to be pure and true,)
"It is time, O passionate heart and morbid eye
That old *hysterical* mock-disease should die."
And I stood on a giant deck and mix'd my breath
With a loyal people shouting a battle-cry,
Till I saw the dreary phantom arise and fly
Far into the North, and battle, and seas of death.

Let it go or stay, so I wake to the higher aims
Of a land that has lost for a little her lust of gold,
And love of a peace that was full of wrongs and shames,
Horrible, hateful, monstrous, not to be told ;
And hail once more to the banner of battle unroll'd !
Tho' many a light shall darken, and many shall weep
For those that are crush'd in the clash of jarring claims,
Yet God's just wrath shall be wreak'd on a giant lair;
And many a darkness into the light shall leap
And shine in the sudden making of splendid names,
And noble thought be freer under the sun,
And the heart of a people beat with one desire;
For the peace that I deem'd no peace is over and done,
And now by the side of the Black and the Baltic deep,
And deathful-grinning mouths of the fortress, flames
The blood red blossom of war with a heart of fire.

Let it flame or fade, and the war roll down like a wind,
We have proved we have hearts in a cause, we are noble still,
And myself have awaked, as it seems, to the better mind ,
It is better to fight for the good, than to rail at the ill ;
I have felt with my native land, I am one with my kind.
I embrace the purpose of God, and the doom assign'd.

Just so : he embraces the purpose of God : how infinitely conde-
scending : the execution of that purpose showing itself in all the horrors
and carnage of war, in depopulated countries, smoking cities, sobbing
widows and wailing, fatherless little ones. And yet, except an occasional
metaphor like "blood-red blossom of war," which is altogether inappropriate and inadequate, the lines are exceedingly fine ; full of a magnificent impetuosity and rush which it is impossible to resist. But the
moral is detestable, and, unfortunately, it is the moral of a large portion
of Tennyson's verse.

Curiously enough, though so clamorous for the fierce delights of
battle, and constantly posing in patriotic attitudes, Lord Tennyson's
National and War songs are among the poorest of his productions.
They have that fatal air of vamped up enthusiasm, and affectation, which
mars so much of his work, and probably forms an almost necessary element in a considerable portion of a Poet Laureates verse : so much of
these having to be written to order. Let me read you two verses from
his "English War Song," and after that an equal number from Thomas
Campbell's "Ye Mariners of England." Tennyson's run as follows :

ENGLISH WAR SONG.

Who fears to die ? Who fears to die ?
Is there any here who fears to die ?
He shall find what he fears ; and none shall grieve
For the man who fears to die :
But the withering scorn of the many shall cleave
To the man who fears to die.

(Chorus.)

Shout for England !
Ho ! for England !
George for England !
Merry England !
England for aye !

*   *   *

There standeth our ancient enemy;
    Hark ! he shouteth—the ancient enemy,
On the ridge of the hill his banners rise !
    They stream like fire in the skies ;
Hold up the Lion of England on high
    Till it dazzle and blind his eyes.

Chorus, etc.

Do you detect the falsetto note ? The sham fervor ? The blatant, Jingo sqeak of the Philistinish, anti-French, Cockney penny trumpet ? If not, contrast with its puny tooting the following trumpet blare from Thomas Campbell ; and as the great lines break upon you like a majestic wave, and thrill you with their magnificently patriotic fire, say which of these poets strike the truer and higher and fuller note.

Yᴱ MARINERS OF ENGLAND.

Ye Mariners of England !
That guard our native seas ;
Whose flag has braved a thousand years
The battle and the breeze !
Your glorious standard launch again
To match another foe !
And sweep through the deep,
While the stormy winds do blow ;
While the battle rages loud and long,
And the stormy winds do blow.
                *   *   *
Brittania needs no bulwarks,
No towers along the steep ;
Her march is o'er the mountain waves,
Her home is on the deep.
With thunders from her native oak
She quells the flood below
As they roar on the shore,
When the stormy winds do blow ;
When the battle rages loud and long,
And the stormy winds do blow.

If you would pursue further the parallel suggested, compare Tennyson's "Charge of the Light Brigade" and his "Charge of the Heavy Dragoons,"—the former among the strongest of all his writings—with Campbell's "Hohenlinden" and the "Battle of the Baltic," or after wading

through his "National Song," and his other so-called patriotic effusions
read aloud Burns' "Scot's Wha Hae," and you will, I think, understand
the difference between the writings of one whose art has been crushed
under a weight of conventionality, over amiable, dilettante refinement
and forms, and one of nature's bards ; and yet Campbell's compositions
present many points of resemblance to Tennyson's, and display the
same consummate art, and labored conscientiousness, the same exquisite
finish and repose, that give so indescribable a charm to "In Memoriam"
and "The Idylls of a King."

How far, this lack of deep, spontaneous, natural emotion is the result
of over-refinement, and the restrictive and self-repressing influence of
Tennyson's monotonously peaceful and luxurious life, or of a natural
coldness of temperment, it is difficult to say.   But if regard be had to
his careful and persistent isolation of himself from the world, and especially from the intrusions of the common herd, one might be led to conclude
to both : that is, to a certain lack of deep emotional earnestness, and an
inevitably imperfect sympathy with common people, their aspirations
and regrets, their sins and sorrows, their laughter and tears.   His "In
Memoriam," with all its wonderful suggestiveness, its depth of thought,
its rich and varied music, its perfection of epithet and trope, its noble
serenity and its triumphant close, is, after all, cold and heartless.   It
speaks from the understanding to the understanding, not from the heart
to the heart.   It is the refined philosophising of an amiable and highly
cultured man of genius, who mourns in exquisitely rounded numbers an
intellectual loss, but never allows his grief to urge him into any natural,
because emotional eccentricity of expression or metre.   It is too calmly
contemplative ; too exquisitely finished ; altogether too elegantly ornate
and chaste to have been inspired by any great passion ; the scholar
throughout is at least as prominent as the poet ; in reading it we do
not think of the promising student who perished in his youth, but of the
middle-aged, comfortably circumstanced poet ; of Alfred Tennyson, not
of Henry Hallam.

And the same fatal over-refinement, and imperfect sympathy with
the toiling masses, detract from the effectiveness of some of his greatest
passages.   We are constantly looking, and looking in vain, in Tennyson,
for that touch of nature that makes the whole world kin.   With him, it
is always the touch of art.   Take, for instance, the famous interview
between Arthur and Guinevere, and the noble farewell speech of the
"blameless King": which I shall read to you presently as illustrating the
highest range of the author's genius.

The speech, though rising easily into the sublime, hardly touches the heart ; and why ? Simply because we doubt its sincerity. It is too over-refined to be human. Arthur, a rude, ignorant chief of half-naked savages, away back in the darkness and mists of the Fourth Century. would have spoken and acted quite differently, and even accepting Mr. Tennyson's highly idealized picture of the blameless King, his parting speech to Guinevere is pitched on an altogether too lofty key. Only the Almighty could have thus forgiven. Just think of it. Here was his wife, Guinevere : whom he had lived with, and loved and implicitly trusted for years ; whom he had never wronged even in thought, and on whom he lavished all the wealth of his kingly heart and royal exchequer. And there was his favorite knight, his bosom friend, his trusted Lancelot, whom he loved with a love surpassing that of woman.

And yet these two unite in deceiving him, and in bringing shame and ruin on himself, the Order and the Kingdom. It is conceivable that, thus doubly wronged, and with impending ruin as the consequence staring him in the face, Arthur could have calmly, coolly, freely forgiven his faithless queen, and that in a set and carefully prepared speech ? Passion is always extempore, and Tennyson never is.

But the greatest fault we have to find with Tennyson is that he has no Gospel—no Message. His genius is rather eclectic than original. He borrows from every poet and from every age ; and whatever he borrows he adorns. But he has no great message of his own to deliver. If he has, I should like to know what it is. We all know, or can know, if we care, what Dante's Gospel was, what Chaucer's, what Spenser's, what Milton's, what Goethe's, what Shelley's, what Wadsworth's and what Carlysle's, but what is Mr. Tennyson's?

His "Idyll's of the King" teach no great lesson; voice the sentiments and character of no great age. They are a bastard attempt to graft upon a barbarous age and savage warriors the refined sentiments and religious atmosphere of the Ninteenth Century. Arthur and Lancelot, and Gawain, and Galahad are monstrous anachronisms, utterly devoid of flesh and blood and real living individuality ; while the sympathies of the reader all go with Lancelot, magnificent even in his great sin, and not with Arthur, uninteresting in spite of his thousand virtues. A hero, especially a King, should be made of sterner stuff, and Tennyson's Arthur is of the very softest possible. He lacks a healthy, muscular vitality : in a word, back-bone. And so does Tennyson.

As to his other works : "In Memoriam" is a magnificent poem of its kind, but that kind can never appeal to any wide range of feeling or

passion, and so far as it is meant to express grief, the brief lament of David over his faithless child, lifts us into a much higher because truer
and more natural atmosphere.   All the passion and sorrow and despair
of a broken heart are summed up in the infinitely sad and simple lament,
"O, Absolom, my son, my son !   Would to God I had died for thee.   O
Absolom, my son !"

From Tennyson's minor pieces, what lesson can we glean ?   What
comfort ?   None.   Perhaps I can emphasize this point better by a reference to some other poet, with whose life and writings you are familiar.
Say we take Longfellow.   His works all breathe an atmosphere of hope
and resignation and patience and comfort and joy.   From their perusal
we rise refreshed ; strengthened, comforted, made hopeful and glad.
Their study is positive health and strength.   Reading Tennyson is a kind
of intellectual dissipation.

I have dwelt thus long on what I take to be the defects and limitations of Mr. Tennyson's writings and genius, because I am anxious to
hold up to you only high and noble standards of criticism.   In these
times, when every woman is a poetess and every man has written a book,
we must guard ourselves against the influence of those local surroundings and conventional judgments that tend to erect false standards of
taste, and substitute for classical ideals those born out of narrow sentiments and personal predilections.   But I should be sorry to let you go
with the idea that I was lacking in genuine admiration for Tennyson,
and if you will kindly bear with me a few minutes longer shall try to do
justice to his many and undeniable excellencies.

And, first, I would direct your attention to the beauty and accuracy
of his descriptions of scenery and plants.   In this respect Tennyson
unites thoughtful accuracy to the sensuousness of Keats and the ideal-
ism of Shelley.   The early poets and dramatists, from Chaucer down-
ward, dealt only in large effects.   Being first in the field, they were naturally struck mainly by general impressions.   Hence, there is an absence
of detail, and minute dwelling on slight differences of color and shade.
If Chaucer had to paint the rising of the sun, and the gladsome appearance of nature in the early dawn, he did it with a broad sweep of the
brush.

"And all the orient laugheth of the light."   So, too, Spenser, all the
Elizabethian writers except Shakespeare—and in this as in everything
he was a great exception—dealt only with broad results.   With the advent of Dryden and Pope nature was banished from the field, and for
200 years descriptions of nature were all after one pattern—stereotyped

into conventional forms. Thomson was the first to revive a love of nature, and base his descriptions on minute, faithful, personal study. Then came Burns and Wordsworth, to invest her with a spirit of all-embracing and loving humanity; to dower the daisy with modesty and give fresh meaning to the primrose by the river's brim. And, finally, followed Alfred Tennyson, whose descriptions unite the scientific accuracy of the botanist with the delicate romantic fancy and glamour of the poet.

But it is to his larger efforts at descriptive painting that I wish more specially to direct your attention. To scientific accuracy of detail he unites a boldness of treatment, and a suggestive breadth of effect, that recall the triumphs of an earlier age, and many of his best descriptions have a dramatic suggestiveness that is distinctly and grandly Homeric. I have not time to illustrate this by many quotations, but the following from Vivien may serve my purpose; as it will also incidentally illustrate another of Tennyson's excellencies, the exceeding richness, delicacy and appropriateness of his metaphors.

While Vivien is tempting Merlin the lightning flashes from out the sky, and a great storm breaks forth. They take shelter in the bole of a giant oak, where the wily beauty twines herself around the hoary Magi, and crying :

> "O Merlin, though you do not love me, save
> Yet save me !" clung to him and hugg'd him close;
> And called him dear protector in her fright,
> Nor yet forgot her practice in her fright,
> But wrought upon his mood and hugg'd him close.
> The pale blood of the wizard at her touch
> Took gayer colors, like an opal warm'd,—
>
> *   *   *   *   *
>
> *   *   and ever overhead
> Bellow'd the tempest, and the rotten branch
> Snapt in the rushing of the river-rain
> Above them; and in change of glare and gloom
> Her eyes and neck, glittering, went and came;
> Till now the storm, its burst of passion spent,
> *Moaning and calling out of other lands,*
> Had left the ravaged woodland yet once more
> To peace; and what should not have been had bee.
> For Merlin, over-talked and over-worn,
> Had yielded, told her all the charm; and slept."

The metaphor I alluded to, is, of course, the pale blood of the wizard taking gayer colors, like the opal warmed, and the particular line in the description of the storm which I have adduced to illustrate Tennyson's occasional daring and Turneresque suggestiveness, is that in which the storm, having spent its force, goes "moaning and calling out of other lands."

Of the dramatic effectiveness of his metaphors I can only afford to give one instance ; it is where Lancelot espies the traitor Sir Modred on the wall, trying to spy some secret scandal which might involve the Queen in ruin.

But much

> "He saw not, for Sir Lancelot, passing by,
> Spied where he couch'd; and as the gardener's hand
> Picks from the colewort a green caterpillar,
> So from the high wall and the flowering grove
> Of grasses Lancelot pluck'd him by the heel,
> And cast him as a worm upon the way. "

At the same time I should warn you that Tennyson is not always so happy as this; and that, especially in his earlier writings, his figures are often too profuse and his metaphors mixed. Take, for example, the poem entitled "The Poet," which opens and closes so finely,—all between, however, being very poor. Talking of the poet, he says :

> The viewless arrows of his thoughts were headed,
> 　　　and winged with flame.

> Like Indian reeds blown from his silver tongue,
> 　　　and of so fierce a flight,
> From Calpe unto Caucasus they sung,
> 　　　Filling with light.

> And vagrant melodies the winds which bore
> 　　　Them earthward till they lit;
> Then, like the arrow-seed of the field flower,
> 　　　The fruitful wit,

> Cleaving, took root, and springing forth anew,
> 　　　Where'er they fell, behold,
> Like to the mother plant in semblance grew
> 　　　A flower all gold.

And bravely furnished all abroad to fling,
The winged shafts of truth,
To throng with stately bowers the breathing spring
Of hope and youth."

Here we have the anomaly of "viewless" arrows "wing'd" and "headed with flame;" changed immediately from Indian reeds blown from a silver tongue; which reeds (not the tongue) at once proceed to sing all the way from Calpe to Caucasus, and not only supply music but light. Then these vagrant melodies are borne earthward, and become metamorphosed into arrow-seeds—whatever these may be—which, taking root, spring up into a gold flower, probably Mr. Wilde's sun-flower—which in its turn proceeds to discharge whole volleys of winged shafts, that somehow or other succeed in crowding with stately bowers the spring of hope and youth.

But this, as I have said, occurs in one of his earlier poems, and you will search in vain for such signs of immaturity in his later and severely accurate productions. And this suggests another of Mr. Tennyson's virtues—his exceeding conscientiousness and care. In this respect he affords a splendid example to all young writers. No author, not excepting Addison, DeBalzac, Hawthorne or Campbell, was ever more careful to elaborate and polish his utterances to the hishest possible degree of excellence. Of all poets Tennyson is the most artistic; a faulty metre, an inappropriate epithet, a careless line, is—in his later works at any rate—so rare as to call for notice only for its exceptionalness. If you would realize the extent to which Tennyson carries this conscientious minuteness of execution and revision, you have only to compare the 1832 edition of his poems with the version as it now stands. Not that his revisions are always for the best. Poetic corrections are not always improvements, and Tennyson's natural tendency to over-refinement, which the circumstances of his education and life have developed into a finicalness that amounts almost to a disease, has helped in some instances to mar the effectiveness of his original work by sacrificing freshness and boldness to elegance and finish. But all the same, the fact deserves to be emphasized, especially in this age of raw haste and imperfect workmanship. And to this anxious carefulness and habit of constant revision, is due, to a large extent, the matchless perfection of the form which his thought almost always takes.

Akin to this, too, is the classical repose of his best work. "Tithonus," "Lucretius," "Ænone" are steeped in the very spirit of Grecian classicalism; and so, in a less degree, are "In Memoriam" and the "Idylls of a King." This, is which, to a large extent, gives so satisfying a charm to his poetry. The atmosphere of his verse is restful. From the distractions and turmoil of every-day life his works offer a grateful refuge, and the soul, fretted and worried by a thousand cares, is glad at times to seek the company of his own lotus-eaters, with them to—

> "Swear an oath, and keep it with an equal mind,
> In the hollow Lotus-land to live and lie reclined
> On the hills like gods together, careless of mankind."

I have already remarked on the eclectic nature of his genius, and closely allied to this, if indeed it be not a manifestation of it, is its flexibility. He adapts himself easily to all circumstances, moods and forms. Now, his verse, in its noble simplicity and strength, reminds the reader of Homer ; anon, by its biting wit and negligent grace, of Horace; and by turns we catch distinct echoes of Wordsworth, Poe, Keats, Byron, Spenser and Dante ; while at all times the influence of Virgil is predominant. He is indeed an English Virgil, with all of Virgil's inimitable grace of expression, and more than Virgil's variety and strength. Is it a ballad—and to the child-like artlessness and naive simplicity of the ballad his peculiar genius is most foreign—he gives us "The Lord of Burleigh ;" a romance, "Elane," or "The Passing of Arthur ;" a fanciful arabesque of delicate satire and graceful fancy, "The Princess;" a sternly simple and moving tale of pathos, "Enoch Arden;" while once or twice, in his shorter pieces, he touches all but the highest limit of poetic feeling, as in that exquisitely suggestive and most perfect of all his songs :

> Break, break, break,
> On thy cold gray stones, O Sea !
> And I would that my tongue could utter
> The thoughts that arise in me.
>
> Oh well for the fisherman's boy,
> That he shouts with his sister at play !
> Oh well for the sailor lad,
> That he sings in his boat on the bay !
>
> And the stately ships go on
> To their haven under the hill !
> But O for the touch of a vanish'd hand
> And the sound of a voice that is still !

Break, break, break,
 At the foot of thy craigs, O Sea !
But the tender grace of a day that is dead
Will never come back to me.

Here Tennyson is at his best, and why ? Because, in addition to his usual perfection of rhythmical form and music, he has that touch of nature the absence of which deprives so much of his verse of human interest. The lines :

"But O for the touch of a vanish'd hand
And the sound of a voice that is still,"

find immediate echo in the heart of every one who has loved and lost, and infinitely to be pitied is the man or woman who has not, and therefore touches a truer and tenderer and deeper chord of feeling than do the most splendid passages in the Arthurian Idylls, or the most thoughtful in "In Memoriam."

I have already referred more than once to the "Idylls of the King," and not always in a complimentary manner, but though legitimate exception may be taken to them as not representing the spirit of any age, and being indeed untrue to the spirit of all ages, artistically they will always rank among the most rounded and complete of all Tennyson's writings. In them we have him at his full strength. The little tricks of speech, the small methods, the elaborate mannerisms, the superabundant metaphor of his earlier productions have been entirely dropped, and one knows not whether more to admire the grace and precision with which the poet moves, or the noble simplicity and strength everywhere so manifest. Of the Idylls, that of "Lancelot and Elaine" is the most sweetly moving and beautiful, "Geraint and Enid" the most interesting, and "Guinevere" and "The Passing of Arthur" the most majestic. Once accept the sentiment as natural, and few passages in English literature can be said to surpass in grandeur and pathos the description of Arthus's final interview with Guinevere, and his farewell speech to the guilty Queen as she grovels prostrate at his feet.

"Yet think not," says the King, "that I come to
urge thy crimes.

I did not come to curse thee, Guinevere,
I, whose vast pity almost makes me die
To see thee. laying there thy golden head,
My pride in happier summers, at my feet.
The wrath which forced my thoughts on that fierce law,
The doom of treason and the flaming death
(When first I learnt thee hidden here) is past.
The pang—which while I weighed thy heart with one
Too wholly true to dream untruth in thee,
Made my tears burn—is also past, in part.
And all is past, the sin is sinn'd, and I,
Lo ! I forgive thee, as Eternal God
Forgives ; do thou for thine own soul the rest.
But how to take last leave of all I loved ?
O golden hair, with which I used to play,
Not knowing ! O imperial-moulded form,
And beauty such as woman never wore,
Until it came a Kingdom's curse with thee—
I cannot touch thy lips; they are not mine,
But Lancelot's : nay, they never were the King's.

I cannot take thy hand ; that too is flesh,
And in the flesh thou has sinn'd ; and mine own flesh,
Here looking down on thine polluted, cries,
I loathe thee ; yet not less, O Guinevere,
For I was ever virgin save for thee,
My love thro' flesh hath wrought into my life,
So far that my doom is, I love thee still,
Let no man dream but I love thee still,
Perchance, and so thou purify thy soul,
And so thou lean upon our fair father Christ,
Hereafter in that world where all are pure
We two may meet before high God, and thou
Wilt spring to me, and claim me thine, and know
I am thine husband—not a smaller soul,
Nor Lancelot, nor another. Leave me that,
I charge thee, my last hope. Now must I hence.
     *   *   *   *
But hither shall I never come again,
Never lie by thy side ; see thee no more—
      Farewell !"

And while she grovell'd at his feet,
She felt the King's breath wander o'er her neck,
And in the darkness o'er her fallen head,
Perceived the waving of his hand that blest.

Finally, and greatest excellence of all, there is the noble seriousness of Tennyson's verse. This it is which gives it so high a place, and this it is that will preserve it, if anything can, to purify and sweeten and delight future generations. All he has written is pure as crystal, clean as the driven snow; and his "In Memoriam" teaches in accents of unfaltering dignity and matchless grace the sublime lesson of trust in God and resignation to his august decrees. Of his dramatic efforts I do not propose to speak, having neither the inclination nor the time. Tennyson lacks the dramatic faculty, and his "Queen Mary" and "Harold" are merely splendid narrative poems, interspersed with long, rhetorical monologues. I should have liked also to quote from his magnificent "Ode on Wellington," perhaps the strongest in its evenly sustained power of all his poems, (though marred by over-elaboration and too-apparent art); and "In Memoriam," in some respects the most notable poem of the last half century, must be dismissed with scant courtesy. But I have already overstepped the limits I had assigned myself at starting, and must haste to bring these scattered coments to a conclusion.

Mr. Taine, in his brilliant though unsatisfactory notice of Tennyson, brings his criticism to a close with a striking parallel between DeMusset and the English poet. A German would have selected Heine; an American, Poe; an Englishman, Hood; and a Scotchman, Burns.

I have no desire to institute harsh comparisons between illustrious men of genius. Tennyson and Burns moved in entirely different spheres; breathed entirely different atmospheres; and their lives and characters were as widely and as fundamentally opposed as their genius. For Tennyson, life, so far as outsiders may judge, has been an unbroken succession of prosperous and happy days. No chill penury ever froze his noble rage; no clamorous dun ever knocked at his door. Nurtured in England's foremost University, and surrounded from the cradle with admirers and friends; brought up in luxury, and having at his disposal all those refinements and conveniencies that minister to life's comfort; his soul untorn by great passion; his life unmarred by any great excesses; crowned with the laurel-wreath of English song; the friend of his Sovereign and beloved of her people, Tennyson has walked through life as through a beautiful garden full of great works of art; of singing-birds and music and flowers; and now that he is approaching the limit of life he stands forth a noble example of an almost ideal respectability, in whose life and writings, ethically at least, detraction itself can find no flaw. And in perfect keeping with this beautifully rounded life is the pure and exquisite perfection of his writings; so full of quiet beauty, of melodious measures, of happy descriptions, of noble sentiment, and informed withal with that high seriousness and classical repose which are among the chief essentials of highest art. All honor, I say, to such a man and such a poem; fit types both of them of the pure and wholesome court whose laureate Tennyson is. But with all these excellencies, there is the unsurmountable fact, that after all he is only a court poet. His excursions are confined to lordly mansions, to well-trimmed lawns, to ancestral gardens made beautiful by all the embellishments of sculpture, and art and song. Into the hut of the peasant, the garret of the starving needle woman, he does not enter. Never has his nice footstep paused by a Bridge of Sighs, or his daintily gloved hand brushed lovingly away the mud-bedraggled hair that hid the worn face of "one more unfortunate." He sings of love, but with an affectation which its ravishing sweetness only half conceals, and such stanzas as

> Ae fond kiss and then we sever !
> Ae farewell, alas, for ever.
>
> Had we never loved sae kindly,
>   Had we never loved sae blindly,
> Never met—or never parted,
>   We had ne'er been broken-hearted !

are worth a hundred "Locksley Halls" and by the soul-thrilling passion of

> "And my fause lover stole the rose,
>   But ah, he left the thorn wi' me,"

the hysterical explosions of "Maud" seem thin and poor. What possible interest can toiling, suffering humanity have in such sentimental abstractions as King Arthur and Sir Galahad? They move, not like real living men, but like the personages of a dream, and on meeting them one feels an almost irresistable impulse to prick them, to see if they are really flesh and blood.

Much other was the lot, and much different the genius, of the Scotch Exciseman. Inured to poverty from the cradle; compelled to support himself for years on less than $50 a year; cursed by constitutional melancholia that sapped the native vigor of his blood; impelled into excesses by the superabundant liveliness of his genius and the passionate yearning to escape from self and sordid and ungenial surroundings; alternately petted and coldly dropped by society; the unwilling recipient of a

thousand dangerous hospitalities; harrassed on his death-bed by an av-
aricious creditor; broken down in body and mind; his wife and children
destitute; his past a dreary blank; his future uncertain and clouded; so
far as the quality and permanence of their fame go I had rather have
been the large-hearted, passionate, chivalrous, free handed, poverty-
stricken, dissipated Scotch Exciseman, who, out of the liberality of his
great nature made all humanity the recipients of his genius, than England's laureate, with his blameless life, unassailed by great temptations
or griefs, surrounded by his aristocratic friends and all the refinements
of Nineteenth Century life, piping melodious measures of entrancing
sweetness, whose notes never reach the heart of the great masses outside.
I have no desire to underrate the quality of Mr. Tennyson's works. For
sweetness, finish, purity of sentiment, noble repose, and perfection of
form, they stand without a rival in literature; but all the same I had
rather go down to posterity as the author of "A Man 's a Man for a'That,"
"Scot's Wha Hae" and "Tam O'Shanter" than of "The Idylls of a King"
and "In Memoriam."

SYNOPSIS LECTURE XXVII.

SUBJECT.—A RAMBLE FROM HERRICK TO WORDSWORTH,

ROBERT HERRICK—1591-1674. A clergyman, song writer and epigrammatist, friend of Ben Jonson; "Gather ye Rosebuds;" "Cherry-ripe;" "To Daffodils;" "Ah Ben."

JASPER MAYNE—"Our Tune Passes."

RICHARD LOVELACE—1618-1684; his "To Lucasta."

MATTHEW PRIOR—1664-1721. The precurser of Tom Moore; his answer to Chloe Jealous.

TOM MOORE—His answer to Chloe Jealous.

THOMAS GRAY—1716-1771. His famous "Elegy;" lines from "Progress of Poesy;" lines from "Ode to Eton."

WILLIAM COLLINS—1720-1759. His odes; unhappy career; his "Oriental Eclogues;" "Dirge in Cymbeline;" "Ode written in 1746;" "How Sleep the Brave;" "Ode to Evening."

JAMES THOMSON—1700-1748. Author of the "Seasons."

COWPER—1731-1800. His love of nature; lines from "On receipt of his Mother's Picture;" "To Mary."

GEORGE CRABBE—1754-1832. "The Village."

SAMUEL TAYLOR COLERIDGE—1772-1834. In foremost rank of lyric poets. "Genevieve;" "Ancient Mariner;" "Christabel;" "Youth and Age;" "Love, Hope, and Patience."

WILLIAM WORDSWORTH—1770-1850. Adversely criticised and much admired. His" Excursion;" "Intimating of Immortality;" "Lines on Tintern Abbey;" "Lavdamia;" "Vernal Ode;" "Ode to Lycoris" and "Dion"—his character; his smaller pieces. "Resolution and Independence;" "The world is too much with us;" "Grasmere Church-yard."

A RAMBLE FROM HERRICK TO WORDSWORTH.

It is at least occasionally delightful to pass from the bright sunshine into the shade; from the broad highway into the by-path; from the rapture of the ocean and the sweeping river to the glen and the bower. There are such quiet resting-places in literature—such inviting retreats; and a ramble for an hour where the streamlet murmurs, the birds sing and the bees hum, may be pleasant.

ROBERT HERRICK.

To pass from Spenser to Herrick is to descend from the heights of poetry to a comparatively lowly level. Herrick lives on the plain. His prettinesses are such as belong to a flat country. His thought is often graceful but is never elevating, and the dainty love-lyrics in which he sings the charms—too minutely specified sometimes—of a score of mistresses are frequently sensual in tone. Hazlitt has pointed out that from Herrick's constant allusion to pearls and rubies one might take him for a lapidary rather than a poet, and it must be allowed that the use he makes of jewelry in celebrating the eyes and teeth and bosoms and lips of fair ladies is not a little wearisome. It is impossible to say of Herrick's poetry that it is a "perpetual feast of nectared sweets, where no crude surfeit reigns." The sweets are to be found in it in such abundance that they are apt to induce satiety, and whilst woman's bodily charms are methodically dwelt on their spiritual features are left out of the catalogue. Rarely does this poet exhibit feeling or pathos, but his command of language is great, and he has the art, which Prior and Tom Moore possessed, of saying pretty things in a pretty way. The following little piece of counsel addressed to girls affords a favorable specimen of his style as a song writer, but his chief strength, perhaps, lies in the epigram :

Gather ye rose-buds while ye may,
Old Time is still a flying;
And this same flower that smiles to-day
To-morrow will be dying.

The glorious lamp of Heaven, the Sun,
The higher he's a-getting,
The sooner will his race be run,
And nearer he's to setting.

That eye is best which is the first,
When youth and blood are warmer;
But being spent, the worse and worse
Times still succeed the former.

Then be not coy, but use your time,
And while ye may, go marry;
For having lost but once your prime
You may forever tarry.

Here is another snatch of song :

Cherry-ripe, ripe, ripe, I cry,
Full and fair ones; come and buy !
If so be you ask me where
They do grow?   I answer, there,
Where my Julia's lips do smile,
There's the land of Cherry isle;
Whose plantations fully show
All the year where cherries grow.

And this is a charmingly pathetic address

TO DAFFODILS :

Fair daffodils, we weep to see
You haste away so soon;
As yet the early rising sun
Has not attained his noon.
     Stay, stay,
Until the hasting day
     Has run
But to the even-song;
And having prayed together, we
     Will go with you along.

We have short time to stay as you,
  We have as short a spring;
As quick a growth to meet decay
  As you, or anything;
    We die
As your hours do, and dry away
Like the Summer's rain,
Or as the pearls of morning dew,
  Ne'er to be found again.

Robert Herrick was born in 1591 and lived into the reign of Charles II. He was educated for the Church, and obtained a living in Devonshire. After about twenty years residence there he was ejected by the storms of civil war. Herrick lived afterwards in Westminster, and, although a clergyman, associated with the jovial sports of the age. He "quaffed the mighty bowl" with Ben Jonson, to whom he addresses the following effusion :

AH, BEN !

Say how or where
Shall we, thy guests,
Meet at those lyric feasts
  Made at the Sun,
The Dog, the Tripple Tun;
We such clusters had
As made us nobly wild, not mad:
  And yet each frolic verse of thine
Outdid the meat, outdid the frolic wine.

MY BEN !

Or come again,
Or send for us
Thy wit's great overplus;
But teach us yet
Wisely to husband it;
Lest we that talent spend;
And having once brought to an end
  That precious stock, the store
Of such a wit, the world should have no more.

JASPER MAYNE.

From a play by Jasper Mayne called "The Amoran's War" this is the 'strophe of a Song :

OUR TIME PASSES.

Time is a feather'd thing,
And whilst I praise
The sparklings of thy looks and call them rays,
Takes wing;
Leaving behind him, as he flies.
An unperceived dimness in thine eyes.
His minutes, whilst they're told,
Do make us old.
And every sand of his fleet glass,
Increasing age as it doth pass,
Insensibly sows wrinkles there,
Where flowers and roses did appear.

Whilst we do speak, our fire
Doth into ice expire:
Flames turn to frost,
And, ere we can
Know how our crow turns swan,
Or how a silver snow
Springs there where yet did grow,
Our fading Spring is in dull Winter lost.

RICHARD LOVELACE.

The verses "To Althea, from Prison," by Richard Lovelace, the pattern of a brilliant cavalier poet of the time of Charles I are too well-known to need quotation, but those "To Lucasta" are so beautiful that one cannot deny himself the pleasure of hoping that they are new to some reader:

TO LUCASTA.—GOING TO THE WAR.

Tell me not, sweet, I am unkind,
That, from the nunnery
Of thy chaste breast and quiet mind,
To war and arms I fly.

True, a new mistress now I chase
The first foe in the field;
And with a stronger faith embrace
A sword, a horse, a shield.

Yet this inconstancy is such
As you too shall adore:
I could not love thee, dear, so much,
Loved I not honor more.

MATTHEW PRIOR.

Many of the pieces of Matthew Prior have a lightness and quickness of fancy which remind one of Tom Moore. The Irish poet was no doubt, in some instances, indebted to his predecessor for the structure of his verse; and readers familiar with the "Melodies," in listening for the first time to some passages in Prior's poems would at once attribute them to Moore. Like the latter, Prior is an apt writer, also, of *vers de société*, and a brilliant epigrammatist; but unfortunately many of his pieces are too coarse to be tolerated in our day. Yet Dr. Johnson, strangely enough declared Prior's poems to be a lady's book. "No lady," he said, "is ashamed of having it standing in her library." The following piece sounds like a song of Moore's, and the fancy exhibited in it is of the artificial kind, in which Moore delighted. It is an answer to Chloe Jealous:

> Dear Chloe, how blubber'd is that pretty face,
> Thy cheek all on fire and thy hair all uncurl'd;
> Pray thee quit this caprice; and as old Falstaff says,
> Let us e'en talk a little like folks of this world.
> * * * * *
> What I speak, my friend Chloe, and what I write, shows
> The difference there is between Nature and Art;
> I count others' verse, but love thee in prose:
> And they have my whimsies, whilst thou hast my heart.
>
> The god of us verse-men (you know, child) the Sun,
> How after his journey he sets up his rest:
> If at mornings o'er earth 'tis his fancy to run,
> At night he reclines on his Thetis' breast.
>
> So when I'm wearied with wand'ring all day
> To thee, my delight, in evening I come;
> No matter what beauties I saw in my way,
> They were but my visits, but thou art my home.
>
> Then finish, dear Chloe, this pastoral war;
> And let us, like Horace and Lydia agree:
> For thou art a girl as much brighter than her
> As he was a poet sublimer than me.

Prior deserves, I think, more praise as a lyrist than he has hitherto received; for, his success, such as it is, was not due to any contemporary influence. The vein of poetry at that period led in another direction;

and when the Queen Anne men attempted the lyric they generally failed. Such labored and conventional odes as those written by Addison, Hughes, and Congrave on "St. Cecilia," or in "Praise of Music," were not in common; but these odes, and there are numbers of equal merit or de- merit, are merely specimens of the verse-makers craft, in an age when the sole execllence of some writers, called poets by courtesy, was mechan- ical skill.

THOMAS GRAY.

Thomas Gray, author of the famous "Elegy Written in a Church- yard," was born, like so many other poets, in London. Charles Dickens once observed of him that a poet never gained a place among the im- mortals with so small a volume under his arm. Yet it is only on a portion of that tiny volume that his fame rests. In "The Progress of Poesy" he thus describes Shakespeare, Milton, and Dryden:

> Far from the sun and summer's gale,
> In thy green lap was Nature's darling laid,
> What time, where lucid Avon strayed,
> To him the mighty mother did unveil
> Her awful face; the dauntless child
> Stretched forth his little arms, and smiled.
> "This pencil take," she said, "whose colors clear
> Richly paint the vernal year;
> Thine, too, these golden keys, immortal boy !
> This can unlock the gates of joy,
> Of Horror that, and thrilling Fears,
> Or ope the sacred source of sympathetic Tears."
>
> Nor second he, that rode sublime
> Upon the seraph-innings of ecstacy,
> The secret of the abyss to spy,
> He passed the flaming bounds of space and time:
> The living throne, the saphire blaze,
> Where angels tremble while they gaze
> He saw; but blasted with excess of light,
> Closed his eyes in endless night.
> Behold where Dryden's less presumtuous car,
> Wide o'er the fields of glory bear
> Two coursers of etherial race,
> With necks in thunder clothed, and long-resounding pace.

"The Progress of Poesy" and "The Bard" are Gray's two most

splendid odes. Dr. Johnson has criticized them severely but somewhat unjustly. The "Hymn to Adversity" and the "Ode to Eton College" are also famous. The concluding verse of the latter may be quoted, the last sentence of which has passed into a proverb:

> To each his sufferings: all are men
> Condemned alike to groan;
> The tender for another's pain,
> The unfeeling for his own.
> Yet, ah ! why should they know their fate,
> Since sorrow never comes too late,
> And happiness too swiftly flies ?
> Thought would destroy their paradise
> No more; where ignorance is bliss
> 'Tis folly to be wise.

Gray's Elegy is at least one of the most popular poems in the English language. It lives in the memory like the sound of church bells, and is part of the valued possessions of the mind for countless throngs. The hold it has upon us is owing to the pensive beauty of the verse, to the naturalness of the thoughts, which are obvious without being commonplace, and to the choice of a subject in which everyone must feel a pathetic interest. When the poem appeared, the leading review of the day observed: "The excellence of this little piece amply compensates for its want of quantity;" and this was all the critic had to say in praise of a poem which ranks with the choicest treasures of poetical literature. In spite of the cold praise of the reviewer the Elegy gained immediate popularity, which Gray imputed to the subject, observing that the public would have received it as well if it had been written in prose; an extraordinary assertion, for there never was a poem that owed more to the melody of the versification, and to the exact adaptation of the metre to the theme. The permanence of Gray's fame depends not on his Odes but on his Elegy; and it is impossible to imagine any progress of thought or society which would make that poem less acceptable to the world. It is founded, to use one of Carlyle's phrases, on the eternal verities.

Collins, who was about four years younger than Gray, died insane at the age of thirty-nine. His history is brief and painful. He was the son of a hatter at Chichester, was educated at Winchester and Oxford. He left Oxford abruptly, considering himself in some way insulted, and repaired to London with rare genius, wild impulses and high ambition. His want was steadiness of purpose and application. In 1746, when twenty-six years old, he published his "Odes," which failed to attract attention. The disappointment utterly unmanned him, and in his depression he took to evil courses. He had good friends, as Thomson, author of the "Seasons," and Horne, author of "Douglas," and he was not without means. In the end he lost his reason and was tended by his sister, in Chichester. At one time he had to be confined in an asylum. His career affords one of the most touching examples of accomplished youth and genius, linked to personal humiliation and calamity, which throw their lights and shades on the annals of literature.

Collins' Odes appeared, like Gray's, to a limited circle of readers; and there are even men of culture and with some love of poetry who are quite unable to to appreciate the peculiar powers of this fine, but occasionally obscure poet. Perhaps the most inadequate criticism to be found in Johnson's "Lives of the Poets" is that bestowed on poor Collins; but the subtle charm of his verse was not likely to be appreciated by one who failed to see the loveliness of "Lycidas." Johnson, strange to say, finds far more to admire in the lyric poetry of Shenstone, whose ideas are commonplace and whose verse is jingling. Regarding the "Odes" of Collins, Southey says: "Silently and imperceptibly they had risen by their own buoyancy, and their power was felt by every reader who had any poetic feeling."

Of his "Oriental Eclogues," published while at Oxford, and then utterly neglected by the university and literary public alike, "Hassan, or the Camel Driver" is the best known. It is a finished picture, impressive and even appalling in its reality. But the three following pieces would be enough to secure Collins' fame:

DIRGE IN CYMBELINE.

To fair Fidele's grassy tomb
　Soft maids and village hinds shall bring
Each opening sweet, of earliest bloom,
　And rifle all the breathing spring.

No wailing ghost shall dare appear,
　To vex with shrieks this quiet grove,
But shepherd lads assemble here,
　And melting Virgins own their love.

No withered witch shall here be seen,
　No goblins lead their nightly crew;
The female fays shall haunt the green,
　And dress thy grave with pearly dew.

The red-breast oft at evening hours
 Shall kindly lend his little aid,
With hoary moss and gathered flowers
 To deck the ground where thou art laid.

When howling winds and beating rain
 In tempest shake thy sylvan cell,
Or midst the chase on every plain
 The tender thought on thee shall dwell.

Each lonely scene shall thee restore,
 For thee the tear be duly shed;
Belov'd till life can charm no more;
 And mourn'd till pity's self be dead.

This "Ode written in the year 1746" is well known, but it is not by any means certain that it is frequently associated with the name or memory of poor, unhappy Collins:

How sleep the brave that sink to rest,
By all their country's wishes blest ?
When Spring, with dewy fingers cold,
Returns to deck their hallow'd mould,
She shall there dress a sweeter sod
Than fancy's feet have ever trod.

By fairy hands their knell is rung;
By forms unseen their dirge is sung;
There Honor comes, a pilgrim gray,
To bless the turf that wraps their clay,
And Freedom shall awhile repair,
To dwell a weeping hermit there.

That surely is a composition which might serve as a model for those wishing to celebrate Commemoration Day in verse.

The "Ode to Evening," it will be observed, is unrymed:

If aught of oaten stop, or pastoral song
May hope, chaste Eve, to soothe thy modest ear
 Like thy own solemn springs,
 Thy springs, and dying gales;

Oh nympn reserved, while now the bright-haired sun
Sits in yon western tent, whose cloudy skirts,
    With brede ethereal wave
    O'erhung his wavy bed.

Now air is hushed, save where the weak-eyed bat
With short shrill shriek, flits by on leathern wing,
    Or where the beetle winds
    His small but sullen horn,

As oft he rises midst the twilight path,
Against the pilgrim borne with heedless hum;
    Now teach me, maid composed,
    To breathe some soften'd strain,

Whose numbers, stealing through the darkening vale,
May not unseemly with its stillness suit,
    As musing slow, I hail
    Thy genial loved return !

For when thy folding-star arising shows
His paly circlet, at his warning lamp
    The fragrant hours, and elves
    Who slept in buds the day,

And many a nymph who wreathes her brows with sedge
And sheds the freshening dew, and lovlier still,
    The pensive pleasures sweet
    Prepare thy shadowy car

Then let me rove some wild and heathy scene,
Or find some ruin midst its dreary dells,
    Whose walls more awful nod
    By thy religious gleams.

Or if still blustering winds, or driving rain,
Prevent my willing feet, be mine the hut
    That, from the mountain side,
    Views wilds, and swelling floods,

And hamlets brown, and dim-discovered spires,
And hears their simple bell, and marks o'er all
    Thy dewy fingers draw
    The gradual dusky veil.

While Spring shall pour his showers, as oft he wont,
And bathe thy breathing tresses, meekest Eve !
    While Summer loves to sport
    Beneath thy lingering light.

While sallow Autumn fills thy lap with leaves,
Or Winter getting through the troublous air,
    Affrights thy shrinking train,
    And rudely rends thy robe :

So long, regardful of thy quiet rule,
Shall Fancy, Friendship, Science, Smiling Peace,
    Thy gentlest influence own,
    And love thy favourite name !

I shall just mention James Thomson, author of the "Seasons," as we pass along. On his death Collins wrote a memorial ode. Thomson's rhetoric in the "Seasons" is not unlike Johnson's in the "Rambler," and reflects one of the passing faults that came of French influence on our literature. But in this style the words, though chosen too exclusively from the Latin side of English, are well chosen; each is used in its true sense, and, under a form of Rhetoric now obsolete there is a love of Nature that has grown from observation, and will forever be as fresh as it is true. Either Thomson or Mallet is the author of "Rule Britannia," and it may be noted here in passing that the best patriotic songs or lyrics in our language, and the best battle songs are the work of Scotchmen —of Burns, and Campbell, of Scott and Allan Cunningham.

Thomson inaugurated a new era in English literature in his admiration for rural or woodland scenery. Cowper's chief merit, it has often been said, is that he freed poetry from the so-called conventional diction popular in his age, and drew his imagery direct from nature. Cowper, often unpoetical and common-place, is never wanting in simplicity, and in his observation of nature he is unerring. He has no fine sense of harmony, none of those exquisite felicities of language which abound in Spenser, Milton and Keats, and which form a striking feature in Tennyson's poetry; but he has great clearness of expression and his pathos is profound. I shall only quote a few lines from those written "On the Receipt of his Mother's Picture:"—

Where once we dwelt our name is known no more,
Children not thine have trod my nursery floor,
And where the gardener Robin, day by day,
Drew me to the school along the public way,
Delighted with my bauble coach and wrapt
In scarlet mantle warm, and velvet capt,
'Tis now become a history little known
That once we called the pastoral house our own.
    *   *   *   *   *

All this, and more endearing still than all,
Thy constant flow of love, that knew no fall,
Ne'er roughened by those cataracts and brakes,
That humor interposed too often makes ;
All this, still legible in memory's page,
And still to be so to my latest age,
Adds joy to duty, makes me glad to pay
Such honors to thee as my numbers may;
Perhaps a frail memorial, but sincere,
Not scorned in heaven, though little noticed here.

And these :

TO MARY.

Autumn, 1793.

The twentieth year is well nigh past
Since first our sky was overcast.
Ah ! would that this might be our last !
                                    My Mary !

Thy spirits have a fainter flow,
I see thee daily weaker grow;
'Twas my distress that brought thee low,
                                    My Mary !

Thy needles, once a shining store,
For my sake restless heretofore,
Now rust disused, and shine no more
                                    My Mary !

For though thou gladly wouldst fulfil
The same kind office for me still,
Thy sight now seconds not thy will,
                                    My Mary !

But well thou play'dst the housewife's part,
And all thy threads, with magic art,
Have wound themselves about my heart,
                                    My Mary !

Thy indistinct expressions seem
Like language uttered in a dream ;
Yet me they charm, whate'er the theme,
                                    My Mary !

Thy silver locks, once auburn bright,
Are still more lovely in my sight
Than golden beams of Orient light,
                                    My Mary !

For, could I view nor them nor thee
What sight worth seeing could I see ?
The sun would rise in vain for me,

My Mary !

Partakers of thy sad decline,
Thy hands their little force resign,
Yet gently pressed, press gently mine,

My Mary !

*   *   *   *

And still to love, though pressed with ill
In wintry age to feel no chill
With me is to be lovely still,

My Mary !

*   *   *   *

And should my future lot be cast
With much resemblance of the past,
Thy worn-out heart will break at last,

My Mary !

Poor, dear Cowper, what a story was yours ! No wonder that Mrs. Browning should shed the abiding tears of genius over your grave !

I would fain pause to speak of George Crabbe, the faithful painter of the miseries and trials of the poor, who, in 1783 gave, in his "Village," a picture of "the cold charities of man to man," and I should like to linger beside many others, but this is a ramble which must have its limits. We have gone mostly by the green lanes and country ways of England, passing many a stately mansion, in the distance, unheeded, and indeed only pausing here and there, and now and then, as inclination prompted. We did not start with the idea of compiling a history or a gazetteer, nor did our ramble pre-suppose the necessity of halting at every door. But I think we cannot do better than call a halt in the lake country where Wordworth rests, and where so many bright spirits have had glorious times.

Cowper died in 1800, when several of the great poets whose works gave such splendor to the first quarter of this century were in the full prime of manhood. Wordsworth was thirty, Walter Scott twenty-nine, Coleridge twenty-eight, and Campbell twenty-three. Shelley, Keats, and Hood were at this date comparative infants, and Byron was a school-boy of twelve. The French Revolution, exciting ardent hopes in some minds and profound disappointment and regret in others, created an

extraordinary movement in intellectual life.   The beautiful but somewhat languid stream of poetry that flowed so calmly in the Eighteenth
Century, burst toward the close of it into a mountain torrent, leaping
and foaming with an impetuous energy that amazed the few so-called
classic verse makers who retained Pope's style, while lacking his vigor
and his wit.   Wordsworth, calmest and least impulsive of poets, has
described what he felt at this period:—

> A glorious time,
> A happy time that was ; triumphant looks
> Were then the common language of all eyes;
> As if, awaked from sleep, the nations hailed
> Their great expectancy.

And Coleridge, inspired by the same hopes, writes:—

> When France in wrath her giant limbs up-reared,
> And with that oath, which smote air, earth and sea,
> Stamped her strong foot and said she would be free !
> Bear witness for me how I hoped and feared !

In speaking of Coleridge and Wordsworth, who were closely associated together, particularly in the "Lyrical Ballads" published in 1798,
some of which were by Coleridge, but the greater number by Wordsworth, I shall only do so from a single point of view, and it would be
obviously impossible at this time to enter into any account of their lives.

If we except Shelley, Coleridge, great in so many ways, takes the
foremost rank in the lyrics amongst the early poets of this Century.
The music of his versification is exquisite; so perfect is it, indeed, at
times, that the most able critic would be doing a rash act were he to alter
a single word.   "Genevieve," for instance, is simply the perfection of a
love poem.   It is a poem written in youth :

GENEVIEVE.

> Maid of my love, sweet Genevieve !
> In bea ty's light you glide along :
> Your eyes are like the star of eve,
> And sweet your voice, as seraph's song
> Yet not your heavenly beauty gives

This heart with passion soft to glow :
Within your soul a voice there lives !
It bids you hear the tale of woe.
When, sinking low, the sufferer wan
Beholds no hand outstretched to save,
Fair as the bosom of the swan,
That rises graceful o'er the wave,
I've seen your breast with pity heave,
And therefore love I you, sweet Genevieve !

In middle life Coleridge wrote a poem entitled "Love," in which the same thought is beautifully elaborated. It 'is much too long to quote now, but a stanza or two will show what I mean :

Few sorrows hath she of her own—
My hope ! my joy ! my Genevieve !
She loves me best when e'er I sing
    The songs that make her grieve.
*   *   *   *   *
All impulses of soul and sense
Had thrilled my guileless Genevieve ;
The music and the doleful tale,
    The rich and balmy eve ;
*   *   *   *
Her bosom heaved—she stepped aside
As conscious of my look she stept
Then suddenly, with timorous eye
    She fled to me and wept.

If you read his "Ancient Mariner" and his "Christabel" the perfect movement of the verse will strike you as much as the dazzling imagination which floods every page with poetic light. Regarding the short poem, entitled "Youth and Age," Leigh Hunt says that its music can only be matched by some of the sweet strains of our early poets :

YOUTH AND AGE.
Verse, a breeze mid blossoms straying,
Where Hope clung feeding like a bee --
Both were mine ! Life went a Maying
    With Nature, Hope, and Poesy,
        When I was young !

When I was young ? Ah, woful when
Ah ! for the change 'twixt Now and Then !
    *   *   *   *

Flowers are lovely; love is flower-like,
  Friendship is a sheltering tree :
O ! the joys that came down shower-like
Of Friendship, Love, and Liberty,
                    Ere I was Old.

Ere I was Old ?   Ah, woful Ere
That tells me Youth's no longer here !
    *   *   *   *
Dewdrops are the gems of morning,
But the tears of mournful eve !
Where no hope is life's a warning
That only serves to make us grieve,
                    When we are Old.

That only serves to make us grieve,
With oft and tedious taking leave,
Like some poor, nigh-related guest,
Who may not rudely be dismist
Yet hath out-stay'd his welcome while,
And tells the jest without a smile.

   Before leaving Coleridge I should like to give you a piece not com—
monly known, but which is at once beautiful and true, and, if one may
be allowed to say so, is equal in value to many sermons.   There is also
deep pathos in it.   The title is

LOVE, HOPE AND PATIENCE IN EDUCATION.

O'er wayward childhood wouldst thou hold firm rule,
And sun thee in the light of happy faces ;
Love, Hope, and Patience, these must be thy graces,
And in thine own heart let them first keep school.
For, as old Atlas on his broad back places
Heaven's starry globe, and there sustains it,—so
Do these upbear the little world below
Of Education, Patience, Love, and Hope.
Methinks I see them grouped in seemly show,
The straightened arms upraised, the palms aslope,
And robes that, touching us as adown they flow,
Distinctly blend, like snow embossed in snow.
Oh, part them never ! If Hope prostrate lie
              Love too will sink and die.
But Love is subtle, and doth proof derive
From her own life that Hope is still alive;

And bending o'er with soul-transfusing eyes
And the soft murmurs of the mother dove,
Woos back the fleeting spirit and half supplies;
Thus Love repays to Hope what Hope first gave to Love.
Yet haply there will come a weary day,
      When, overtasked at length,
Both Love and Hope beneath the load give way,
Then with a statue's smile, a statue's strength
Stands the mute sister, Patience, nothing loth,
And both supporting does the work of both.

Wordsworth has been the subject of much adverse criticism, and of much admiration, and he has deserved them both, but chiefly the latter. He has written a good deal that is not child-like, but simply childish. In that vein he suggests those foolish persons who attempt to get down to the young by talking baby-talk. But after all, that is a small part of him, and one could readily explain it from the simple, remote life he led. Wordsworth was by no means a smart man, but he was a good man and a man of genius. In his "Excursion" he is often tedious, and often prosaic, but what a glorious work that still is. How often does he in it, to use his own words—

Add the gleam
The light that never was on sea or land
The consecration and the poet's dream,

to the object of his thought. No man in later years has had a greater number of devoted admirers amongst those whose admiration is worth having.

His "Intimations of Immortality" and "Lines on Tintern Abbey" exhibit imagination of the highest order. His "Lavdamia," "Vernal Ode," "Ode to Lycoris and Dion" are fine and richly classic poems, in conception and diction. His sonnets take the first rank in that difficult species of composition in which success has been so seldom attained, whilst some of his shorter pieces are gems. His whole nature is well set forth by his own lines :

My heart leaps up when I behold
A rainbow in the sky:
So was it when my life began;
So it is now I am a man;

> So be it when I shall grow old,
>   Or let me die !
> The child is father to the man;
> And I could wish my days to be
> Bound each to each by natural piety.

One could quote many beautiful shorter pieces.   The only difficulty is to select.   Some may be indicated, as "She was a phantom of delight," "Oh, Nightingale," "Lucy," "Nutting," "I wandered lonely as a cloud," "Ruth."

There is one piece for which I have had a great affection for many years, and which does not seem to have attracted ordinary attention.   I may quote a few lines here and there, but it is too long to give as a whole. The title is

RESOLUTION AND INDEPENDENCE.

> There was a roaring in the woods all night;
> The rain came heavily and fell in floods;
> But now the sun is rising calm and bright:
> The birds are singing in the distant woods;
> Over its own sweet voice the stock dove broods;
> The jay makes answer while the magpie chatters;
> And all the air is filled with pleasant noise of waters.
> All things that love the sun are out of doors;
> The sky rejoices in the morning's birth;
>   *   *   *   *
> I was a traveller then upon the moor.
>   *   *   *   *
> My old remembrances went from me wholly
> And all the ways of men so vain and melancholy.
>   *   *   *   *   *
> As high as we have mounted in delight
> In our dejection do we sink as low.
>   *   *   *   *
> I thought of Chatterton, the marvelous Boy,
> The sleepless Soul that perished in his pride;
> Of him who walked in glory and in joy,
> Following his plow along the mountain side:
> By our own spirits we are defied;
> We Poets in our youth begin in gladness,
> But thereof come in the end despondency and madness.

But there came no madness to Wordsworth.   He lived to a good old age.

Of Wordsworth's Sonnets, which form so considerable a portion of his works, many of which are of such excellence, a single example must suffice, but it is one of great beauty and deep significance.

> The world is too much with us; late and soon
> Getting and spending, we lay waste our powers:
> Little we see in Nature that is ours;
> We have given our hearts away—a sordid boon !
> This sea that bears her bosom to the moon;
> The winds that will be howling at all hours,
> And are upgathered now like sleeping flowers;
> For this, for everything we are out tune;
> It moves us not. Great God ! I'd rather be
> A Pagan suckled in a creed outworn;
> So might I, standing on this pleasant lea,
> Have glimpses that would make me less forlorn;
> Have sight of Proteus rising from the sea.
> Or hear old Triton blow his wreathed horn.

Wordsworth is buried in Grasmere Churchyard, according to his own wish, not far from the beautiful little lake Grasmere that sleeps among the gentle hills. I stood by his tomb a few years ago on a quiet Sunday morning, before entering the little church. It is almost overgrown with grass, and at first one felt indignant. But the wiser and better thought came that most probably he would have had it so. He who loved nature so dearly would rather rest with her undisturbed.

And here we part. We have come a long way, from Devonshire and Herrick to the English Lakes and Wordsworth. It is not the distance or the time that is all. He who will carefully reflect, even on the slight materials which has now been afforded him, will note a change and a progress in thought and sentiment far more astonishing than can be afforded by time or space. Thank God it is for the better and towards the best

SYNOPSIS LECTURE XXVIII.

SUBJECT—COWLEY—WALLER—MILTON.

Remarks on the restoration of the Drama; reinstated under Charles II; Davenant and his set.

ABRAHAM COWLEY, 1618–1667; the most popular part of his day; Pope's lines; Cowper's regret; unhappy life; buried with pomp; his works; "The Wish;" Tribute to Bacon.

EDMUND WALLER, 1605–1687. Smooth and refined verse; born to a fortune; his character; imprisoned; dies at Beaconsfield; opinion of his contemporaries; Go, Lovely Rose; Old Age and Death.

JOHN MILTON, 1608–1674, the greatest poet of his time; in the first rank of all poets; his youthful surroundings; influence of his father upon him; musical talent; education; Coleridge's criticism; career at Cambridge; Hymn on the Nativity; lives with his father in the country; writes "Arcades," "Comus," Lycidas"; quotation from last; goes abroad; visits Galileo; L'Allegro and Penseroso; "Paradise Lost;" his blindness; retirement; his youthful ambition; his ambition in 1641; notice of Paradise Lost; Milton's Devil; compared with Goethe's Mephistopheles; Paradise Regained and Samson Agonistes; criticism of his genius; Dryden's lines; the Drama again; Milton's place in his age; Wordsworth's Sonnet; extracts from Milton's poems.

THREE POETS OF THE REVOLUTION AND RESTORATION.

The Drama of the Restoration is generally said to have flourished from 1660 to 1700. As a rough statement this is well enough, and it is quite true also that a certain similarity of sentiment and style characterizes the period. A Gallican vein runs through the tragedy and comedy just as surely as an Italian vein runs through the Elizabethan drama. From Davenant to Cibber the aims are the same, the ideal the same, and the poetic sentiment the same. But when we look a little closer we are ready to forget that this coincidence exists. When the drama was publicly reinstated, under Charles II., it was a pompous and gorgeous thing with a new panoply of display. Under the auspices of Davenant, a set of fashionables wrote stilted pieces of parade which hardly belonged to literature at all. Literature had indeed taken another form and the best minds were interested in other employments than writing plays, and we proceed to say something of three poets of the time:

ABRAHAM COWLEY.

Abraham Cowley, the posthumous son of a London grocer, was born in 1618. He was educated at Westminster, and afterwards at Cambridge. He published a volume of poems in his thirteenth year. He became the most popular poet of his days. Pope writes of him:

> Who now reads Cowley? If he pleases yet
> His moral pleases, not his painted wit;
> Forgot his epic, nay Pindaric art,
> But still I love the language of his heart.

Cowper has also sketched Cowley in "The Task," where he laments that "his splendid wit" should have been "entangled in the cobwebs of the schools." His life was in many respects not a happy one, but when he died in 1667, the year that saw the publication of "Paradise Lost," he was buried with great pomp in Westminster Abbey. "The King himself", says Sprat, "was pleased to bestow on him the best epitaph, when, upon the news of his death, his majesty declared that Mr. Cowley had not left a better man behind him."

His poetical works are divided into four parts,—"Miscellanies," the "Mistress or Love Verses," "Pindaric Odes," the "Davideis, an Heroical Poem of the Troubles of David."

The following is entitled.—

THE WISH.

Well, then, I now do plainly see
This busy world and I shall ne'er agree;
The very honey of all earthly joy
   Does of all meats the soonest cloy.
   And they, methinks, deserve my pity,
Who for it can endure the stings,
The crowd, and buzz, and murmurings
   Of this great hive, the city.

Ah! yet ere I descend to th' grave,
May I a small house and large garden have,
And a few friends, and many books, both true,
   Both wise, and both delightful too!
   And, since love ne'er will from me flee,
A mistress moderately fair
And good, as guardian angels are,
   Only beloved, and loving me!

O fountains! when in you shall I,
Myself, eased of unpeaceful thoughts espy?
O fields! O woods! when, when shall I be made
   The happy tenant of your shade?
   Here's the spring-head of Pleasure's flood;
Where all the riches lie, that she
   Has coined and stamped for good.

Pride and ambition here
Only in far-fetched metaphors appear;
And naught but winds and hurtful murmurs scatter,
   And naught but Echo flatter.
   The gods, when they descended hither
From heaven, did always choose their way;
And therefore we may boldly say
   That 'tis the way too thither

How happy here should I,
And one dear she, live, and embracing die !
She, who is all the world, and can exclude
　In deserts solitude.
　I should have then this only fear,—
Lest men, when they my pleasures see,
Should hither throng to live like me,
　And so make a city here.

His tribute to Lord Bacon is admirable and wonderfully just,—

BACON.

From these and all long errors of the way,
In which our wandering predecessors went,
And like the old Hebrews many years did stray
In deserts but of small extent,
Bacon, like Moses, led us forth at last;
The barren wilderness he passed,
Did on the very border stand
Of the blest promised land,
And from the mountain's top of his exalted wit
Saw it himself, and showed us it.
But life did never to one man allow
Time to discover worlds and conquer too;
Nor can so short a line sufficient be,
To fathom the vast depths of nature's sea :
The work he did we ought to admire,
And we're unjust if we should more require
From his few years, divided 'twixt the excess
Of low affliction and high happiness;
For who on things remote can fix his sight,
That's always in a triumph or a fight ?

EDMUND WALLER.

Edmund Waller, 1605–1687, a courtly and amatory poet, stood next in rank to Cowley, so far as public estimation went. His verse is smooth and refined, and he did much for poetical diction, going on writing about love until he was over eighty years of age. He was born to a fortune of $15,000 a year. His mother was a sister of the celebrated John Hampden. The poet himself was not a man of much principle, and pushed his way along in a very prosaic way. He was easy and accomplished, and many of his witty sayings are recorded. He was imprisoned at one time for treason, and at last died at Beaconsfield in 1687, where he was interred in the same churchyard as that in which Edmund Burke sleeps.

He was much praised by his contemporaries as the "maker and model of melodious verse," an opinion favored afterwards by Dryden and Pope, but now he is seldom read. A good example of his style at its best is a song,—

GO, LOVELY ROSE.

Go, lovely rose !
Tell her that wastes ner time and me
That now she knows,
When I resemble her to thee
How sweet and fair she seems to be.

Tell her that's young,
And shuns to have her graces spied,
That had'st thou sprung
In deserts, where no men abide,
Thou must have uncommended died.

Small is the worth
Of beauty from the light retir'd.
Bid her come forth,
Suffer herself to be desir'd
And not blush so to be admir'd.

Then die ! that she
The common fate of all things rare
May read in thee,
How small a part of time they share
That are so wondrous sweet and fair.

The following also is well worthy of being quoted,—

OLD AGE AND DEATH.

The seas are quiet when the winds give o'er,
So calm are we when passions are no more.
For then we know how vain it was to boast
Of fleeting things too certain to be lost.
Clouds of affection from our younger eyes
Conceal that emptiness which age descries.

The soul's dark cottage, batter'd and decay'd
Lets in new light through chinks that time has made;
Stronger by weakness, wiser men become,
As they draw near to their eternal home.
Leaving the old, both worlds at once they view,
That stand upon the threshold of the new.

JOHN MILTON.

Incomparably the greatest poet of his time, and in the very first rank of any age, is John Milton, who was born in London, in 1608, and who, as was said, produced his "Paradise Lost" the year that Cowley died. How much surrounding circumstances colored his genius, and what he would have been had he entered the world half a century earlier, it would be difficult to estimate, but the world has no reason to regret that he lived in gloomy and troublous times. His father came of an ancient Catholic family, but was disinherited on becoming a Protestant. His father's sufferings, in this way, would undoubtedly affect the disposition of the son. At any rate, Milton was all for freedom of opinion in religious matters. Another circumstance to be taken into account is that the elder Milton was distinguished as a musical composer and the son was well skilled in the practice of music. Coleridge styles Milton a musical and not picturesque poet, a criticism probably suggested by this fact, and having no great depths of observation in it. In the most musical passages in Milton the pictures presented are as vivid and distinct as the paintings of Titian or Raphael. As this,—

Sabrina fair,
Listen where thou art sitting
Under the glassy, cool, translucent wave,
In twisted braids of lilies knitting
The loose train of thy amber-dropping hair.

Or this picture of a morning in May,—

Now the bright morning star, day's harbinger
Comes dancing from the east, and leads with her
The flowery May; who from her green lap throws
The yellow cowslip and the pale primrose.
Hail bounteous May! that dost inspire
Mirth and youth and warm desire;

> Woods and groves are of thy dressing,
> Hill and dale doth boast thy blessing.
> Thus we salute thee with our early song
> And welcome thee and wish thee long.

At the age of fifteen young Milton was sent to St. Paul's School, London, and two years afterwards to the University of Cambridge. He was a good student and splendid scholar, of a haughty temper, and from his graceful features and bearing called "the lady of Cambridge." Before he was twenty-one he had composed his exquisite "Hymn on the Nativity." After leaving the university he went to reside with his father, who had retired from business and was living in the country. During five years' residence there he studied classical literature and wrote his "Arcades", "Comus", and "Lycidas." The first two of these are masques, a kind of drama, in which, on account of the allegorical characters introduced, the actors had to wear masques. "Comus" was founded on an actual occurrence, and was presented at Ludlow Castle in 1634 before the Earl of Bridgewater, the president of Wales. "Lycidas" was the result of the death of Edward King, a friend of Milton's, who was drowned in crossing the Irish channel. It is a charming monody, loftily sad, a noble tribute to a much loved friend. It contains many powerful as well as pathetic passages, and attacks a corrupted clergy. There are the well-known lines,—

> Alas what boots it with incessant care
> To tend the homely slighted shepherd's trade
> And strictly mediate the thankless muse.
> Were it not better done as others use
> To sport with Amaryllis in the shade,
> Or with the tangles of Neara's hair?
> Fame is the spur that clear spirit doth raise—
> (That last infirmity of noble minds)
> To scorn delights and live laborious days;
> But the fair guerdon when we hope to find
> And think to burst out into sudden blaze,
> Comes the blind Fury with the abhorred shears
> And slits the thin-spun life. * * * —

Here too are lines which Ruskin somewhere quotes with admiration,—

        *   *   * Call the vales and bid them hither cast
Their bells, and flowerets of a thousand hues,
Ye valleys low, where the mild whispers use
Of shades, and wanton winds, and gushing brooks
On whose fresh lap the twart-star sparely looks ;
Throw hither all your quaint enamelled eyes
That on the green turf suck the honeyed showers
And purple all the ground with vernal flowers,
Bring the rathe primrose that forsaken dies
The tufted crow-toe, and pale jessamine,
The white pink, and the pansy streaked with jet.
The glowing violet,
The musk-rose, and the well-attered woodbine,
With cowslips wan that hang the pensive head ;
And every flower that sad embroidery wears :
Bid Amaranthus all his beauty shed
And daffodillies fill their cups with tears
      To strew the laureate hearse where Lycid lies.

I have quoted at some length from Lycidas because it is not nearly so well known, and ought to be. Indeed it may be doubted if readers of good literature, men of poetry, are not somewhat frightened at the very thought of Milton. The idea of "Paradise Lost" has no doubt terrified many a one. But readers should begin with the shorter works, and if they never get the length of "Man's first disobedience and the fruit of the forbidden tree" they will at least not have denied themselves a singular pleasure and a great benefit.

In 1638 Milton went abroad, and traveled for fifteen months in France and Italy. He met with and was made much of by "the choicest Italian wits," then a prisoner of Inquisition.

Nothing could be more appropriate than that I should give Milton's own words as to his upbringing and early career. In the case of some even this might be dangerous, even were they great men, on account of an unconscious vanity which leads to bias ; but here we are not only safe, but it is most pleasant, bringing us, as it were, into his very presence and company, instead of permitting us merely to hear of him. He writes then, as his "Second Defence of the people of England",— "I will now mention who and whence I am. I was born at London, of an honest family. My father was distinguished by the undeviating integrity of his life ; my mother by the esteem in which she was held, and the alms which she bestowed. My father destined me as a child to the pursuits of literature ; and my appetite for knowledge was so vora-

cious that, from twelve years of age, I hardly ever left my studies or
went to bed before midnight. This primarily led to my loss of sight.
My eyes were naturally weak, and I was subject to frequent headaches,
which, however, would not chill the ardor of my curiosity, or retard the
progress of my improvement. My father had me daily instructed in
the grammar school, and by other masters at home. He, then, after I
had acquired a proficiency in the various languages, and had made a
considerable progress in philosophy, sent me to the University of Cambridge, there I passed seven years, in the usual course of instruction
and study, with the approbation of the good, and without any stain upon
my character, till I took the degree of Master of Arts.

"After this I did not, as this miscreant feigns, run away into Italy,
but of my own accord retired to my father's house, whither I was accóm-
panied by the regrets of most of the fellows of the college, who showed
me no common marks of friendship and esteem. On my father's estate,
where he had determined to pass the remainder of his days, I enjoyed
an interval of interrupted leisure, which I entirely devoted to a perusal
of the Greek and Latin classics ; though I occasionally visited the
metropolis, either for the sake of purchasing books, or of learning
something new in mathematics, or in music, in which I, at that time,
found a source of pleasure and amusement. In this manner I spent five
years, till my mother's death ; I then became anxious to visit foreign
parts, and particularly Italy.

"My father gave me his permission and I left home with one servant. On my departure the celebrated Henry Wootton, who had been
King James' ambassador at Venice, gave me a signal proof of his regard
in an elegant letter which he wrote, breathing not only the warmest
friendship, but containing some maxims of conduct, which I found very
useful in my travels. The noble Thomas Scudamore, King Charles'
ambassador, to whom I carried letters of recommendation, received me
most courteously at Paris. His lordship gave me card of introduction
to the learned Hugo Grotius, at that time ambassador from the Queen
of Sweden to the French court, whose acquaintance I eagerly desired,
and to whose house I was accompanied by some of his lordship's
friends. A few days after, when I set out for Italy, he gave me letters
to the English merchants on my route, that they might shew me any civ-
ilities in their power. Taking ship at Nice I arrived at Genoa, and
afterwards visited Leghorn, Pisa and Florence. In the latter city, which
I have always more particularly esteemed for the elegance of its dialect,
its genius, and its taste, I stopped about two months ; when I contracted

an intimacy with many persons of rank and learning, and was a constant attendant at their literary parties, a practice which prevails there, and tends so much to the diffusion of knowledge and the preservation of friendship.

"From Florence I went to Sienna, thence to Rome, where, after I had spent about two months viewing the antiquities of that renowned city, where I received the most friendly attention from Lucas Holstein and other learned and ingenious men, I continued my route to Naples. There I was introduced to a certain recluse, with whom I had traveled from Rome, to John Baptista Manso, Marquis of Villa, a nobleman of distinguished rank and authority, to whom Tasso, the illustrious poet, inscribed his book on friendship. During my stay he gave me singular proofs of his regard ; he himself conducted me round the city, and to the palace of the Viceroy, and more than once paid a visit to my lodgings. On my departure he gravely apologized for not having shown me more civility, which he said he had been restrained from doing because I had spoken so unreservedly on matters of religion.

"When I was preparing to pass over into Sicily and Greece, the melancholy intelligence which I received of the civil commotions in England, made me alter my purpose ; for I thought it base to be traveling for amusement abroad, while my fellow-citizens were fighting for liberty at home. While I was on my way back to Rome, some merchants informed me that the English Jesuits had formed a plot against me, if I returned to Rome, because I had spoken too freely on religion, but, if any questions were put to me concerning my faith, to declare it without reserve or fear. I nevertheless returned to Rome. I took no steps to conceal either my person or my character, and for about the space of two months, I again openly defended, as I had done before, the reformed religion in the very metropolis of popery.

"By the favor of God I got back safe to Florence, where I was received with as much affection as if I had returned to my native country. There I stopped as many months as I had done before, except that I made an excursion for a few days to Lucca ; and, crossing the Appenines, passed through Bologna and Ferrara to Venice. After I had spent a month in surveying the curiosities of that city, and had put on board a ship the books which I had collected in Italy, I proceeded through Verona and Milan, and along the Leman Lake to Geneva. The mention of this city brings to my recollection the slandering More, and makes me again call the Deity to witness that in all those places, in which vice meets with so little discouragement, and is practiced with so little shame, I never once deviated from the paths of integrity and virtue, and perpetually reflected that, though my conduct might escape the notice of men, it could not elude the inspection of God. At Geneva I held daily conferences with John Deodati, the learned professor of theology. Then, pursuing my former route through France, I returned to my native country, after an absence of about one year and three months, at the time when Charles, having broken the peace, was renewing what is called the Episcopal war with the Scots ; in which the royalists being routed in the first encounter, and the English being universally and justly disaffected, the necessity of his affairs at last obliged him to con-vene a Parliament. As soon as I was able I hired a spacious house in the city for myself and my books, where I again with rapture renewed my literary pursuits, and where I calmly awaited the issue of the con-test, which I trusted to the wise conduct of Providence and to the cour-age of the people. The vigor of Parliament had begun to humble the pride of the bishops. As long as the liberty of speech was no longer subject to control, all mouths began to be opened against the bishops ; some complained of the vices of the individuals, others of those of the order.

"They said that it was unjust that they alone should differ from the model of other reformed churches, and particularly the Word of God. This awakened all my attention and zeal. I saw that a way was open-ing for the establishment of real liberty ; that the foundation was lay-ing for the deliverance of man from the yoke of slavery and supersti-tion ; that the principles of religion, which were the first objects of our care, would exert a salutary influence on the manners and constitution of the republic ; and, as I had from my youth studied the distinctions between religious and civil rights, I perceived that, if I ever wished to be of use, I ought, at least, not to be wanting to my country, to the Church, or to so many of my fellow-Christians, in a crisis of so much danger. I therefore determined to relinquish the other pursuits in which I was engaged, and to transfer the whole force of my talents and my industry to this one important subject."

This to me is the most interesting passage in Milton's autobiog-raphy. It mirrors the man so distinctly and clearly ; and, further it so unerringly predicts his future career. It needs no comment, speaking as it does, beyond the eloquence of words, for itself.

Before this period of travel, he had, as well as the works already mentioned, composed and written his "L'Allegro" and "Il Penseroso." These are probably the best known and most appreciated of his works.

With his public employment under Cromwell, as Latin Secretary to the Council State ; with his private life and his domestic troubles ; or with his prose works, which themselves are a monument of genius ; I cannot now deal. I pass on to consider "Paradise Lost." This immortal work was begun in 1658, and was completed in 1665. For many years the poet's sight had been failing, and by the close of 1652 he was totally blind. The Restoration deprived Milton of his public employment, and even exposed him to danger, but it is said that through the interest of Davenant and Marvell his name was included in the general amnesty. He retired to the country to realize in blindness and bereavement the high ambition of his youth. What that was he himself tells us in a College Exercise written in his nineteenth year. He would choose such a subject—

> Where the deep transported mind may soar
> Above the wheeling poles, and at heaven's door
> Look in.

In 1641, after his return from Italy, and when he was thirty-three years of age, he hopes ' he might perhaps leave something so written in after-times as they should not willingly let die," and he goes on to say that his ambition is "to be an interpreter and relater of the best and sagest things among mine own citizens, throughout this Island, in the mother dialect;—that what the greatest and choicest events of Athens, Rome, or modern Italy, and those Hebrews of old did for their country, "I, in my proportion, with this over and above, of being a Christian, might do for mine ; not caring to be once named abroad, though perhaps I could attain to that, but content with these British Islands as my world. Something of highest hope and hardest attempting, whether in epic poem as exemplified by Homer, Virgil and Tasso, or after the dramatic wherein Sophocles and Euripides reign, or in the style of those magnific odes and hymns of Pindarus and Calimachus; not forgetting that, of all these kinds of writing, the highest models are to be found in the Holy Scriptures—in the Book of Job, in the Song of Solomon, and the Apocalypse of St. John, in the frequent songs interspersed throughout the Law and the Prophets." He ends thus : "The thing which I had to say, and those intentions which have lived within me, ever since I could conceive myself anything worth to my country, I return to crave excuse that urgent reason hath plucked from me by an abortive and fore-dated discovery. And the accomplishment of them lies not but in

a power above man's to promise ; but that none hath by more studious
ways endeavoured, and with more unwearied spirit that none shall, that
I dare almost over of myself ; as far as life and free leisure will extend ;
and that the land had once enfranchised herself from this impertinent
yoke of prelaty, under whose inquisitorial ánd tyrannical duncery no
free and splendid wit can flourish.   Neither do I think it shame to cov-
enant with any knowing reader, that for some few years yet I may go on
trust with him toward the payment of what I am now indebted ; as being
a work not to be raised from the heat of youth or the vapors of wine,
like that which flows at waste from the pen of some vulgar amourist, or
the trencher fury of a rhyming parasite ; nor to be obtained by the invocation of Dame Memory and her Siren daughters ; but by devout
prayer to that eternal Spirit, who can enrich with all utterance and knowledge, and send out his Seraphim, with the hallowed fire of his altar, to
touch and purify the lips of whom he pleases.   To this must be added
industrious and select reading, steady observation, insight into all seemly
and generous arts and affairs.   Till which in some measure he accomplished, at mine own peril and cost, I refuse not to sustain this expectation from as many as are not loth to hazard as much credulity upon the
best pledges I can give them."

And how nobly Milton kept his promise all the world knows.   "Paradise Lost" is a work unparalleled of its kind.   It may be excelled in
some respects by Homer's Iliad, but in its own field it rises high "above
all Greek, above all Roman fame."   The subject is the origin of evil.
The first book of "Paradise Lost" is one of the sublimest pictures ever
drawn by mortal pen.   The delineation of Satan, and the fallen angels,
"hurled headlong flaming from the ethereal sky", and their parliament
in the fiery gulf underneath Chaos is a magnificent effort of genius.
The fourth book is equally noticeable for its grace and luxuriance of
imagination.

Milton's Devil is a distinct creation of his own.   Satan's idea of
existing ever afterwards as a Devil, and that not from necessity but
choice is a splendidly daring conception of the poet's.   A striking picture has been brought out by contrasting and comparing Milton's Satan
and Goethe's Mephistopheles :—Satan is a collosal figure ; Mephistopheles an elaborate portrait.   Satan is a fallen archangel scheming
his future existence ;   Mephistopheles is the modern Spirit of Evil.
Mephistopheles has a distinctly marked physiognomy ; Satan has not.
Satan has a sympathetic knowledge of good ; Mephistopheles knows
good only as a phenomenon.   Much of what Satan says might be spoken

by Raphael; a devilish spirit runs through all that Mephistopheles says. Satan's bad actions are preceded by noble reasonings; Mephistopheles does not reason ; Satan's bad actions are followed by compunctious visitings ; Mephistopheles never repents. Satan conducts an enterprise ; Mephistopheles enjoys an occupation. Satan has strength of purpose ; Mephistopheles is volatile. Satan feels anxiety; Mephistopheles lets things happen. Satan's greatness lies in the vastness of his motives; Mephistopheles' in his intimate acquaintance with everything. Satan has a few sublime conceptions ; Mephistopheles has accumulated a mass of observations. Satan may end in being a devil ; Mephistopheles is one irrevocably.

Adam and Eve are drawn very beautifully, and their residence in Paradise is described charmingly ; they have our interest and sympathy all the time ; but Milton's hero is the ruined archangel.

"Paradise Regained" and "Samson Agonestes" followed the poet's noblest work, and they are great in comparison with anything but it.

Milton's genius was not dramatic. His character was too strong, his mind too lofty and unbending, to allow him to stoop and take hold of everything and be interested in everything as the dramatist must do. We cannot imagine him proposing to himself to create a Falstaff or Bobadil or Pistol or Doll Taresheet. His vast scholarship; haughty genius; and his religious and ascetic tendencies all pointed to the epic as the form his great creations would take. His greatest achievement has characteristics of its own ; he was self-conscious, and you discover himself ever again in "Paradise Lost." You discover him even in his own Satan. That is not Homeric, but in some respects Milton surpasses Homer, and the lines of Dryden, as they have been remembered, are worthy of being so:

> Three poets, in three distant ages born,
> Greece, Italy and England did adorn.
> The first in loftiness of thought surpassed,
> The next in majesty ; in both the last.
> The force of nature could no farther go
> To make a third, she join'd the other two.

Milton died without a struggle, on Sunday, the 8th November, 1674.

I began by speaking of the re-establishment of the drama, and wish now, in a few words to allude to the Restoration Dramatists, especially in connection with Milton ; for they formed a feature in the age of which he is now, in literature, the most striking figure. I spoke of Davenant and his followers.   Out of the ashes of that rustling, silken school sprang Dryden, and, in company with Etheredge and Shadwell, recalled the drama to something at least of decency and good sense. Between 1670 and 1675 this group received a sudden accession of numbers so remarkable that it has had no parallel since the days of Marlowe. Within four years Crowne, Wycherly, Mrs. Aphra Behn, George, Duke of Buckingham, Lacy, Settle, Otway and Lee, published their first plays, and with these more or less distinguished individuals, a whole array of now forgotten playwrights burst upon the world.   Again between 1693 and 1700 there ripened a new crop of ornaments—Congreve, Cibber, Mary Pix, Vanbrugh, Farquhar and Rowe. These then are the genius of the Drama of the Restoration. Their plays are very immoral, and their genius of no very high order. Excepting Dryden, they are all but forgotten. Lee is remembered by one line. They form mostly the dark background to the brilliant and lofty genius of Milton.

The Puritans had set their faces against all those practices which were supposed to be essential to the life of the Drama.   Even in Shakespeare, and much more in Ben. Jonson, Beaumont, and Fletcher, and others, may be traced this opposition to the Puritanical spirit.   That literary crusade against the Puritans as canting, sour-visaged, mirth-forbidding, art-abhorring religionists, which came to its height when Butler wrote his "Hudibras" and Wycherley his plays, was already hot when the wits of King James' days used to assemble after the theatre in their favorite taverns. By considering this matter we shall recognize how Milton was *the* poet of that intermediate era, which came between the age of Shakespeare and Elizabeth and the age of Dryden and the second Charles.   He represented, although in some senses not a Puritan, all that was best in Puritanism, and deepest in English Society. We may then understand Wordsworth's noble sonnet :

Milton, thou shouldst be living at this hour
England hath need of thee ; she is a fen
Of stagnant waters ; altar, sword and pen
Fireside, the heroic wealth of hall and bower,
Have forfeited their ancient English dower
Of inward happiness. We are selfish men ;
Oh ! raise us up, return to us again ;

And give us manners, virtue, freedom, power,
Thy soul was like a star and dwelt apart ;
Thou hadst a voice whose sound was like the sea,
Pure as the naked heavens—majestic, free,
So didst thou travel on life's common way
In cheerful godliness ; and yet thy heart
The lowliest duties on herself didst lay.

FROM MILTON'S POEMS.

HYMN ON THE NATIVITY.

*   *   *   *

No war or battle sound
Was heard the world around ;
The idle spear and shield were high uphung;
The hooked chariot stood
Unstained with hostile blood;
The trumpet spake not to the armed throng ;
And Kings sat still with awful eye,
As if they surely knew their sov'reign lord was by.

But peaceful was the night
Wherein the Prince of Light
His reign of peace upon the earth began :
The winds, with wonder whist,
Smoothly the waters kiss'd
Whispering new joys to the mild Ocean,
Who now hath quite forgot to rave,
While buds of calm sit brooding on the charmed wave.

The stars, with deep amaze,
Stand fix'd in steadfast gaze,
Bending one way their precious influence;
And will not take their flight,
For all the morning light,
Or Lucifer that often warn'd them thence·
But in their glimmering orbs did glow,
Until their Lord himself bespake and bid them go.

The shepherds on the lawn,
Or ere the point of dawn,
Sat simply chatting in a rustic row;
Full little thought they then
That the mighty Pan
Was kindly come to live with them below;
Perhaps their loves or else their sheep,
Was all that did their silly thoughts so busy keep.

When such music sweet
Their hearts and ears did greet
As never was by mortal finger strook,
Divinely warbled voice
Answering the stringed noise,
As all their souls in blissful rapture took.
The air such pleasure loath to lose,
With themes and echoes still prolongs the heavenly close.

*   *   *   *   *

Such music as 'tis said,
Before was never made,
But when of old the sons of morning sung,
When the Creator great
His constellations set,
And the well-balanced world on hinges hung,
And cast the dark foundations deep,
And bid the weltering waves their oozy channels keep.

Ring out ye chrystal spheres,
Once bless our human ears,
If ye have power to touch our senses so;
And let your silver chime
Move in melodious time;
And let the base of heaven's deep organ blow;
And with your ninefold harmony
Make up full concert to the angelic symphony.

*   *   *   *   *

But see the Virgin blest
Hath laid her babe to rest,
Time is, our tedious song should have an ending;
Heaven's youngest-teemed car
Hath fix'd her polish'd car,
Her sleeping Lord with handmaid lamp attending;
And all about the courtly stable
Bright harness'd angels sit in order serviceable.

FROM L' ALLEGRO.

And ever against carking cares,
Lap me in soft Lydian airs,
Married to immortal verse,
Such as the meeting soul may pierce,
In notes, with many a winding bout,

Of linked sweetness long drawn out,
With wanton heed and giddy cunning
The melting voice through mazes running;
Untwisting all the charms that tie
The hidden soul of harmony.

FROM IL PENSEROSO.

But let my dear feet never fail
To walk the studious cloister's pale;
And love the high embowed roof,
With antic pillars massy proof,
And storied windows richly dight
Casting a dim religious light,
There let the pealing organ blow
To the full-voiced quire below,
In service high, and anthems clear.
As may with sweetness, through mine ear,
Dissolve me into ecstacies,
And bring all heav'n before mine eyes.

PARADISE LOST.

SATAN'S ADDRESS TO THE SUN.

O thou, that with surpassing glory crown'd,
Look'st from thy soul dominion like the God
Of this new world ; at whose sight all the stars
Hide their diminish'd heads ; to thee I call,
But with no friendly voice; and add thy name,
O Sun, to tell thee how I hate thy beams,
That bring to my remembrance
I fell, how glorious once,—above thy sphere;
Till pride and worse ambition threw me down,
Warring against heaven's matchless King.

ASSEMBLING OF THE FALLEN ANGLES.

Ten thousand banners rise in the air
With orient colors waving : with them rose
A forest of huge spears ; and thronging helms
Appeared, and serried shields in thick array,
Of depth immeasurable: anon they move
In perfect phalanx to the Dorean mood
Of flutes and soft recorders; such as rais'd
To height of noblest temper heroes old
Arming to battle; and, instead of rage,
Deliberate valour breath'd, firm and unmov'd.

THE GARDEN OF EDEN.

And higher than that wall a circling row
Of goodliest trees, loaden with fairest fruit,
Blossoms and fruits at once of golden hue,
Appear'd, with gay enamel'd colours mix'd;
Of which the sun more glad unpress'd his beams
Than in fair evening cloud, or humid bow,
When God hath shower'd the earth; so lovely seem'd
That landscape; and of pure, now purer air
Meets his approach; and to the heart inspires
Vernal delight and joy, able to drive
All sadness but despair; now gentle gales
Fanning their odoriferous wings, dispense
Native perfumes, and whisper whence they stole
Those balmy spoils.

ADAM AND EVE LEAVE PARADISE.

The world was all before them where to choose
Their place of rest, and Providence their guide,
They, hand in hand, with wandering steps andslow,
Through Eden took their solitary way.

"PARADISE REGAINED."

CHRIST OVERCOMES THE TEMPTER.

So Satan fell: and straight a fiery globe
Of angels on full sail of wing flew nigh,
Who on their plumy vans receiv'd him soft
From his uneasy station, and upbore,
As on a floating couch through the blithe air;
Then in a flowery valley sit him down
On a green bank, and set before him spread
A table of celestial food, divine,
Ambrosial, fruits fetch'd from the Tree of Life
And from the Fount of Life ambrosial drink,
That soon refresh'd him wearied, and repair'd
What hunger, if aught hunger had impair'd,
Or thirst; and as he fed, angelic quires
Sung heavenly anthems of his victory
Over temptation, and the Tempter proud.

"SAMSON AGONESTES."

(Samson's Soliloquy.)

"But chief of all
O loss of sight, of thee I most complain,

Blind among enemies : O worse than chains,
Dungeon, or beggary, or decrepit age !
Light, the prime work of God, to me is extinct,
And all our various objects of delight
Annulled, which might in part my grief have eased,
Inferior to the vilest now become
Of man or worm, the vilest here excel me :
They creep, yet see ; I, dark in light, exposed
To daily fraud, contempt, abuse, and wrong
Within doors or without, still as a fool
In power of others, never in my own,—
Scarce half I seem to live, dead more than half,
Oh dark, dark, dark, amid the blaze of noon,
Irrecoverably dark, total eclipse
Without all hope of day !
Oh first created beam, and thou great Word,
'Let there be light, and light was over all,'
Why am I thus bereav'd thy prime decree ?
The sun to me is dark
And silent as the moon
When she deserts the night,
Hid in her vacant interlunar care,
Since light so necessary is to life,
And almost life itself, if it be true
That light is in the soul,
She all in every part, why was the sight
To such a tender ball as the eye confin'd,
So obvious and so easy to be quench'd,
And not, as feeling, through all parts diffus'd,
That she might look at will through every pore ?
Then had I not been thus exiled from light,
As in the land of darkness; yet in light,
To live a life half dead, a living death,
And buried ; but, O yet more miserable !
Myself my sepulchre, a moving grave.

SONNETS.

(On reaching his twenty-third year.)

How soon hath Time, the subtle thief of youth,
Stol'n on his wing my three and twentieth year !
My hast'ning days fly on with full career,
But my late spring no bud or blossom sheweth,
Perhaps my semblance might deceive the truth,
That I to manhood am arriv'd so near ;
And inward ripeness, doth much less appear,
That some more timely happy spirits indueth,

Yet be it less or more, or soon or slow,
It shall be still in strictest measure ev'n
To that same lot, however mean, or high,
Toward which Time leads me, and the will of heav'n ;
All is if I have grace to use it so,
As ever in my great Task-Master's eye.

ON HIS DETRACTORS.

I did but prompt the age to quit their clogs,
By the known rules of ancient liberty,
Where straight a barbarous noise environs me
Of owls and cookoos, asses, apes and dogs,
As when those hinds as were transform'd to frogs
Rail'd at Latona's twin-born progeny,
Which after held the sun and moon in fee.
But this is not by casting pearls to hogs,
That brave for freedom in their senseless mood,
And still revolt when truth would set them free.
Licence they mean when they cry liberty ;
For who loves that, must first be wise and good :
But from that mark how far they rose we see,
For all this waste of wealth and loss of blood.

ON HIS BLINDNESS.

When I consider how my light is spent
Ere half my days, and in this dark world and wide,
And that one talent, which is death to hide,
Lodg'd with me useless, tho' my soul more bent
To serve therewith my Maker, and present
My true account, lest He, returning, chide ;
"Doth God exact day-labor, light denied ?"
I fondly ask ; but Patience, to prevent
That murmur, soon replies, "God doth not need
Either man's work or his own gifts ; who best
Bears His mild yoke, they serve Him best ; His state
Is Kingly; thousands at His bidding speed,
And post o'er land and ocean without rest ;
They also serve who only stand and wait."

SYNOPSIS LECTURE XXIX.

Seven and seventy years ago, in a thriving sea-port in Maine, a child was born into the world, to whose cradle the seven fairies repaired, to "shower upon it their benefactions." Longfellow, poet, lived so familiarly in our midst, in such constant and open communication to us through his writings, that we came to be more familiar with his private life and ways than we are of our next door neighbor. His poetry has been translated into almost every civilized tongue, and, to an unprecedented degree, has touched the sympathies of two hemispheres. His very presence breathed an atmosphere of "peace on earth—good will to men." The day Longfellow died we all felt that we had lost a near and dear friend.

HENRY WADSWORTH LONGFELLOW.

Seven and seventy years ago, in a thriving sea-port in Maine, a child was born into the world, to whose cradle the seven fairies repaired, to "shower upon it their benefactions." The First, on whose face shone the light that never was on sea or land, brought—Genius ; that perilous gift, with which to move the hearts of men. The Second, of serious and most divine aspect, added—Temperance ; the better to restrain the quick impulses of a fine nature, and shape them to sweet and noble issue. The Third, from out whose deep-set eyes peered the experience of the Ages—Wisdom. The Fourth, with eyelids modestly downcast—Reverence. The Fifth, beautiful with a beauty transcending that of mortal—Love ; and the Sixth, breathing the freshness of perpetual youth—Length of Days. Lastly, the Seventh stepped forward, a "daughter of the gods, divinely tall, and most divinely fair, and circling the infant brow with the radiant nimbus of Immortality, said :

"Go forth, O poet soul, brave of heart, quick of sympathy, strong of purpose ; go forth into the world, and with sweet words of comfort and of song, cheer the hearts of the suffering and the heavy laden, crown labour with new dignity, inspire thy fellows with fresh hope and lofty ambitions,—so shall the nations hail thee as the Healer of Hearts ; and so, in the far distant ages, when Father relates to son the story of thy career and writings, the 'Golden Legend' of thy cunning brain, shall be eclipsed in all men's minds, by the Golden Legend of thy blameless life !"

And thus equipped with Genius, Temperance, Wisdom, Reverence, Health and Love, the Poet soul went forth, and far and wide sped his winged words of wisdom and of cheer, of comfort and of hope, until in the process of years the entire globe recognized in him a personal friend, and enthroned in their hearts, as Laureate of the Household, gentle historian of the human heart—the name of Henry Wadsworth Longfellow

I shall not detain you with biographical details. Indeed, Longfel-

low, poet, lived so familiarly in our midst, in such constant and open
communication with us through his writings, and all his movements were
so carefully noted by the newspapers, that we came to be more familiar
with his private life and ways than we are of those of our next-door
neighbor.   We love to pry into the kitchens of great men ; to assure
ourselves of the fact that with all their greatness they are human ; that,
after all, they live and love, rejoice and sorrow, suffer and toil, in much
the same way as do less gifted mortals.   And surely never was life more
freely open to a world's scrutiny!   And surely never was scrutiny re-
paid by sight more wholesome and peaceful and pure ; than that presented by the life and walk of Longfellow.   And here, on the threshold
of our study, we are brought face to face with the question—what is the
secret of the deep, tender and wide-spread source of sorrow and bereavement, with which at the time of his removal smote the civilized world ?
I say 'world', for his was no merely national reputation.   His poetry
has been translated into almost every civilized tongue, and, to an unprecedented degree, has touched the sympathies of two hemispheres.
Other deaths had occurred but a short time before his,—some of men of
more commanding position, and whose lives will bulk more largely in
history than Longfellow's, but none of those touched the heart of the
people like his.   When that Scotch Diogenes, the cross-grained but
large-hearted seer of Greenwich, Thomas Carlisle, died, the pulse of humanity maintained unmoved its even beat, and while yet the funeral
services were ringing in their ear, biographer, relatives and critics were
snarling and fighting over his scarce-closed grave.   Lord Beaconsfield
passed away in the ripe splendor of his magnificently rounded and imperial career, but the event caused hardly a ripple in domestic circles.
George Eliot, the world's most gifted Englishwoman, the only legitimate
successor of the many-sided genius of Avon, passed from our midst, to
be lamented keenly, it is true, but only by a select and cultured circle ;
and the sudden fall of the late President Garfield owed much of its
tragic interest to the dramatic circumstances attending the "deep dam-
nation of his taking off."   But, Garfield's excepted, not one of these deaths
can be said to have moved the general public with a sense of personal
bereavement.   The day Longfellow died, however, we all felt that we had
lost a near and dear friend ; in millions of households, from Sacramento
to Japan, there was next morn an empty chair,—at the table an unoccu-
pied place.   And it is this universality of deep, individual sorrow that
arrests our attention and demands an explanation of a circumstance so
exceptional.

And first, as to his personal character. Of Longfellow it may be truly said that the calm, mild beauty of his face, the loving expression of the bright-blue eyes, reflected a chrystalline purity of soul, that, in turn, found faithful reflex in rounded music of his sweetly flowing and hopeful verse. His very presence breathed an atmosphere of "peace on earth—good will to men," and a glance from those loving eyes—eyes whose brightness no lapse of years ever dimmed—fell upon the troubled soul, as the cool hand of a Florence Nightingale on the throbbing temples of the fevered soldier. From that serene presence Impurity shrank abashed, and Vice, spite all his impudence, was fain to hide his brazen forehead. And all this, with the most complete geniality and manliness and masculine strength of carriage and purpose ; and utterly without conscious or apparent effort. Peace and goodness seemed to emanate from him, and make themselves subtily felt, as warmth from sunlight—as odor from flowers. Like Una, wherever he went, he made a sunshine in the shady place.

The author of "Hohenlinden" has finely remarked of Sir Philip Sidney, that his life was poetry in action. This, and more, may with all truth be said of Longfellow, whose life was not only a poem, but a poem wedded to the most harmonious music ; a full and rounded strain of linked sweetness long drawn out ; a "Psalm of Life," now fused and blended into the fuller and more joyous strain of a "Psalm of Eternity." I know of no poetry in which art and ethics are so harmoniously wedded ; no author whose spiritual nature, writings and life are in more complete accord. All three make indeed but one poem, and it is impossible to dissociate them. Patience, modesty, gentleness, love, and withal self-reliance, courage and strength,—all were his ; united to a deeply-rooted belief in the ultimate apotheosis of humanity, and the all-encircling protection and love of an all-wise and all-benificent Creator. Through all his poems runs this note of trustfulness and confidence in the race. It never deserts him. Even in those dark hours in 1838, when a terrible accident snatched from him the partner of his life, he never lost heart, or bated one jot of courage ; and while so sorely in need of sympathy himself, was prodigal in the extension of it to all the world. And it is this large faith, this capacity for sympathizing, this earnest, resolute cheerfulness, that gives him his hold on the hearts of the people. Into all our domestic trials he enters with the self-abandonment of a dear friend who knowing the bitterness of having loved and lost still cherishes the sweet conviction that " 'Tis better to have loved and lost than never to have loved at all."

He is above all things the Poet of the Fireside. For him there was indeed no place like Home. To use his own words :

'By the fireside there are peace and comfort,
Wives and children, with fair, thoughtful faces,
Waiting, watching
For a well-known footstep in the passage.

Each man's chimney is his Golden Mile-stone ;
Is the central point, from which he measures
Every distance
Through the gateways of the world around him."

Other poets have been dear to us, but none so dear as he ; others have stirred us to more thrilling ecstacies of sympathetic passion, but none nestled so close to our affections as this gentle singer with the child-like heart. To the rebellious, defiant spirit, which a sense of wrong or the pressure of grief has hardened into selfish and indifference and coldness, he comes with noiseless step, and laying his hand upon the frozen heart, melts it into tears. He captures our affections unawares, and steals with the softness of sunshine into our affections. An air of domestic repose and peace breathes through all his writings. He is never wearied of the fireside, the prattle of young lips, the joyous distractions of the nursery. The childish talk in the "Golden Legend" is one of the pleasantest features in that most charming of mediæval stories.

It is told of a kindred spirit,—that brave, loving, patient, noble heart, which no sickness or misfortune could sour, but which dissolved in tears at the sight of another's misery, and finally broke in an anguish of grief over the sorrows of the poor needle-woman, in the "Song of the Shirt" —I say, it is told of Tom Hood that, even when racked with pain, and in the presence of inevitable death, he would steal into his children's room, in the early dawn, to lay some humorous sketch or poem upon their pillows, with which to gladden them when they awoke. And so with Longfellow. He is always stealing into the children's room,— never so much at home as when in the nursery ; never more truly divine than when hovering on noiseless pinions around the cradle, or by the open grave :

CHILDREN.

Come to me, O ye children !
  For I hear you at your play,
And the questions that perplexed me
  Have vanished quite away.

Ye open the eastern windows
  That look towards the sun,
Where thoughts are singing swallows
  And the brooks of morning run.

In your hearts are the birds and the sunshine,
  In your thoughts the brooklets flow, .
But in mine is the wind of Autumn,
  And the first fall of the snow.

Ah ! what would the world be to us
  If the children were no more ?
We should dread the desert behind us
  Worse than the dark before.

What the leaves are to the forest
  With light and air for food,
Ere their sweet and tender juices
  Have been hardened into wood—

That to the world are children ;
  Through them it feels the glow
Of a brighter and sunnier climate
  Than reaches the trunks below.

Come to me, O ye children !
  And whisper in my ear
What the birds and the winds are singing
  In your sunny atmosphere.

For what are all our contrivings
  And the wisdom of our books
When compared your caresses,
  And the gladness of your looks?

Ye are better than all the ballads
  That ever were sung or said ;
For ye are living poems,
  And all the rest are dead.

Nor does he spare time or pains because it is for children he
writes, as witness the verses " To a Child," in which he lavishes
upon them such a wealth of fancy and learning, and embellishes with
all the wonderful but unobtrusive riches of his reading, a simple nursery
chimney tile,—

TO A CHILD.

Dear child ! how radiant on thy mother's knee,
With merry-making eyes and jocund smiles,
Thou gazest at the painted tiles,
Whose figures grace,
With many a grotesque form and face,
The ancient chimney of thy nursery !
The lady with the gay macaw,
The dancing girl, the grave bashaw
With bearded lip and chin ;
And, leaning idly o'er his gate,
Beneath the imperial fan of state, the Chinese mandarin.

With what a look of proud command
Thou shakest in thy little hand
The coral rattle with its silver bells,
Making a merry tune !
Thousands of years in Indian seas
That coral grew by slow degrees,
Until some deadly, wild monsoon
Dashed it on Coromandel's sand !
Those silver bells
Reposed of yore,
As shapeless ore,
Far down in the deep-sunken wells
Of darksome mines,
In some obscure and sunless place,
Beneath huge Chimborazo's base,
Or Potosi's o'erhanging pines !
And thus for thee, O little child,
Through many a danger and escape,
The tall ships passed the stormy cape;
For thee in foreign lands remote,
Beneath a burning, tropic clime,
The Indian peasant, chasing the wild goat,
Himself as swift and wild,
In falling, clutched the frail arbute,
The fibres of whose shallow root,
Uplifted from the soil, betrayed
The silver veins beneath it laid,
The buried treasures of the miser, Time.

But, lo ! thy door is left ajar!
Thou hearest footsteps from afar !
And, at the sound,
Thou turnest round
With quick and questioning eyes,
Like one, who, in a foreign land,
Beholds on every hand
Some source of wonder and surprise !
And, restlessly, impatiently,
Thou strivest, strugglest, to be free.
The four walls of thy nursery
Are now like prison walls to thee.
No more thy mother's smiles,
No more the painted tiles,
Delight thee, nor the playthings on the floor,
That won thy little, beating heart before;
Thou strugglest for the open door.

Through these once solitary halls
Thy pattering footsteps falls.
The sound of thy merry voice
Makes the old walls
Jubilant, and they rejoice
With the joy of thy young heart,
O'er the light of whose gladness
No shadows of sadness
From the sombre background of memory start.

Once, ah, once, within these walls,
One whom memory oft recalls,
The Father of his Country, dwelt.
And yonder meadows broad and damp
The fires of the besieging camp
Encircled with a burning belt.
Up and down these echoing stairs,
Heavy with the weight of cares,
Sounded his majestic tread;
Yes, within this very room
Sat he in those hours of gloom,
Weary both in heart and head.

But what are these grave thoughts to thee?
Ont, out ! into the open air,
Thy only dream is liberty,
Thou carest little how or where.
I see thee eager at thy play,

Now shouting to the apples on the tree,
With cheeks as round and red as they;
And now among the yellow stalks,
Among the flowering shrubs and plants,
As restless as the bee.
Along the garden walks,
The tracks of thy small carriage-wheels I trace;
And see at every turn how they efface
Whole villages of sand-roofed tents,
That rise like golden domes
Above the cavernous and secret homes
Of wandering and nomadic tribes of ants.
Ah, cruel little Tamerlane,
Who, with thy dreadful reign,
Dost persecute and overwhelm
These hapless Troglodytes of thy realm !

What !   tired already ! with those suppliant looks,
And voice more beautiful than a poet's books,
Or murmuring sound of water as it flows,
Thou comest back to parley with repose !
This rustic seat in the old apple tree,
With its o'erhanging golden canopy
Of leaves illuminate with autumnal hues,
And shining with the argent light of dews,
Shall for a season be our place of rest.
Beneath us, like an oriole's pendent nest,
From which the laughing birds have taken wing,
By thee abandoned, hangs thy vacant swing.
Dream-like the waters of the river gleam ;
A sailless vessel drops adown the stream,
And like it, to a sea as wide and deep,
Thou driftest gently down the tides of sleep.

O child ! O new-born denizen
Of life's great city ! on thy head
The glory of the morn is shed,
Like a celestial benison !
Here at the portal thou dost stand,
And with thy little hand
Thou openest the mysterious gate
Into the future's undiscovered land.
I see its valves expand,
As at the touch of Fate !
Into those realms of love and hate,
Into that darkness blank and drear,

By some prophetic feeling taught,
I launch the bold, adventurous thought,
Freighted with hope and fear;
As upon subterranean streams,
In caverns unexplored and dark,
Men sometimes launch a fragile bark,
Laden with flickering fire,
And watch its swift-receding beams,
Until at length they disappear,
And in the distant dark expire.

By what astrology of fear or hope
Dare I to cast thy horoscope!
Like the new moon thy life appears;
A little strip of silver light,
And widening outward into night
The shadowy disk of future years;
And yet upon its outer rim,
A luminous circle, faint and dim,
And scarcely visible to us here,
Rounds and completes the perfect sphere;
A prophecy and intimation,
A pale and feeble adumbration,
Of the great world of light, that lies,
Behind all human destinies.

Ah, if thy fate, with anguish fraught,
Should be to wet the dusty soil
With the hot tears and sweat of toil,
To struggle with imperious thought,
Until the overburdened brain,
Weary with labor, faint with pain,
Like a jarred pendulum, retain,
Only its motion, not its power,—
Remember, in that perilous hour,
When most afflicted and oppressed,
From labor there shall come forth rest.

And if a more auspicious fate
On thy advancing steps await,
Still let it ever be thy pride
To linger by the laborer's side ;
With words of sympathy or song
To cheer the dreary march along
Of the great army of the poor,

O'er desert sand, o'er dangerous moor.
Nor to thyself the task shall be
Without reward ; for thou shalt learn
The wisdom early to discern
True beauty in utility;
As great Pythagoras of yore
Standing beside the blacksmith's door,
And hearing the hammers, as they smote
The anvils with a different note,
Stole from the varying tones, that hung
Vibrant on every iron tongue,
The secret of the sounding wire,
And formed the seven-chorded lyre.

Enough ! I will not play the Seer;
I will no longer strive to ope
The mystic volume, where appear
The herald Hope, forerunning Fear,
And Fear the pursuivant of Hope.
Thy destiny remains untold;
For, like Acestes' shaft of old,
The swift thought kindles as it flies,
And burns to ashes in the skies.

I have quoted these lines partly to illustrate their author's fondness for children, and partly to call attention to the wideness of his reading, and the exactness and breadth of his scholarship. As a linguist he had few equals, and the literature of foreign countries were as familiar to him as his own. In the exact sciences he was always a diligent student, and with one hand in that of his dearly beloved friend Agassiz, and the other laying friendly hold by Chaucer, he sang his way from the daisies to the stars. Of him we may truly say, as Tennyson has so finely remarked of his brother-in-law, Dr. Lushington, late Professor of Greek in Glasgow University,—

"He wears his weight of learning lightly,
  As a flower."

Like the great Baptist orator, Robert Hall, Longfellow was never happier than when tumbling on the rug ; his finest sonnet was inspired by a child's playthings ; and the pleasantest hour of the day for him was what, in one of his most charming songs, he calls the "Children's Hour." The former of these is steeped in the quiet beauty and philosophic calm of Wordsworth :

NATURE.

"As a fond mother, when the day is o'er,
   Leads by the hand her little child to bed,
   Half-willing, half-reluctant to be led,
And leaves his broken playthings on the floor,
Still gazing at them through the open door,
   Nor wholly reassured and comforted
   By promise of others in their stead,
   Which, though more splendid, may not please him more;
So Nature deals with us, and takes away
   Our playthings one by one, and by the hand
Leads us to rest so gently that we go
Scarce knowing if we wish to go or stay,
Being too full of sleep to understand
How far the unknown transcends the what we know."

The other I mentioned, "The Children's Hour," has always been my favorite, among all Longfellow's poems. The sentiment is so delicate, the humor so exquisitely tender,—I know not where to find its equal,—

THE CHILDREN'S HOUR.

Between the dark and the daylight,
   When the night is beginning to lower,
Comes a pause in the day's occupations,
   That is known as the Children's Hour.

I hear in the chamber above me
   The patter of little feet,
The sound of a door that is opened,
   And voices soft and sweet.

From my study I see in the lamplight,
   Descending the broad, hall stair,
Grave Alice, and laughing Allegra,
   And Edith, with golden hair.

A whisper, and then a silence:
  Yet I know by their merry eyes
They are plotting and planning together
  To take me by surprise.

A sudden rush from the stairway,
  A sudden raid from the hall!
By three doors left unguarded
  They enter my castle wall!

They climb up into my turret,
  O'er the arms and back of my chair;
If I try to escape, they surround me;
  They seem to be everywhere.

They almost devour me with kisses,
  Their arms about me entwine,
Till I think of the Bishop of Bingen,
  In his Mouse-Tower on the Rhine!

Do you think, O blue-eyed banditti,
  Because you have scaled the wall,
Such an old mustache as I am
  Is not a match for you all!

I have you fast in my fortress,
  And will not let you depart,
But put you down into the dungeon
  In the round-tower of my heart.

And there will I keep you forever,
  Yes, forever and a day,
Till the walls shall crumble to ruin,
  And moulder in dust away!

Akin to this love of children are his deep admiration and respect
for true womanhood.   Never since Dan Chaucer sang the sufferings of
the divinely patient Constance has the winning purity of maiden's
soul, the unconquerable strength of woman's devotion, the inexhaustible
patience of woman's love, been more feelingly portrayed, than in the
idyl of the black-eyed, brown-haired Evangeline, in her Norman cap
and kirtle of blue.   And they are all of a kind,—the coy, naive, warm-
hearted little Quaker maiden Priscilla, the May-flower of Plymouth;

Elsie, sublime in her quenchless love and deathless devotion; and Min-nehaha, "Laughing Water," "handsomest of all the women."

Then, again, marked the catholicity of the sentiment. We have here no hint of illiberality, or the narrow distinctions of sect or school. There is no heterodoxy in the "Psalm of Life." Pagans, Schoolmen, Puritans, Quakers, Priests, jongleurs, jesters, Jesuits and Jews, pass by turn across the stage, and are drawn with tender and impartial art. Whatever his religious beliefs may have been on matters of less than vital importance, they are not obtruded here. Trust in the ultimate destinies of the human race, and love for God and man,—are his all-embracing creed. The moral of his song is ever, "Heart within and God o'erhead," "Art is long and time is fleeting, and the grave is not its goal," "Work, Work, Work," "Patience and abnegation of self, and devotion to others," "Let us be patient; these severe afflictions

> Not from the ground arise,
> But oftentimes celestial benedictions
> Assume this dark disguise."

These and "the nobility of labor—the long pedigree of toil," are among the lessons which he most earnestly enforces, and which find perhaps most popular expression in the "Psalm of Life," "Excelsior," the "Village Blacksmith," and "The Builders."

His whole philosophy is one of charity, resignation and cheerful-ness,—a cheerfulness that is born of love and faith, not of indifference to any form of human suffering. He has warm, strong sympathies with his brother man all the world over, and to each and every one he stretches forth the hand of a hearty fellowship. He feels deeply, and he thinks earnestly, but he does not in consequence thereof indulge in fruitless complaint and dissatisfied murmurs; for, amid prosperity and adversity, through sunshine and through cloud, he recognizes the truth that a "good God reigneth over all."

> "For this he knows, in joys or woes,
> That saints *will* aid if men will call,
> For God's blue sky bends over all."

Finally, with all his gentleness, and sweet humanity, Longfellow was no mere theorist—no dilletante. He preached the gospel of hard

work, but, like Chaucer's good Parson, he first followed it himself. His
life, though unshaken by many great sorrows, and flowing placidly along
from cradle to grave, was one of unceasing work.   More than most men
he "scorned delights and lived laborious days," and even when,
crowned with the white blossoms of three score and ten, he met his old
fellow-students of '25, his noble greeting to them was full of courage
and hope, and his "Morituri Salutamus" breathes the most resolute
spirit of true manhood.   He and his class-mates of Bowdoin were old:—

> What then? Shall we sit idly down and say,
> The night hath come; it is no longer day?
> The night hath not yet come ; we are not quite
> Cut off from labor by the falling light;
> Something remains for us to do or dare;
> Even the oldest tree some fruit may bear;
> Nor Œdipus Coloneous, or Greek Ode,
> Or tales of pilgrims that in morning rode
> Out of the gateway of Tabard Inn,
> But other something, would we but begin;
> For age is opportunity no less
> Than youth itself, though in another dress,
> And as the evening twilight fades away
> The sky is filled with stars, invisible by day.

Before passing to a critical consideration of his works I would call
attention to the refined spiritualism that underlies much of Longfellow's
verse; as in "Resignation," "Footsteps of the Angels," "Haunted
Houses," and "Evangeline."   Who is not familiar with the lines :

> The spirit world around this world of sense
>   Floats like an atmosphere, and everywhere
> Wafts through these earthly mists and vapors dense
>   A vital breath of more ethereal air,
>
> Our little lives are kept in equipoise
>   By opposite attractions and desires;
> The struggle of the instinct that enjoys,
>   And the more noble instinct that aspires.
>
> These perturbations, this perpetual jar
>   Of earthly wants and aspirations high
> Come from the influence of an unseen star,
>   An undiscovered planet in our sky.

And as the moon from some dark gate of cloud
Throws o'er the sea a floating bridge of light,
Across whose trembling planks our fancies crowd
Into the realm of mystery and night,—

So from the world of spirits there descends
A bridge of light, connecting it with this,
O'er whose unsteady floor that sways and bends,
Wander our thoughts above the dark abyss.

And again, in the memorial lines to James T. Fields, where the poet expresses the secretly cherished and sweetly consoling conviction of many a bereaved heart:

'It were a double grief, if the departed,
Being released from earth, should still retain
A sense of earthly pain;
It were a double grief, if the true-hearted,
Who loved us here, should, on the further shore,
Remember us no more.''

A passing reference, too, may be permitted to Longfellow's delicate Pantheism, traces of which we also catch in portions of Mr. Tennyson's less artless verse. Thus, where Longfellow says:

''And the Poet, faithful and far-seeing,
Sees, alike in stars and flowers, a part
Of the self-same, universal being,
Which is throbbing in his brain and heart.''

CHRISTMAS BELLS.

I heard the bells on Xmas day
Their old, familiar carols play,
And wild and sweet
The words repeat
Of peace on earth, good-will to men !

And thought how, as the day had come,
The bellfries of all Christendom
Had rolled along
The unbroken song
Of peace on earth, good-will to men !

Till, ringing, singing on its way,
The world revolved from night to day,
    A voice, a chime,
    A chant sublime
Of peace on earth, good-will to men !

Then from each black, accursed mouth
The cannon thundered in the South,
    And with the sound
    The carols drowned
Of peace on earth, good-will to men !

It was as if an earthquake rent
The hearthstones of a continent,
    And made forlorn
    The household born
Of peace on earth, good-will to men !

And in despair I bowed my head ;
"There is no peace on earth," I said ;
    "For hate is strong,
    And mocks the song
Of peace on earth, good-will to men !"

Then pealed the bells more loud and deep ;
"God is not dead ; nor doth he sleep !
    The Wrong shall fail,
    The Right prevail,
With peace on earth, good-will to men !"

Longfellow's works fall to be considered under the five heads of : Narrative Poems, Ballads and Songs, Dramatic Sketches, Translations, and Prose Writings. These are as pure as was his life. In all these many hundred pages there is not a line which cannot be read aloud in the family circle. Not much to boast of, you may think, but when we remember how many an otherwise noble page is smudged and smeared by indecency and irreverence; how, from Ovid, Boccaccio and Chaucer, to Swinburne, Whitman and Zola, many a fair tale and stately poem bear the mark of the serpent's trail ; how the severe purity of Browning even is at times obscured, as in "Pippa Passes," the reference may be excused. In keeping with this kind of purity of thought, accompanied as it is with a complete absence of sneering or ill-nature, are the grace and simplicity of expression. Every word is chosen with the nice skill of a master of his art, and yet so naturally do they fall into their places, that of art there is no suggestion. I can call to mind no English poet, of equal fertility, whose workmanship is so uniformly excellent, and not many,—among the exceptions being Gray, Campbell, Landor, Poe, Tennyson and Rosetti—whose poems show as few traces of carelessness or haste. About his verse, too, there hangs a delightful old world flavor and quaintness. Like most Americans, Longfellow was deeply impressed by the relics of old days. *In* the New World, but not wholly of it, he dwells with almost wearisome fondness on the word old, and among other favorites are : mediæval, missal, mystic, haunts, "castled Rhine," lore, cloister, belfry, old cathedral, scroll, old-fashioned, etc. Sometimes, as in "Sandalphon,"

> "It is but a legend, I know,
> A fable, a phantom, a show,
>   Of the ancient Rabbinical lore ;
> Yet the old mediæval tradition,
>   But haunts me and holds me the more."

At other times, he turns lovingly to some

> "Old legends of the monkish page,
> Traditions of the saint and sage,
> Tales that have the rime of age
>   And chronicals of eld."

"His fancy," remarks his friend and critic, Professor John Nichol, "recrosses the Atlantic for the inspiration which many derive from the past. Now and then he gives us glimpses of the hoar frost silvering his native pines, or, heaping the logs on the hearth, sits down to tell us a New England tale; but most of his minor poems are drawn from the same experiences and memories as his *Hyperion* and *Outre-Mer*. Like Irving, in the variety of his culture, superior in genius, his imagination is rather Tuetonic than English. Cut Germany out of his volume and you cut out nearly half. He lingers in feudal towers or Flemish towns, and chooses for his emblem of life's river, not the Ohio, or the Hudson, or the Assabeth, but 'the Moldan's rushing stream.' "

He enters thoroughly into the romance and poetry of the times of chivalry, and loves to wander through—

"Old towns, whose history lies hid
  In monkish chronicle or rhyme—
Burgos, the birthplace of the Cid,
Zamora and Valladolid,
Toledo, built and walled amid
  The wars of Wamba's time."

NUREMBERG.

In the valley of the Pegnitz, where across broad meadow-lands
Rise the blue Franconian mountains, Nuremberg, the ancient, stands.

Quaint old town of toil and traffic, quaint old town of art and song,
Memories haunt thy pointed gables, like the rooks that round them throng.

Memories of the Middle Ages, when the emperors, rough and bold,
Had their dwelling in thy castle, time-defying, centuries old;

And thy brave and thrifty burghers boasted, in their uncouth rhyme,
That their great imperial city stretched its hand through every clime.

In the court-yard of the castle, bound with many an iron band,
Stands the mighty linden planted by Queen Cunigunde's hand;

On the square the oriel window, where in old heroic days
Sat the poet Melchior singing Kaiser Maximilian's praise.

Everywhere I see around me rise the wondrous world of Art:
Fountains wrought with richest sculpture standing in the common mart;

And above cathedral doorways saints and bishops carved in stone,
By a former age commissioned as apostles to our own.

In the church of sainted Sebald sleeps enshrined his holy dust,
And in bronze the Twelve Apostles guard from age to age their trust;

In the church of sainted Lawrence stands a pix of sculpture rare,
Like the foamy sheaf of fountains, rising through the painted air.

Here, when Art was still religion, with a simple, reverent heart,
Lived and labored Albrecht Durer, the Evangelist of Art;

Hence in silence and in sorrow, toiling still with busy hand,
Like an emigrant he wandered, seeking for the Better Land.

Emigravit is the inscription on the tombstone where he lies;
Dead he is not, but departed,—for the artist never dies.

Fairer seems the ancient city, and the sunshine seems more fair,
That he once has trod its pavement, that he once has breathed its air!

Through these streets so broad and stately, these obscure and dismal lanes,
Walked of yore the Mastersingers, chanting rude poetic strains.

From remote and sunless suburbs came they to the friendly guild,
Building nests in Fame's great temple, as in spouts the swallows build.

As the weaver plied the shuttle, wove he too the mystic rhyme,
And the smith his iron measures hammered to the anvil's chime;

Thanking God, whose boundless wisdom makes the flowers of poesy bloom
In the forge's dust and cinders, in the tissues of the loom.

Here Hans Sachs, the cobbler poet, laureate of the gentle craft,
Wisest of the Twelve Wise Masters, in huge folios sang and laughed.

But his house is now an alehouse, with a nicely sanded floor,
And a garland in the window, and his face above the door;

Painted by some humble artist, as in Adam Puschman's song,
As the old man gray and dove-like, with his great beard white and long.

And at night the swart mechanic comes to drown his cark and care,
Quaffing ale from pewter tankards, in the master's antique chair.

Vanished is the ancient splendor, and before my dreamy eye
Wave these mingling shapes and figures, like a faded tapestry.

Not thy Councils, not thy Kaisers, win for thee the world's regard;
But thy painter, Albrecht Durer, and Hans Sachs, thy cobbler-bard.

Thus, O Nuremberg, a wanderer from a region far away,
As he paced thy streets and court-yards, sang in thought his careless lay:

Gathering from the pavement's crevice, as a floweret of the soil,
The nobility of labor,—the long pedigree of toil.

He visits Nuremberg : 'quaint old town of toil and trafic'; and there his imagination is haunted by "memories of the middle-ages", whose wondrous treasures of printing, sculpture, and architecture, even now recall the time when "art was still religion." And amidst the warm, bright light that rests so lovingly upon the "pointed gables" of that "great emperial city', the poet beholds, in fancy, the heroes of the ancient days —"Melchior, singing Kaiser Maximilian's praise"; Albrect Dürer, the painter ; Hans Sachs, the "cobler bard"; the master-singers, chanting rude poetic strains,—and as he gazes, lo, before his

> ——"dreamy eye
> Wave these mingling shapes and figures, like a faded tapestry."

Had Longfellow lived on the Scottish border eighty years ago he would probably have turned out anothor Walter Scott, in his love for romantic lore and in the composition of original ballads. His own efforts in this department are among the most successful in modern literature. Always excepting Coleridge's "Ancient Mariner," I know not where to seek a more weird and effective ballad than that of the "Skeleton in Armor," and hardly less striking, though in a different vein, is the ever popular "Wreck of the Hesperus."

In the use of tropes, Longfellow is profuse and usually successful ; Evangeline especially is full of happy metaphor and dainty conceit.

Now, the stars shine over her "the thoughts of God in the heavens," and, again, they blossom "the forget-me-nots of the angels"; while, at another time, he reverses the figure, and the flowers become immortalized in their turn, when :

> "Everywhere about us are they glowing,
>   Some like stars to tell us Spring is born,
> Others, like blue eyes with tears o'erflowing,
>   Stand, like Rnth amid the golden corn."

Who, too, has not admired the picture of the maiden :

> "Standing with reluctant feet,
>   Where the brook and river meet,
>   Womanhood and childhood fleet !"
>   *   *   *

"And whose smiles, like sunshine, dart
Into many a sunless heart,
For a smile of God thou art !"

Contrast, again, the boldness and delicacy of the two following :

"From the bleak shores of the sea to the lands where the Father of waters
Seizes the hills in his hands, and drags them down the ocean."

And this :

"Talk not of wasted affection, affection never was wasted ;
If it enrich not the heart of another, its waters, returning
Back to the springs, like the rain, shall fill them full of refreshment."

There is strength, too, and a sort of quaint humor in calling the
"grim, taciturn bear, the anchorite monk of the desert."

In descriptions of scenery, Longfellow belongs to the school of
Scott, rather than of Spenser ; of Linnel than of Turner. He paints
nature as it is, not as we should like it to be, and he is most successful
in describing scenery of a vast and imposing kind. His sight, however,
though uncommonly accurate and sharp, does not pierce much beyond
the more salient features of the landscape, and his scenery sometimes
approaches perilously near to the merely illustrative style. As a rule,
while his descriptions are inferior in luxuriance to those of " Enoch
Arden," in subtlety to Browning's Italian pictures, they are superior in
simplicity. They do not adorn Nature as a mistress, in the manner of
Chateaubriand, with the subjective fancies of a lover : they bring her
before us a faithful nurse, careful of her children.

Of his longer poems, "Hiawatha" shows most creative or dramatic
power. In it, Longfellow has expanded, out of a small germ of Indian
tradition, an altogether unique story,—a strange mixture of mythology,
romance, and fable, as unlike all poems that preceded it as a savage is
unlike all civilized people, and full of vigorous pictures of forest life
and scenery, and a certain soft and noiseless grace like that of the
people it describes. It is unique, also, among Longfellow's poems, as
having a certain, indescribable humor of its own, which none of his
other works possesses. Next in order of merit, I am disposed to place
his "Evangeline ;" that tale of "love in Acadia ;" of the "affection that
hopes, and endures, and is patient ;" of the "beauty and strength of

woman's devotion." The description of Evangeline's meeting with her dying love, after years of separation and trials had bowed and wasted both, is deeply affecting, and rises into a height that makes hostile criticism an impertinence.

Of his Tales, it need only be said, they are all eminently readable, fluent, interesting, and gracefully told, but lacking the breadth, humor, and sap, of the works of him who wrote the "Canterbury Tales." Of the translations, and these are from almost every known European tongue, it is sufficient to say that they stand unsurpassed ; perhaps the most successful being the ballads from the German ; which are not so much translations as transfusions of the poetic spirit of one language into another. While his "Dante" is generally acknowledged to be easily first amid a host of claimants to that honor.

Longfellow's principal prose works are "Hyperion" and "Kavanagh." The former, though called a romance, possesses none of the elements of the ordinary novel. As a story, it is incomplete, its conclusion being tantalizingly abrupt. Regarded as a kind of poem, however, the book is charming, being a magnificent reflex of the many-colored lights that flash across a poet's mind, like the strange, rich, dreamy splendors that stream through the painted windows of some old cathedral.

But it is in his short, original, swallow-flights of song that the poet shows to most advantage, and has won his most enduring laurels. It is the office of the poet to gladden and to elevate the heart of man ; to whisper consolation to the sorrowing ; to breathe words of hope and joy to the downcast and despairing ; and to endeavor, as far as in him lies, to build up again the broken foundations of belief in the good, the beautiful, the perfect, and the true. Thus, as Longfellow tells us:

> "God sent his singers upon earth
> With songs of sadness and of mirth,
> That they might touch the hearts of men,
> *And bring them back to heaven again.*"

In order to accomplish this great end, the poet must be true to himself. Receiving his gift from above reverently, with pure hands, and a lowly, trustful spirit, he must "look into his heart and write." When Longfellow does this, his minstrelsy rings most sweetly and clearly, and it is in his shorter poems that he speaks most directly out of the fullness of his own heart, and therefore touches to finest issues the hearts of his readers.

Finally, we cannot claim for Longfellow that he is one of

> "the grand old masters,
> One of the bards sublime,
> Whose distant footsteps echo
> Through the corridors of Time."

He seldom stirs within us the fountains of deep thought, nor does he often arouse us to strange vague speculations upon the more solemn mysteries of our being and destiny. He rather resembles the "humble poet,

> Whose songs gushed from his heart,
> As showers from the clouds of summer,
> Or tears from the eyelids start.

> Who, through long days of labor,
> And nights devoid of ease,
> Still heard in his soul the music
> Of wonderful melodies.

> Such songs have power to quiet
> The restless pulse of care,
> And come like the benediction
> That follows after prayer."

In reading Longfellow we are never perplexed with misgiving or doubt. For him, life has no riddle; honest labor, and faith in God, are the means by which to work out a man's redemption. And this suggests one secret of his phenomenal popularity: he is intelligible to the humblest understanding. The moral and intellectual quality of his verse is such as appeals to the sympathies, and falls within the easy comprehension of every reader. They are written from what may be called everybody's point of view: they express, always neatly, sometimes gracefully, and now and then beautifully, what the generality of readers think and feel on the subject, or rather what they know they ought to think and feel. It is this somewhat common cast of intellectual character that gives so much directness and sureness of aim to

Longfellow's appeals, and insures for them at least an intelligent hearing. At the same time we must beware of confounding, as some of
Longfellow's critics *do* confound, the common with the commonplace.
All that is best in life and nature, and mostly all that is highest in art,
is common. Such are joy and sorrow, regret and hope, hate and love,
sunshine and shadow, ripple of stream and song of bird, beauty of
woman and wealth of color, and all the infinite variations of the divine
harmonies of nature and life. But, are they commonplace ?

And so with those thoughts that find immediate echo in the universal heart of humanity. They do so, not because commonplace, but because they are in such perfect accordance with those elemental truths
which lie deep at the foundation of nature and art, that the soul
instinctively recognizes the harmony, and leaps to assimilate them
to itself. The truth is, that Longfellow has suffered from the injudi-
cious eulogy of his friends, who have claimed for him a preeminent
place among the *Du Majores* of song, and not, where he rightly belongs,
to a lofty place among the *minores*. And this unwise overpraise has
helped to drive, into the opposite extreme, lets enthusiastic critics, who,
because Longfellow occasionally lapsed into Tupperisms, and was guilty
of so unnatural, stilted and theatrical a piece of rhetorical clap-trap as
"Excelsior," have not hesitated to degrade him into a kind of superior
Tupper, or rhyming "A. K. H. B." "He has not," acknowledges Mr.
Nichol, "intensity enough to take rank with the *Du Majores*, but his
writings are deeper than they seem; because every sentence he has
penned is as clear as crystal and as pure as snow. There are reasons in
this over-wrought, over-educated, over-examined age, when we prefer
his company to that of the "grand old masters," when we turn from Dante
and Milton, even from Keats and Tennyson, to "songs that have power
to quiet the restless pulse of care"—songs which are likely to appeal to
human hearts when the louder and more pretentious rhapsodies of
many contemporaries shall have passed like a purple smoke away.

To speak more definitely, Longfellow's intellectual sweep is not
wide. His genius moves with clipped wings within a charmed circle of
thought. You remember what Tennyson says of him : "I hold it truth
with him who sings. On one clear chord with divers tones," etc. Inside
these limits, he is perfect ; but when he attempts to soar into the rare
altitudes of metaphysical speculation, which is the native air of creations
like Faust and Hamlet, or of ecstatic passion, as depicted in "Othello"
or "The Duchess of Malfi," he fails, like Icarus, and tumbles earth-ward,
and his limitation of range is largely "because he is dowered with neither

hate nor scorn. Singing glory to God, good will to men," "His ways are ways of pleasantness, and all his paths are peace." Standing before the arsenal his fancy hears

'The bursting shell, the gateway wrenched asunder,
The rattling musketry, the clashing blade,
And ever and anon in tones of thunder
The diapason of the canonade."

But he turns from those discordant noises into the track of his perpetual beneficence—

"Were half the power that fills the world with terror,
Were half the wealth bestowed on camps and courts
Given to redeem the human mind from error
There were no need of arsenals and forts.

"Down the dark future, through long generations
The echoing sounds grow fainter, and then cease,
And like a bell with solemn, sweet vibrations
I hear once more the voice of Christ say, Peace.

"Peace ! and no longer from its brazen portals
The blast of war's great organ shakes the skies,
But beautiful as songs of the immortals
The holy melodies of Love arise."

His poetry, also, though not his prose, lacks humor, although those who knew him intimately will tell you how much true humor, and even fun, underlay his habitual seriousness. *Apropos* of this : You are perhaps familiar with an anecdote of the poet that will, however, bear repetition. When traveling in Switzerland with Mr. Nathan Appleton, Longfellow had been extortionately charged at Zurich, by the landlord of the hostlery called "The Raven"; whereupon he wrote upon the book of the inn :

"Beware of the Raven of Zurich :
'Tis a bird of omen ill,
With an ugly, unclean nest,
And a very, very long *bill.*

Which reminds one of Burns's retaliatory impromptu, in similar circumstances, where he wrote on the window of an Inn in Inverary :

> "There's næthin here but hielan' pride,
>   Hielan' scab and hunger,
> If God Almighty sent me here
> 'Twas surely in an anger."

On another occasion, some twenty years ago, when the Appleton's
were living at Lynn, Longfellow's son Charles called on them in his boat,
one day. The surf running high, the boat was capsized, and he was
thrown into the water. Captain Nathan Appleton rigged him out afresh,
but, not having a fitting pair of shoes, loaned him slippers. These, the
poet returned some days later, with this parody of one of the best known
of his own verses :

> "Slippers that perhaps another,
>   Sailing o'er the Bay of Lynn,
> A forlorn or shipwrecked nephew,
>   Seeing, may purloin again."

It has sometimes been objected, notoriously by Poe, whose criticisms,
however, in spite of their acuteness, are generally beneath notice—that
Longfellow lacked originality and force, and keen-nosed critics have
picked out some stray lines and expressions that appear to echo some
other poet. It would be surprising if so receptive and sympathetic a
genius as Longfellow, one of the most widely read and scholarly men of
this century, did not reflect an occasional ray from some one of the
many orbs whose sunshine had been the chief solace of his life : and, at
times, the quick ear of the student will catch in his song a familiar note.
Thus in the poems entitled "The Spirit of Poesy" and "Sunrise on the
Hills," and in the verse :

> "The green trees whispered low and mild :
>   It was a sound of joy !
> They were my playmates when a child,
> And rocked me in their arms so wild,
> Still they looked at me and smiled,
>   As if I were a boy;"

—though the words are the words of Longfellow, the voice is that of Wordsworth. So, too, the line, "Look, then, into thine heart, and write," is an echo of Sidney; in "The Ladder of St. Augustine" there is a suggestion of Tennyson ; in "Sandalphon" a hint of Poe ; in the "Slave's Dream" a faint reflection of Byron ; and Bryant's clear and thoughtful note is distinctly audible in the lines—

> "O what a glory doth this world put on
> For him who, with a fervent heart, goes forth
> Under the bright and glorious sky, and looks
> On duties well-performed, and days well spent !
> For him the wind,—ay, and the yellow leaves,
> Shall have a voice, and give him eloquent teachings.
> He shall so bear the solemn hymn that Death
> Has lifted up for all, that he shall go
> To his long resting place without a tear."

But what of these faint and broken reflections, if reflections they are, when compared with the far-extending sunshine of his verse? What two poems in modern literature can lay claim to greater originality than "Hiawatha" and "Evangeline," and what short piece, since Gray's "Elegy," has furnished the world with more memorable lines than the "Psalm of Life?"

As to the charge of want of strength, it arises largely from a confounding of simplicity with weakness, purity and sweetness with want of virility and force. But, except a very rare and exceptional lapse into feebleness, though never into the puerilities which make ridiculous certain portions of Wordsworth, and even Tennyson, Longfellow's verse is uniformly even and strong. Certainly, we are never startled by dramatic climaxes of passion as in Webster or Byron, emotional ecstacies of feeling as in Shelley and Bailey, melodious paroxysms of sound and fury as in Swinburne, sublime imaginative flights as in Milton, "mighty lines" as in Marlowe, nebulous transcendentalism as in Blake and Emerson, or metaphysical riddles and syntactical conumdrums as in Browning,—but eccentricity is not strength, and because Longfellow was never eccentric it were foolish to call him weak. His strength is calm, even, well-sustained and full ; always suggestive of a reserve force behind. It is not, like Carlyle's, the strength of the thunderbolt, that shatters and appals, but rather of the light which impregnates the dull clod with vitality and warmth, that slowly develope into green grass, flowers and fruit, and fields of golden grain. Longfellow, too, could always rise to the occasion, us witness the Miltonic strength and loftiness of the peroration of the "Building of the Ship," and the compactness and vigor of such poems as "Victor Galbraith," "The Warden of the Cinque Ports," "A Ballad of the French Fleet," and "Paul Revere's Ride."

Lastly, Longfellow's dramatic talent was of the poorest and thinnest quality. His personages are theatrical lay figures ; with conventional costumes, conventional names, conventional speeches, and conventional sentiments. In "The Courtship of Miles Standish," for instance, the personages of the story are made up of cheap and second-hand historical material : the rugged and religious Puritan captain, "clad in doublet and hose and boots of Cordovan leather," who is introduced "striding," of course, "with a martial air ;" John Alden,

> " * * * his friend and household companion,
> Writing with diligent speed at a table of pine
>   by a window,
> Fair-haired, azure-eyed,"—

a sort of Cromwell and Milton, in fact, — these and the "Puritan maiden, Priscilla," are all lay figures. They are, in short, puppets; moved from without, not from within ; having their actions shaped by extraneous and visible agencies, not by the spontaneous and natural, generative forces of their own nature. But, making due allowance for these defects, and limitations of genius, how much remains that calls for nothing but praise. The first reading of the "Psalm of Life" has marked an epoch in many a young man's career, and, with all its sentimental shoddyism, it is a fact that many a weary traveler's hope has been rekindled, and his courage fired, by the example of the

> " * * * youth, who bore, 'mid snow and ice,
> A banner, with the strange device,
>   Excelsior !"

The influence of Longfellow's life and works upon his age and upon literature can hardly be over-stated. So the grasping, selfish, money-making, materialistic spirit of the times, with its tawdry sentiment, its venal politics, its mean ambitions, and heartless slang, its hopeless pessism, his pure and unselfish life and hopeful utterances, were a continual and silent, but withal potent protest ; while the simple directness of his diction, and the purity of his thought, are in wholesome contrast to the affected, sensuous, and spasmodic rhetoric of those "too" erotic bards whom Mr. Robert Buchanan once dubbed the "Fleshly" school of poets. Purity of the lives of American authors—Poe the solitary exception. It is surely not without significance that, in a high-pressure age like this, when men rush to fortunes on railways and electric wires, and the possibilities of man's soul bid fair soon to be resolved into formulas of profit and loss, God should raise up four such men and poets as Bryant, Longfellow, Emerson and Whittier. Three of this noble quartette have now gone, each to take—

"His chamber in the silent halls of death."

SEA-WEED.

When descends on the Atlantic
       The gigantic
Storm-wind of the equinox,
Landward in his wrath he scourges
       The toiling surges,
Laden with sea weed from the rocks:

From Bermuda's reefs; from edges
       Of sunken ledges,
In some far-off, bright Azore;
From Bahama, and the dashing,
       Silver-flashing
Surges of San Salvador;

From the tumbling surf, that buries
       The Orkneyan skerries,
Answering the hoarse Hebrides;
And from wrecks of ships, and drifting
       Spars, uplifting
On the desolate, rainy seas;—

Ever drifting, drifting, drifting
       On the shifting
Currents of the restless main;
Till in sheltered coves, and reaches
       Of sandy beaches,
All have found repose again.

So when storms of wild emotion
    Strike the ocean
Of the poet's soul, erelong
From each cave and rocky fastness,
    In its vastness,
Floats some fragment of a song:

From the far-off isles enchanted,
    Heaven has planted
With the golden fruit of Truth;
From the flashing surf, whose vision
    Gleams Elysian
In the tropic clime of youth;

From the strong Will, and the Endeavor
    That forever
Wrestles with the tides of Fate,
From the wreck of Hopes far-scattered,
    Tempest-shattered,
Floating waste and desolate;—

Ever drifting, drifting, drifting
    On the shifting
Currents of the restless heart;
Till at length in books recorded
    They, like hoarded
Household words, no more depart.

RAIN IN SUMMER.

How beautiful is the rain!
After the dust and heat,
In the broad and fiery street,
In the narrow lane,
How beautiful is the rain!

How it clatters along the roofs,
Like the tramp of hoofs!
How it gushes and struggles out
From the throat of the overflowing spout!

Across the window pane
It pours and pours;
And swift and wide,
With a muddy tide,
Like a river down the gutter roars
The rain, the welcome rain!

The sick man from his chamber looks
At the twisted brooks;
He can feel the cool
Breath of each little pool;
His fevered brain
Grows calm again,
And he breathes a blessing on the rain.

From the neighboring school
Come the boys,
With more than their wonted noise
And commotion;
And down the wet streets
Sail their mimic fleets,
Till the treacherous pool
Ingulfs them in its whirling
And turbulent ocean.

In the country, on every side,
Where far and wide,
Like a leopard's tawny and spotted hide,
Stretches the plain,
To the dry grass and the drier grain
How welcome is the rain!

In the furrowed land
The toilsome and patient oxen stand;
Lifting the yoke-encumbered head,
With their dilated nostrils spread,
They silently inhale
The clover scented gale,
And the vapors that arise
From the well watered and smoking soil.
For this rest in the furrow after toil
Their large and lustrous eyes
Seem to thank the Lord,
More than man's spoken word.

Near at hand,
From under the sheltering trees,
The farmer sees
His pastures, and his fields of grain,
As they bend their tops
To the numberless beating drops
Of the incessant rain.
He counts it as no sin
That he sees therein
Only his own thrift and gain.

These, and far more than these,
The Poet sees!
He can behold
Aquarius old
Walking the fenceless fields of air;
And from each ample fold
Of the clouds about him rolled
Scattering everywhere
The showery rain,
As the farmer scatters his grain.

He can behold
Things manifold
That have not yet been wholly told,—
Have not been wholly sung nor said.
For his thought, that never stops
Follows the water-drops
Down to the graves of the dead,
Down through chasms and gulfs profound,
To the dreary fountain-head
Of lakes and rivers under ground;
And sees them, when the rain is done,
On the bridge of colors seven
Climbing up once more to heaven,
Opposite the setting sun.

Thus the Seer,
With vision clear,
Sees forms appear and disappear,
In the perpetual round of strange,
Mysterious change
From birth to death, from death to birth,
From earth to heaven, from heaven to earth;

Till glimpses more sublime
Of things, unseen before,
Unto his wondering eyes reveal
The Universe, as an immeasurable wheel
Turning forevermore
In the rapid and rushing river of Time.

THE ARROW AND THE SONG.

I shot an arrow into the air,
It fell to earth, I knew not where;
For, so swiftly it flew, the sight
Could not follow it in its flight.

I breathed a song into the air,
It fell to earth, I knew not where;
For who has sight so keen and strong,
That it can follow the flight of song?

Long, long afterward in an oak
I found the arrow, still unbroke;
And the song, from beginning to end,
I found again in the heart of a friend.

THE TWO ANGELS.

Two angels, one of Life and one of Death,
   Passed o'er our village as the morning broke;
The dawn was on their faces, and beneath,
   The sombre houses hearsed with plumes of smoke.

Their attitude and aspect were the same,
   Alike their features and their robes of white,
But one was crowned with amaranth, as with flame,
   And one with asphodels, like flakes of light.

I saw them pause on their celestial way;
   Then said I, with deep fear and doubt oppressed,
Beat not so loud, my heart, lest thou betray
   The place where thy beloved are at rest!"

And he who wore the crown of asphodels,
   Descending, at my door began to knock,
And my soul sank within me, as in wells
   The waters sink before an earthquake's shock.

I recognized the nameless agony,
   The terror and the tremor and the pain,
That oft before had filled or haunted me,
   And now returned with threefold strength again.

The door I opened to my heavenly guest,
   And listened, for I thought I heard God's voice;
And, knowing whatso'er he sent was best,
   Dared neither to lament nor to rejoice.

Then, with a smile, that filled the house with light,
   "My errand is not Death, but Life," he said;
And ere I answered, passing out of sight,
   On his celestial embassy he sped.

Twas at thy door, O friend! and not at mine,
   The angel with the amaranthine wreath,
Pausing, descended, and with voice divine,
   Whispered a word that had a sound like Death.

Then fell upon the house a sudden gloom,
   A shadow on those features fair and thin;
And softly, from that hushed and darkened room,
   Two angels issued, where but one went in.

All is of God! If he but wave his hand,
   The mists collect, the rain falls thick and loud,
Till, with a smile of light on sea and land,
   Lo! he looks back from the departing cloud.

Angels of Life and Death alike are his;
   Without his leave they pass no theshold o'er
Who, then, would wish or dare, believing this,
   Against his messengers to shut the door?

THE LIGHTHOUSE.

The rocky ledge runs far into the sea,
    And on its outer point, some miles away,
The Lighthouse lifts its massive masonry,
    A pillar of fire by night, of cloud by day.

Even at this distance I can see the tides,
    Upheaving, break unheard along its base,
A speechless wrath, that rises and subsides
    In the white lip and tremor of the face.

And as the evening darkens, lo! how bright,
    Through the deep purple of the twilight air,
Beams forth the sudden radiance of its light
    With strange, unearthly splendor in the glare!

Not one alone; from each projecting cape
    And perilous reef along the ocean's verge,
Starts into life a dim, gigantic shape,
    Holding its lantern o'er the restless surge.

Like the great giant Christopher it stands
    Upon the brink of the tempestuous wave,
ading far out among the rocks and sands,
    The night-o'ertaken mariner to save.

And the great ships sail outward and return,
    Bending and bowing o'er the billowy swells,
And ever joyful, as they see it burn,
    They wave their silent welcomes and farewells.

They come forth from the darkness, and their sails
    Gleam for a moment only in the blaze,
And eager faces as the light unveils,
    Gaze at the tower, and vanish while they gaze.

The mariner remembers when a child,
    On his first voyage, he saw it fade and sink;
And when, returning from adventures wild,
    He saw it rise again o'er ocean's brink.

Steadfast, serene, immovable, the same
    Year after year, through all the silent night
Burns on forevermore that quenchless flame,
    Shines on that inextinguishable light!

It sees the ocean to its bosom clasp
    The rocks and sea-sand with the kiss of peace;
It sees the wild winds lift it in their grasp,
    And hold it up, and shake it like a fleece.

The startled waves leap over it; the storm
    Smites it with all the scourges of the rain,
And steadily against its solid form
    Press the great shoulders of the hurricane.

The sea-bird wheeling round it, with the din
    Of wings and winds, and solitary cries,
Blinded and maddened by the light within,
    Dashes himself against the glare, and dies.

A new Prometheus, chained upon the rock,
    Still grasping in his hand the fire of Jove,
It does not hear the cry, nor heed the shock,
    But hails the mariner with words of love.

"Sail on!" it says, "sail on, ye stately ships!
    And with your floating bridge the ocean span;
Be mine to guard this light from all eclipse,
    Be yours to bring man nearer unto man!"

————

THE GOLDEN MILE-STONE.

Leafless are the trees; their purple branches
Spread themselves abroad, like reefs of coral,
    Rising silent
In the Red Sea of the winter sunset.

From the hundred chimneys of the village,
Like the Afreet in the Arabian story,
    Smoky columns
Tower aloft into the air of amber.

At the window winks the flickering firelight;
Here and there the lamps of evening glimmer,
    Social watch-fires
Answering one another through the darkness.

On the hearth the lighted logs are glowing,
And like Ariel in the cloven pine-tree
    For its freedom
Groans and sighs the air imprisoned in them.

By the fireside there are old men seated,
Seeing ruined cities in the ashes,
    Asking sadly
Of the Past what it can ne'er restore them.

By the fireside there are youthful dreamers,
Building castles fair, with stately stairways,
    Asking blindly
Of the Future what it cannot give them.

By the fireside tragedies are acted
In whose scenes appear two actors only,
    Wife and husband,
And above them God the sole spectator.

By the fireside there are peace and comfort,
Wives and children, with fair, thoughtful faces,
    Waiting, watching
For a well-known footstep in the passage.

Each man's chimney is his Golden Mile-stone
Is the central point, from which he measures
    Every distance
Through the gateways of the world around him.

In his farthest wanderings still he sees it;
Hears the talking flame, the answering night-wind,
    As he heard them
When he sat with those who were, but are not.

Happy he whom neither wealth nor fashion,
Nor the march of the encroaching city,
    Drives an exile
From the hearth of his ancestral homestead.

We may build more splendid habitations,
Fill our rooms with paintings and with sculptures,
     But we cannot
Buy with gold the old associations !